CW00350456

Dressing the Dead
In Classical Antiquity

EDITED BY

Maureen Carroll & John Peter Wild

AMBERLEY

Front cover: Lazarus, still wrapped for burial, is raised from the dead by Christ in this biblical miracle on an ivory diptych (Andrews diptych) of the early ninth century from Italy. Photo by Victoria and Albert Museum.

First published 2012

Amberley Publishing
The Hill, Stroud
Gloucestershire, GL5 4EP

www.amberley-books.com

Copyright © Maureen Carroll & John Peter Wild 2012

The right of Maureen Carroll & John Peter Wild to be identified
as the Author of this work has been asserted in accordance with the
Copyrights, Designs and Patents Act 1988.

All rights reserved. No part of this book may be reprinted
or reproduced or utilised in any form or by any electronic,
mechanical or other means, now known or hereafter invented,
including photocopying and recording, or in any information
storage or retrieval system, without the permission in writing
from the Publishers.

British Library Cataloguing in Publication Data.
A catalogue record for this book is available from the British Library.

ISBN 978 1 4456 0300 1

Typeset in 10pt on 12pt Sabon.
Typesetting and Origination by Amberley Publishing.
Printed in the UK.

CONTENTS

ABOUT THE AUTHORS

Dimitra Andrianou received her BA from the University of Athens, her MA from the University of Pennsylvania and her PhD from Bryn Mawr College. After a post-doctoral fellowship in 2003 at the American School of Classical Studies at Athens, she became a researcher at the National Hellenic Research Foundation. She has excavated extensively in the Mediterranean and has taught various archaeological courses at the University of Pennsylvania and Bryn Mawr College. She was a research assistant at the Institute for the Study of Aegean Prehistory (INSTAP) and an intern at the University of Pennsylvania Museum. In 2010 she was awarded a prize by the Academy of Athens for her monograph *The Furniture and Furnishings of Ancient Greek Houses and Tombs* (2009).

Lucy Audley-Miller is a Junior Research Fellow at Somerville College, University of Oxford. She held a Wiener-Anspach postdoctoral research fellowship at the Université Libre de Bruxelles in 2010–2011, having taught Classical Archaeology as a Junior Teaching Fellow at St John's College, University of Oxford from 2007–2010. She received her MPhil and DPhil from the University of Oxford and her BA in Archaeology and Ancient History from the University of Newcastle-upon-Tyne.

Maureen Carroll is Reader in Roman Archaeology at the University of Sheffield. She received her BA from Brock University (Canada), and her MA and PhD in Classical Archaeology from Indiana University (USA) and the Free University in Berlin. Before coming to Sheffield, she worked for many years for the state archaeological services in Germany and taught at the University of Cologne. She has excavated widely in Europe, and specialises in Roman death, burial, and commemoration. She is the director of the British project associated with *Clothing and Identities. New Perspectives on Textiles in the Roman Empire (DressID)*, funded by the European Union.

Emilia Cortes is Associate Conservator at The Metropolitan Museum of Art in New York. Since 1995 she has been responsible for the textile collection in Egyptian Art, having first been an Andrew W. Mellon Fellow between 1991 and 1993 in the Textile Conservation Department under Nobuko Kajitani. Since 2001 she has been a member of the Egyptian Art Expedition to Dahshur. From Bogotá, Colombia, Cortes graduated in graphic design in Bogotá and textile design in Como and Florence, having also trained in conservation in Italy, the USA and Peru. Currently she is completing her MA in Museum Anthropology at Columbia University in New York.

John Drinkwater, MA Cambridge, DPhil Oxford, FSA, is Emeritus Professor of Roman Imperial History at the University of Nottingham. Before moving to Nottingham he was lecturer in the former Department of Ancient History and Classical Archaeology at the University of Sheffield. His main field of research has been Roman Gaul, in the context of which he has investigated the likely shape and socio-economic impact of the wool-textile industry of Gallia Belgica. In 2007 he published *The Alamanni and Rome* (Oxford). He is currently working on a study of Nero.

Mary Harlow received her PhD from the University of Leicester. She is Senior Lecturer in Roman History at the Institute of Archaeology and Antiquity, University of Birmingham. She was Assistant Director of the Institute from 2002–2005 and has held various posts dealing with undergraduate studies. She is currently a Research Associate at the Centre for Textile Research, Saxo Institute, at the University of Copenhagen. Her main areas of research are Roman dress, and the study of gender, age and ageing in Roman society.

Sylvia Mitschke graduated from the Institute of Conservation Sciences, University of Applied Sciences in Cologne, in 2000 with a dissertation on textiles from a Merovingian cemetery in Eltville (Rheingau-Taunus-Kreis). Since then, she has been employed as a textile conservator and scientist at the Reiss-Engelhorn-Museums in Mannheim where she specialises in analytical methods, using the facilities of the Curt-Engelhorn-Centre for Archaeometry. Since 2007 she has been a member of *DressID* and is currently a PhD candidate at the University of Tübingen working on *Textile raw materials and processing in the Roman epoch using the example of the finds from Mainz*.

Annette Paetz gen. Schieck received her MA and PhD in Classical Archaeology from Cologne University, Germany. Her research focuses on Roman architecture and on the investigation of ancient textiles and their pictorial sources. She has designed and organised two exhibitions on Coptic textiles: 'Aus Gräbern geborgen' at the Deutsches Textilmuseum in Krefeld (2003) and 'Die koptischen Textilien of Kolumba', at the Erzbischöfliches Diözesanmuseum in Cologne (2005). From 2007 to 2012 she was the project manager of a research and exhibition project on Roman identity and dress (*DressID*), financed by the European Commission (www.DressID.eu). She is now director of the Deutsches Textilmuseum in Krefeld.

Jane Rempel studied archaeology in Canada (BA, Wilfrid Laurier University), England (MSt, Oxford) and the United States (MA, PhD, University of Michigan). She is currently a Lecturer in Classical Archaeology at the University of Sheffield, and her research focuses on Greek colonisation and cultural interaction in the north Black Sea region, with a special interest in landscape and funerary archaeology. She is co-editor of *Living through the Dead. Burial and Commemoration in the Classical World* (2011, with M. Carroll).

Kristin H. South studied Near Eastern Languages and Civilizations at Yale University, receiving her BA and MA in 1993. She has since excavated at Fag el-Gamus, in Egypt's Fayum, as well as at Palmyra (Syria) and at Petra (Jordan). She has worked in the Anthropology Division of the Peabody Museum at Yale University and as a conservation assistant in the Yale Art Gallery. She has taught in the Honours programme at Brigham Young University since 2008.

Annemarie Stauffer obtained her PhD from the Department of Art History at the University of Bern (Switzerland). She was a fellow of the Swiss Institute in Rome. Her principal field of research is textiles of Classical Antiquity and the Middle Ages, and she is the author of many publications on this topic, including *Die Textilien von Palmyra. Alte und Neue Funde* (2000, with A. Schmidt-Colinet), and *Textilien in der Archäologie* (2012, with J. Kunow). She was involved in a conservation and research project in Palmyra from 1990–1994. In 1994 she took up a professorial post at the University of Applied Sciences in Cologne.

John Peter Wild read Classics at Downing College, Cambridge, wrote a doctoral dissertation in Bonn and Cambridge on provincial-Roman textile manufacture and has lectured in Archaeology at the University of Manchester since 1965. He has studied, and is currently preparing reports for publication on, Roman-period textiles from Vindolanda on Hadrian's Wall and on Berenike and Qasr ibrim in Egypt. He is a Fellow of the Society of Antiquaries of London and Corresponding Member of the German Archaeological Institute.

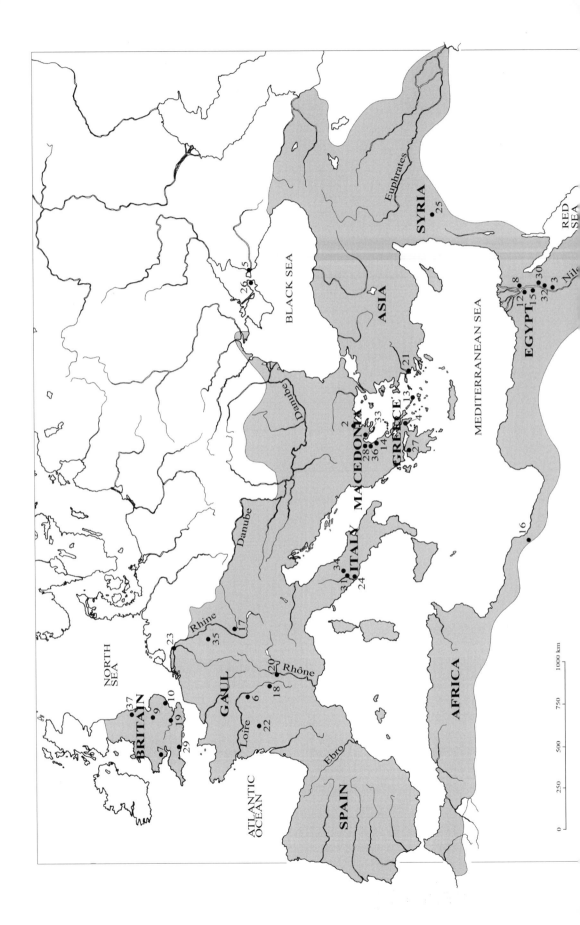

NORTH SEA

ATLANTIC OCEAN

BRITAIN

37

9

10

19

29

GAUL

Loire

6

18

22

35

23

Rhine

17

20

Rhône

SPAIN

Ebro

AFRICA

MEDITERRANEAN SEA

ITALY

24

34

31

MACEDONIA

2

28

36

14

33

GREECE

27

13

4

21

BLACK SEA

Danube

Danube

ASIA

SYRIA

Euphrates

25

EGYPT

12

15

8

32

30

3

Nile

RED SEA

16

5

26

0   250   500   750   1000 km

1	ALEXANDRIA
2	AMPHIPOLIS
3	ANTINOE
4	ATHENS
5	BOLSHAIA BLIZNITSA, S. RUSSIA
6	BOURGES
7	CAERLEON
8	CAIRO
9	CASTOR, PETERBOROUGH
10	COLCHESTER (STANWAY)
11	CORFU
12	DAHSHUR
13	DELOS
14	DION, MACEDONIA
15	FAG EL-GAMUS
16	GHIRZA, LIBYA
17	HOCHDORF, BADEN-WÜRTTEMBERG
18	LES MARTRES-DE-VEYRE
19	LONDON (SPITALFIELDS)

20	LYON
21	MILETUS
22	NAINTRÉ
23	NIJMEGEN
24	OSTIA
25	PALMYRA
26	PANTIKAPAION
27	PATRAS
28	PELLA
29	POUNDBURY, DORSET
30	QARARA
31	ROME
32	SHARUNA
33	THESSALONICA
34	TIVOLI
35	TRIER
36	VERGINA
37	YORK

Preface

Maureen Carroll and John Peter Wild

The papers in this volume stem from an international conference entitled 'Dressing the Dead. Clothing, Textiles and Bodily Adornment from Funerary Contexts in the Graeco-Roman World', held at the University of Sheffield in May 2010, with an additional commissioned paper on textiles in Late Classical and Hellenistic Greece. It was a very interesting and fruitful conference, which pursued a multidisciplinary approach to the role and importance of clothing and textiles in the context of death and burial from the fifth century BC to the fifth century AD, from the Near East, the Mediterranean and Europe.

Investigations of funerary rituals traditionally have focused on grave markers, burial ritual and grave goods and analyses of human skeletal material, while the roles of clothing and textiles in these rituals are less well understood. The conference provided an important opportunity to investigate these issues. This volume reflects that opportunity, and the papers here use a variety of different types of evidence: textiles in graves, such as shrouds or coverlets or the clothing in which the dead were dressed; clothing and textiles associated with death rituals; funerary portraits in sculpture or painting that depict the deceased in order to convey messages about identities; jewellery and dress accessories worn in death and included in the grave; and written documentation on clothing and textiles in funerary contexts.

We would like to thank many people who made the conference and the book possible. Our speakers and authors are to be congratulated on their valuable contributions. Rachel Symonds played an important role as editorial assistant, for which we are grateful. All participants at the conference added to the debates and discussions on dressing the dead. Financial contributions to the conference were provided by the University of Sheffield and the EU-project *DressID*. Jerneja Willmott has demonstrated her skill in archaeological illustration in painstakingly producing images for the book. We should like to thank the museums, universities, archives and other institutions which supplied images or granted permission to publish them. We are also very grateful to John Drinkwater, an excellent colleague and friend, who so admirably summed up the contributions and results of our authors in his introduction. We had the benefit of initial advice and guidance from Alan Sutton, and wish to record our thanks to the editors at Amberley Publishing for facilitating this volume.

Introduction

John F. Drinkwater

Naked we come into the world, but we are extraordinarily unlucky if naked we leave it. As **Wild**, the doyen of ancient textile studies, observes at the start of this volume: 'it is a human reaction to cover [the dead] with textiles'. Bodies prepared for cremation, the collected remains of cremation and interred corpses have commonly been shown respect by being in some way wrapped or clothed. **Wild's** point is here confirmed for the modern world by **Carroll's** reference to contemporary Tanzanian burials, and for the ancient by **Mitschke and Paetz gen. Schieck's** identification of likely Roman plague-burials. All this reminds us of the perennial presence and importance of textiles. As **Andrianou** demonstrates, the ancients, like us, lived in a world made immensely easier by clothes, coverings and draperies in a host of materials, weaves, textures and hues. One thinks, for example, of the scandal caused in Italy in AD 69 by the sight of a Roman general sporting a Gallic tartan cloak (Tacitus, *Histories* 2.20.1). Despite this, ancient textiles have tended to be neglected because, again as **Wild** reminds us, they were highly perishable. They survive best in funerary contexts: the living did not on death lose all right to such amenities. However, as most of the papers presented here demonstrate, their study is complex and demanding.

In the course of archaeological excavation it is difficult simply to recognise finds as textiles. Once recognised, they have to be isolated, stabilised and conserved in a process which nowadays involves a wide range of sophisticated, expensive and preferably non-invasive scientific techniques. After conservation, other scientific methods have to be used to determine the composition of their yarns and threads, how these were woven, and how the resulting fabrics were finished (including their dyeing and decoration). Then follows identification of the garments and draperies into which these cloths were cut and sewn, and what their forms and colours meant. At its most basic, 'meaning' here concerns the categorization of various funerary articles such as winding-cloths, shrouds, and face-coverings, or of normal clothing. It may be expanded to cover the extent to which these garments and the manner of their deposition allow insights into the funerary practices of those involved, and of their relationship to religious beliefs. Still more widely, and extending beyond purely funerary matters, textiles, as clothes and soft-furnishings, may give us a sense of the appearance and fashions of a society, its economic activities, and the attitudes and aspirations of the deceased and of those who disposed of their bodies. Other than through archaeological excavation, textiles are accessible in descriptions found in ancient writings, and as shown on statues, reliefs, mosaics and wall paintings, etc. Though perhaps not quite as acutely as textile remains, these descriptions still offer problems of recognition, stabilisation and conservation. They also have their own difficulties. It is not always easy to say what a description or depiction signifies in terms of textile-history – for example, the precise type of garments and what these are made from. However, information that descriptions and depictions yield may also be used to answer questions concerning funerary rites, religious beliefs, the economy and society. Indeed, perhaps better than even deposed textiles, funerary monuments served the main interest of most parties at the grandest burials which was, again in **Wild's** words, 'to draw attention to the social standing of the deceased' – even in the fleeting moments of display to public gaze of the sculpted and painted contents of **Andrianou's** Greek tombs.

The preceding points are all drawn from papers presented in this volume. The various authors focus on different aspects of each in different ways, depending on their subject matter and what they wish to derive from it. The best-known, because most common, archaeological source of funerary textiles are the mummy-burials of the eastern Mediterranean, here dealt with by **Cortes** and **South**. **Cortes** considers later Roman mummy-textiles found at Dahshur, Egypt. She gives close attention to the details of their production, and presents a magisterial lesson in the handling, conservation and interpretation of ancient textiles and human remains, based on extensive field experience. She outlines the evolution of a set of techniques which combine extensive planning, a rigorous code of practice and the utmost respect for the dead with necessary flexibility and innovation. The material result of her survey is a classification of textiles as shrouds or binding-tapes. In line with her title, **Cortes** constantly stresses the need to consider context: of the relation of finds to each other on the same site, to those of other sites, and to similarly conserved material elsewhere. This, the red-and-white binding-tapes, and her notice of head- and feet-packing, link her paper to that of **South**, on textiles from late-Roman shaft-burials in the Fayum, Egypt. **South** also gives great attention to the techniques of textile production, but her main concern is funerary ritual, and how textiles allow the identification of a new burial practice in the Fayum in the late Roman/Byzantine period. Her mummies are distinctive in having thick textile face-paddings and in having their binding finished off with purpose-made, mostly red-and-white ribbons or tapes. Context is again important. **South** notes that such burials are not unique but, as **Cortes's** finds confirm, extend to the north and south of the Fayum. However, the Fayum discoveries provide the key to recognising and confirming the emergence of a new funerary practice. Funerary textiles usually bring to mind Egypt or Syria, but in the right conditions they can survive elsewhere (as **Wild** reminds us, even Britain), and **Mitschke and Paetz gen. Schieck** describe the discovery, handling and analysis of finds in the city of Rome. They pay particular attention to textiles found in catacomb burials. One set of such burials suggests mass death from a single cause, perhaps plague. It is significant here that, despite the likely grim circumstances of their passing and the haste of the disposal of their bodies, all these people were covered or clothed. The catacomb material was scanty and difficult to work with, but scientific investigation illuminated the nature and quality of the cloths found, and how these were used for funerary purposes. The occurrence of muslin and silk indicates the burial of rich people. In the richest catacomb burial, in a sarcophagus, wrappings were also clearly tailored to fit the corpse. **Mitschke and Paetz gen. Schieck** also consider a mid-first-century urn-cloth – used to wrap cremated remains, but before this employed as a spread on which to prepare the corpse for burning.

The gap between funerary textiles 'as found' and 'as depicted' is bridged by the contributions of **Andrianou, Carroll** and **Harlow**. **Andrianou** demonstrates how literary, archaeological, and especially, visual evidence shows the profusion of high-quality textiles in many forms, in funerary use in late Classical and Hellenistic Greece: dressing the dead and their tombs, or being offered to their spirits. This in turn confirms literary testimony as to how essential textiles – clothing and soft-furnishings (tapestries, mats, and especially, bed-coverings) – now lost, were to the lives of contemporaries. They created the everyday 'comfort' of the title of her article, which the living wished to extend forever to the dead. **Carroll** is likewise interested in textiles both 'found' and 'depicted' as a reflection of the living's concern for the dead. She poses a simple question. Were dead infants given the scant funerary care that Roman tradition and law prescribed? This she answers firmly in the negative, pointing out the direct evidence for respectful child-burials, indicated precisely by the use of textiles: swaddling-clothes for babies and, as for adults, clothes for young children. In this, like **Mitschke and Paetz gen. Schieck**, she notes the occurrence of some very rich burials, with finds of silk. Respect suggests a sense of loss, and Carroll perceives further baring of adult distress – whether for the disappearance of a beloved offspring as an individual or for the family's ruined aspirations for the son or daughter concerned – in tomb-monuments of older children. As in other developed pre-industrial societies, children were valued both for themselves and as an investment in the future. In a similar vein, though focusing on a single sex and a slightly older age-group, **Harlow** notices wealthy imperial-period burials of young women, apparently in their betrothal or wedding dresses, in and around the city of Rome. Though the fabric of these dresses has seldom survived, and where it has survived has been poorly conserved and examined, their function is indicated by other finds, in particular engagement rings and the remains of special hair nets known to be associated with betrothal and marriage. 'Betrothal/wedding' burials are also often found with dolls in their grave goods. **Harlow** suggests that they are the last resting places of girls who had experienced a tragically abbreviated 'life course', dying after betrothal but before they could proceed to become wives and mothers. Their lavish funerals, which centred on a long laying-out, were again, like **Carroll's** child-burials, a means of proclaiming family status. However, they were also a heart-broken admission of a family's blighted hopes – for valuable dynastic alliances thwarted and for grandchildren who could now never be born.

Stauffer concentrates more on textiles 'depicted' than as 'found' in her study of the funerary reliefs and wall-paintings of clan-tombs located around second- and third-century AD Palmyra, Syria. Though not primarily concerned with the actual remains of the deceased, most of which have vanished, she notes that from what remains, it is clear that corpses were mummified but not dressed or provided with textiles as soft-furnishings for their tombs. With regard to depiction, she demonstrates that close examination allows the determination of the general types and styles – Graeco-Roman, Palmyrene and Parthian – of the garments shown, and even of their changing fashions. Again, rare surviving mummy-wrappings, cut from discarded cloaks, etc., confirm that these representations are of everyday garments, not the products of artistic licence. They illustrate what was being worn in high Roman Palmyra, and bring to life the bustling streets of this bustling frontier city, a major conduit of east-west commerce. At first glance, Palmyrene clothing appears to have been anarchically eclectic, a sartorial mish-mash which signified no personal ethnicity or political affiliation. However, **Stauffer** points out that the highest ranking males and females are usually shown only in local dress and that, whatever they wear, their clothes are less decorated than those of the rest. She sees this as confirming the hypothesis that the city's leading, priestly, families provided an important element of cultural continuity and stability in a society constantly exposed to foreign influences. 'Dress as depicted' as a reflection of reaction to changing economic and social circumstances also forms the basis of **Audley-Miller's** examination of Libyan funerary sculpture at Ghirza, Tripolitania. Like other contributors, she sees the clothes of the dead as indicators of status and aspiration in the world of the living. In her study of garments and personal adornment (including hairstyles) she discovers a society in which, like our own, economic and social pressures and demands did not stand still. The early third-century monuments suggest people wanting to be part of the Roman world. Those of the fourth century advertise the arrival of a harsher and more restricted age, one not of imperial globalisation but of local self-help. As Roman power declined, regional 'big men', projecting their power through the adoption of pseudo-military dress, came to the fore.

A number of contributors, such as **Harlow**, **Stauffer** and **Audley-Miller**, closely associate textiles and personal adornment. **Rempel** concentrates on adornment by taking as her subject not so much textiles as decorations attached to textiles and the historical lessons to be drawn from these and other related artefacts. She examines small gold plaques on the costume of a late fourth-century BC priestess of the Bosporan kingdom, buried in a set of rich tombs at Bolshaia Bliznitsa on the Taman peninsula (between the Black Sea and the Sea of Azov). She notes their depiction of Demeter, Persephone and Hercules and links them to an associated tomb-painting of Demeter or Persephone, and to other funerary ceramic objects and jewellery, indicating the worship of these deities. Referring to contemporary economic, political and cultural movements that were bringing the Black Sea communities into increasingly close contact with those of the Aegean, she proposes that in this period the worship of Demeter of Eleusis spread to the Bosporus.

The range and depth of the papers presented here answer many questions but also generate others. For example, since, along with **Stauffer**, many contributors corroborate another of **Wild's** observations – that the ancient dead were usually covered but not clothed – one wonders what lay behind the phenomenon. One can think of good economic reasons for preferring coverings to clothes. Pre-industrial societies were desperately poor compared to industrial, and so disinclined to indulge in the routine squandering of high-grade manufactured articles by, for example, burning or burying them. The dead have to be decently clad, but wrappings are cheaper than clothes, especially if these too can be provided relatively inexpensively. The occurrence of second-hand materials in mummy-burials is not unusual, which underlines the significance of **South's** new, purpose-made tapes. Cremations and inhumations in which premium textiles were effectively lost to society need, therefore, to be taken very seriously. In a world short of 'stuff', this reflects the huge lengths to which a few – not always the richest – were prepared to go to honour the dead and make a claim for the standing of their family. Similarly, one is drawn to wonder why early Roman restrictions on the burial of infants and young children failed. Or rather, given natural, human parental love, which no force on earth could prevent from being expressed as grief on the death of an infant or a child, one wonders why restrictions were instituted in the first place. Was it again a matter of cost? Are we in the presence of a particularly poor pre-industrial society that felt that it could not afford the loss of any wealth – in finished goods or even time – in mourning? Somewhat differently, reference to the preparation of bodies for cremation led me to ask myself why the living bothered to go to such expense. One answer must, again, be that embalming signified wealth and status. But why did the practice begin in the first place? Did it derive, perhaps, from the combination of Mediterranean heat and funerary rituals, which, as in the case of Rome, extended over several days before the final disposal of the corpse?

These are specific questions from specific points made by contributors. There are also, however, more general issues. For example, at the beginning of this introduction I mentioned the possibility that the study of funerary textiles may offer insights into ancient ritual and religious beliefs. A number of contributors strike out in this direction. **Andrianou** hazards a guess that tomb textile patterns could have served as *aides-mémoire* for the souls of the deceased in their dealings with powers beyond the grave. **Rempel** argues that not only did the worship of Demeter of Eleusis spread to the Bosporan kingdom but also that it won such support that local priestess integrated it into their cult of the indigenous Great Goddesses of the Steppe. **Harlow's** eerie but pathetic junior 'Miss Havishams', long in advance of *Great Expectations*, amount to a new funerary ritual at the centre of the Empire. **South**, against the background of the strong evangelisation of late Antique Egypt, proposes that new funerary practices may have developed in order to express Christian symbolism or to establish a Christian identity. But none of this is straightforward. **Andrianou** is diffident in what she says. **Rempel** allows that the Demeter artefacts are very much in the minority; that there are many signs in the Bosporan kingdom of religious development from indigenous traditions; that the plaques, etc., may just be local use of Greek imagery; and generally, that integration, though possible, is not proven. Similarly, **Harlow** concedes that the ritual significance of her graves as those of 'failed' brides is possible but 'not unproblematic'. Finally **South** concedes that context makes it more likely that what we see is just a development in funerary fashion with its roots in the pre-Christian era: so again, custom and usage, not religious belief. Other contributors, even **Mitschke and Paetz gen. Schieck** whose title promises some investigation of ritual, steer clear of ritual and religion. This reminds us how difficult it is, without supplementary explanatory text, to use funerary textiles and funerary archaeology generally, to reconstruct funerary ritual and religious belief. One suspects that archaeologists of the very distant future would, lacking such text, be baffled by the cope, mitre and pectoral cross of a Christian bishop, and even more so by **Carroll's** Tanzanian wrapping. As I have done in other contexts, I cite a fascinating article by John Morris (in B. Levick (ed.), *The Ancient Historian and his Materials. Essays in Honour of C. E. Stevens*, 1975). Having described the all-pervasive but sedulously secretive worship of the goddess Kali in contemporary central India, Morris continues (p.240):

> The moral of the unadvertised worship of Kali is twofold. It illustrates the capacity of a dominant culture and religion to absorb, countenance and contain alien practices ... But it also warns of the important elements in the life and thought of a simple rural economy that archaeological enquiry cannot hope to discover; for the flimsy shrines of Kali rarely contain anything more durable than a rag doll image, coloured black or blue, and can leave no more permanent traces than cremation on a low river bank.

On the other hand, what funerary textile studies are peculiarly able to determine, can tell us much of importance about ancient societies. The technical investigation of the plethora of threads, weaves, clothing-types, etc., points at the very high level of expertise and numbers of people involved in the ancient textile industry, and confirms the great economic importance of cloth-production in the Graeco-Roman world, noted by **Andrianou**. Such production may even have spread to Christian monasteries in Egypt, involved in making new mummy-tapes. Funerary textile studies also vividly demonstrate how closely the Graeco-Roman economy and society were linked to the wider world, in a web of commerce and technology-transfer. Muslin found in Roman catacombs appears to have been an Egyptian copy of Indian originals (**Mitschke and Paetz gen. Schieck**); and silk, woven in Palmyra or Gaul (**Carroll**), was of course imported from China.

A final thought returns us to the start of this introduction. Most dead were equal in being decently covered. In the end however, all contributors suggest an underlying inequality. The deceased rich had a much better chance of survival – of their remains or, in the case of monuments, of their memories – than the deceased poor. And so one wonders how many of the deceased poor were, in dire emergency, such as chronic plague or warfare, tossed naked into a pit.

The textile archaeology of Roman burials: Eyes Wide Shut

John Peter Wild

The excavation of a Roman cemetery presents the archaeologist with a series of particular challenges: the list seems to lengthen by the year, not least in response to today's heightened sensitivities with regard to the treatment of the dead. Some problems, however, are of longer standing. In situations where textile remains might be, or might have been, present, Roman archaeologists seem too often to suffer from a form of myopia, not contracted from leading lights in other periods (Walton Rogers 2007; Stutz 2003, 295–304). It is symptomatic perhaps that in the archaeological literature the expression 'unaccompanied burial' regularly crops up – that is, a grave containing no readily recognisable grave goods, e.g. pottery, glass vessels or metalwork. But we know from our own experience that even in disaster situations – like the 2010 earthquake in Haiti – the dead are rarely 'unaccompanied', it is a human reaction to cover them with textiles. The archaeologically attested burial of naked bodies can be regarded as a deliberate ritual act, as in the case of the North European bog-bodies, like Lindow Man (Stead *et al.* 1986; Turner, Scaife 1995; Joy 2009). So, is the excavator of 'unaccompanied burials' missing something?

Adjacent to the small Roman town of Ashton in Northamptonshire, a 'managed' inhumation cemetery of some 200 graves was excavated in 1983 in advance of road building (Frere 1984, 301 fig. 17; Frere 1985, 288; Dix 1984, 26–27; Upex 2008, 82, col.pl. 22). Most were at first sight empty, apart from the skeleton. The grave in Fig. 1, for example, had a stone revetment, possibly once retained by planking. There were no grave goods, but the attitude of the skeleton, its arms crossed, suggests that it was originally confined in a textile wrapping. How should that be visualised? How can one record a negative? Therein lies a problem.

Decaying organic materials have a better chance of being recognised and understood in an enclosed context, such as in the late fourth-century lead coffin found in 1998 within a stone sarcophagus at Spitalfields, London (Thomas 1999; Wild, forthcoming). Thanks to the persistence of a conservator, who had noted the glint of gold thread in the sludge on the bottom of the inner coffin, the contents were saved at the eleventh hour and examined in detail in the laboratory: not just gold, but damask silk was eventually identified.

By contrast, as is well known, in the Roman-period cemeteries on the desert fringes of the Nile Valley, there is far better preservation of textile material. There, the problem is one of inadequate recording by the excavator rather than lack of imagination. Albert Gayet is pilloried for his efforts at Antinoe a century ago (Calament 2005, 163–189, figs16a, 18a, 18b; Nauerth 2006), and he certainly had a flare for publicity, but in terms of recording and publication he was not so much worse than his contemporaries.

Fig. 1. Inhumation burial in the
late Roman cemetery at Ashton,
Oundle, Northamptonshire
(photo by J. P .Wild).

There is still room for improvement in the field of Egyptology. The fate of the Roman-period mummy no. 1770 in Manchester Museum has not been a happy one. In 1975 her wrappings were unceremoniously hacked off, without any archaeological three-dimensional recording, in pursuit of other lines of scientific enquiry. Making sense of the original textiles, including parts of a tunic, has been extremely difficult (David 1979).

It is easy to be critical. Let me now try to be more constructive, and turn to some of the textile situations which a rather less myopic archaeologist might be asked to bear in mind while digging.

I will look first at the practice of cremation burial, which is of more concern in the western Roman provinces, where it has a long prehistory (Philpott 1991, 8, 217–222), and then at inhumation burial, which is empire-wide and correspondingly multifarious in character.

Burial practice was governed by locally valid cultural constraints. At each funerary event there were arguably three principal interested parties: the burial subject (the deceased), the burial agents (the family, with perhaps a master of religious ceremony) and the burial observers (the community). Their common interest was to draw attention to the social standing of the deceased, and that could be achieved by the conspicuously high quality of the grave goods, among them textiles, deposited with the dead.

In the funerary rite of cremation there were two opportunities for the introduction of textiles into the chain of events. Initially, the body of the deceased on the bier and on the pyre would be clad and wrapped in textiles. Later, after the heat of the pyre had died down, the larger cremated bone fragments would be gathered from the ashes for interment, either directly into a pottery or glass vessel or into a cloth or bag (Cool 2004, 444; Gleba 2008, 87–88), which might or might not be put into another container. A piece of linen tabby from one such bag, for example, preserved by the lead salts leaching from the unusual lead canister in which it was found, came from an early second-century grave near the legionary fortress at Caerleon in South Wales (Wheeler 1929; Boon 1959).

In more elaborate chamber tombs, all manner of further textile items might be added alongside the familiar grave goods made of inorganic materials.

The cremation practices of the late Iron Age and early Roman periods in the western Roman provinces were particularly complex (Pearce 1998; Niblett 2004; Philpott 1991, 217–222; Heinzelmann *et al.* 2001; Koster 2010). Textiles play a prominent role. An aristocratic grave of about AD 40–50 at Stanway near Colchester, arguably the burial of a druid, can serve as an example (Crummy *et al.* 2007, 201–253). The rectangular mortuary pit held an array of grave goods including a gaming board (on which the cremated bone had been placed), a set of surgical instruments, a set of divining rods and feasting paraphernalia. A wool cloak in fine diamond twill, with a suggestion of purple, seems to have been spread below the instruments, rods and gaming board, and folded back over them (Wild 2007, 347–348; Crummy *et al.* 2007, figs 102, 103). That at least appears to be a plausible interpretation of the tiny scraps of fabric adhering to the metal objects, but one has to remember, as a possible alternative, the earlier Iron Age custom of wrapping each object separately in cloth before burial. Almost everything in the princely burial chamber at Hochdorf in Baden-Württemberg was wrapped in cloth (Banck-Burgess 1999, 21–28), and there are signs of the practice in Britain too (Burns *et al.* 1996, 109, figs 75a, 75b).

On the actual funeral pyre of course, the clothing and textiles on or over the deceased will go up in smoke (Cool 2004, 438–440). Indeed, in the later second century an anonymous wealthy Lingonian in Gaul made explicit provision for that in his will: 'I want all my gear to be cremated with me ... and the textiles in weft-faced compound tabby (*polymita*) and tapestry (*plumaria*) ... that I have left behind' (Le Bohec 2003, 353–356; on dating, see Le Bohec 1991, 44–46).

If the tapestry incorporated gold thread, however, something might survive the flames. That was the case at Nijmegen in the Netherlands just after AD 100 when a prominent local lady was cremated with a textile that incorporated gold thread, perhaps a garment, or more likely a soft furnishing (Koster 2010, 41–45 (grave 9); Wild 2010). Tiny fragments of gold clearly affected by the heat were found among the cremated bone in a glass bottle (Koster 2010, 44, pl. 37). The thread had been Z-twisted from a gold ribbon only 0.18 mm wide. Scanning electron micrographs (Fig. 2) show traces of the original core thread (possibly silk) adhering to the inside of the spiral (Cooke, Lomas 2010; Wild 2010).

Inhumation burial, practically universal across the Empire by the end of the third century, is relatively kind to organic materials, but presents the archaeologist with greater challenges. I shall do no more here than present a check-list of possible scenarios. Inevitably one turns to the Syrian deserts and the Nile Valley for the most satisfactory surviving evidence, though one has to be aware of their regional idiosyncrasies.

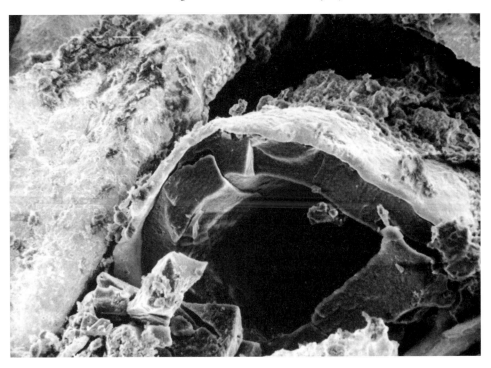

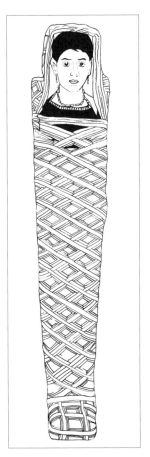

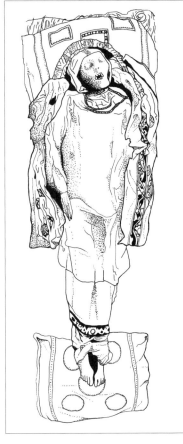

Above: Fig. 2. Scanning electron microscope image of twisted gold ribbon from cremation grave 9 at Nijmegen West (photo by W. D. Cooke).

Far left: Fig. 3. Mummy of young woman, probably from Antinoe, now in Musée du Louvre, Paris (inv. no. AF 6882), showing mitred wrapping with linen strips (drawing by Priscilla Wild).

Left: Fig. 4. Clothed body of 'Euphemia' from Antinoe, now in Musées Royaux d'Art et d'Histoire, Brussels (inv. no. E.1045) (drawing by Priscilla Wild).

At one end of the spectrum stands the wrapped mummy (Fig. 3): at the other the corpse dressed in Sunday-best clothes (Fig. 4) – Euphemia from Antinoe in this case (Calament 2005, 123, 547, 364–365), who has recently been deconstructed by Mark Van Strydonck and his colleagues (Van Strydonck *et al.* 2011).

Mitred wrapping of the mummified body (eg Walker, Bierbrier 1997, 38 n. 11, 107, no. 99) was a job for professionals (Fig. 3): the cost to the family for new and recycled linen was considerable (Montserrat 1997, 37, 41; Wessely 1922, no. 56). The mummy might be covered with a painted linen shroud (Walker, Bierbrier 1997, 120), itself bound into position (Walker, Bierbrier 1997, 149). But the outward form might be built on a host of textile oddments inside. The iconoclastic bishop Epiphanius on his travels in Syria took a dislike to a dyed and painted curtain (perhaps like the Artemis hanging in Riggisberg) (Schrenk 2004, 82–88): 'I tore it and recommended the custodians of the place to wrap the body of some poor man in it and bury him' (Epiphanius, *Epist. ad Johann. Episc. Hierosol.* IX; Migne 1864, 390). The cross-binding is still visible on a piece of curtain in Cairo (De Moor, Fluck 2009, 104, fig. 6) and there are parallels elsewhere (De Moor, Fluck 2009, 91, fig. 2). Large pieces of sailcloth complete with their original reinforcing strips and even an attached brailing ring were used to pad out a late Ptolemaic mummy, now in Lyon (Wild 2001, 215–217).

Bodies wrapped in linen cloth, bound overall with tape (often red or red-striped) or secured with rope like a parcel, were often buried without any further protection and seem to be a feature of late antiquity (Huber 2006, 60 fig. 2; Calament 2005, 272). Schematised binding with rope is shown in a delightful sketch from the catacomb of Commodilla in Rome: the grave-digger with his miner's pick and hanging lamp on a chain stands guard over a trussed corpse (Nicolai *et al.* 1999, 160, pl. 164). Lazarus, too, is conventionally depicted in early Christian art as a neat parcel (Beckwith 1958, pl. I).

The quality of the wrappings, even in secondary use, seems to have mattered. The wealthier Palmyrenes opted for torn-up silk (Schmidt-Colinet *et al.* 2000, 5, 55–57). The desiccated body of Bishop Paulinus, transported back to Trier in AD 386 (Boppert 1990, 238), was wrapped in silk, and an outer layer of silk is claimed to have been wrapped around his cedarwood coffin, converting the whole assemblage into a relic (Schaaffhausen 1884, 238–242; Schneider 1884, 177–178; Dreyspring, Schrenk 2007).

At a number of urban centres across the Empire, bodies were sealed in plaster, usually within a coffin. The corpse was first wrapped in recycled linen of various sorts, without additional binding. An example is the burial of a mother and child at York, wrapped together in household towelling (Henshall 1962, 108–109, pl. 33; see Carroll, this volume and pl. 21). Grave 99 at Poundbury near Dorchester shows similar negative impressions in the plaster – but the occupant of this sarcophagus had his feet covered with some fabric that contained gold thread (Crowfoot 1993).

In contrast to such mortuary packaging, it became increasingly common in later Roman times to inter the dead fully clothed (Fig. 4). Actually, to be more precise, the principal garments were mostly spread out *over* the body, followed sometimes by the entire contents of their clothes chest. How often the corpse was enclosed *within* a garment is a moot point that requires further investigation.

Tomb D in a small cemetery with exceptionally well-preserved organic remains at Les Martres-de-Veyre in Central Gaul, dating to about AD 180, held a pinewood coffin containing the remains of a girl dressed in a breast-band or girdle, a wide fitting Gallic coat of wool tabby and a pair of twill stockings (Audollent 1923, 13–14, 27, 44–46; Romeuf 2001, 11; Van Driel-Murray 1999). There was a basket of fruit, but no extra textiles. The precise depositional facts, alas, were not recorded. A much more complex situation obtains for the rich coffined burials from a mortuary chapel attached to St Maximinus' church in Trier (Reifarth 2005). The deceased were members of the imperial court circle of late Roman Trier. The burials are being studied by Nicole Reifarth using 3D scans, high-resolution digital mapping and a video microscope, to peer into the recesses of the encrusted remains – all non-invasive techniques (Reifarth *et al.* 2006; Reifarth 2007; Dreyspring 2002). In grave 279, for instance, the outline of the body is visible, the collapsed skull and a scatter of pine shavings intended to soak up bodily fluids. On top of the body lay a violet-coloured undergarment and above that, a red silk damask tunic. A wool blanket had been spread over everything.

The cemeteries of Antinoe in Gayet's brief accounts reveal great variety in burial practice, which he struggled to classify. In many cases, the deceased were interred in their own clothes, supplemented sometimes by the deposition of extra garments and/or additional shroud-like wrappings and bindings (Calament 2005, 276, 278). Gayet was fascinated by questions of identity, and the origin of a group of apparently 'intrusive' burials with atypical dress forms (Calament 2005, 280–293).

Textile accessories for the comfort of the deceased are another possible feature to be aware of. Cushions are currently exhibited with Euphemia in Brussels (Fig. 4). Heads might rest on pillows or cushions (Schieck 2009), and the body might be laid on a pile mat or rush mat (Fujii *et al.* 1989, 128; Ogawa, Naruse 1976, 127, 198–199) or a blanket (Reifarth 2005, Grab 249).

To round off this brief tour of the horizon, I turn to a sarcophagus uncovered in a field at Castor near Peterborough, Cambridgeshire in 1968. It was my first textile test as an excavator. The sarcophagus had already lost part of its lid to the plough. The content was at first sight uninspiring: it was 'empty', apart from a thick layer of mud at the bottom containing a few bone fragments. With some care we removed the mud, recording and retaining any items obvious to the naked eye (pl. 1). With hindsight – and techniques have moved on vastly in the past forty years – that was a mistake. We were simply jettisoning vital evidence along with the mud. But we found *in situ* a pair of gold earrings, a silver fibula, sundry other grave goods and a copper-alloy bangle of twisted wire, still around what was left of the lady's right arm. Attached to it were metal-replaced remains of a linen textile (pl. 2), which I only noticed because I was half-expecting it. I thought at the time that it might represent clothing, but it could equally be the remains of cloth wrapping or binding – in fact there are now so many other possibilities to consider that I am almost glad that, so far, the grave remains unpublished!

Acknowledgements

I am grateful to Melanie Giles for the reference to Stutz 2003 and to Christopher Sparey-Green for information about the Poundbury cemetery.

J.P.Wild.58@cantab.net

Bibliography

Audollent 1923: A. Audollent, *Les Tombes gallo-romaines à Inhumation des Martres-de-Veyre, Puy-de-Dôme*, Mémoires présentés à l'Académie des Sciences et Belles-Lettres XIII, Paris

Banck-Burgess 1999: J. Banck-Burgess, *Hochdorf IV: Die Textilfunde aus dem späthallstattzeitlichen Fürstengrab von Eberdingen-Hochdorf (Kreis Ludwigsburg) und weitere Grabtextilien aus hallstatt- und latènezeitlichen Kulturgruppen*, Stuttgart

Beckwith 1958: J. Beckwith, *The Andrews Diptych*, London

Boon 1959: G. C. Boon, 'Cloth from the Caerleon "pipe-burial", 1927', *Antiquaries Journal* XXXIX, 288–289

Boppert 1990: W. Boppert, 'Die Anfänge des Christentums', in H. Cüppers (ed.), *Die Römer im Rheinland-Pfalz*, Stuttgart, 233–257

Burns *et al.* 1996: B. Burns, B. W. Cunliffe, H. Sebire, *Guernsey: An Island Community of the Atlantic Iron Age*, Oxford University Committee for Archaeology Monograph 43, Oxford

Calament 2005: F. Calament, *La Révélation d'Antinoé par Albert Gayet. Histoire, Archéologie, Muséographie*, Institut français d'Archéologie Orientale, Bibliothèque d'Études coptes 18, 1–2, Cairo

Carroll 2006: M. Carroll, *Spirits of the Dead. Roman Funerary Commemoration in Western Europe*, Oxford

Cooke, Lomas 2010: B. Cooke, B. Lomas, 'Examination of the gold thread', in A. Koster, *Het Grafveld van Noviomagus en de rijke Graven van de stedelijke Elite*, Nijmegen, 191, figs 115–120

Cool 2004: H. E. M. Cool, *The Roman Cemetery at Brougham, Cumbria*, Britannia Monograph 21, London

Crowfoot 1993: E. Crowfoot, 'Textiles and gold thread', in D. E. Farwell, T. I. Molleson, *Poundbury: Volume 2: The Cemeteries*, Dorchester, 111–113

Crummy *et al.* 2007: P. Crummy, S. Benfield, N. Crummy, V. Rigby, D. Shimmin, *Stanway; An Elite Burial Site at Camulodunum*, Britannia Monograph 24, London

David 1979: A. R. David (ed.), *Manchester Museum Mummy Project: Multidisciplinary Research on Ancient Egyptian Mummified Remains*, Manchester

De Moor, Fluck 2009: A. De Moor, C. Fluck (eds), *Clothing the House. Furnishing Textiles in the 1st Millennium AD from Egypt and Neighbouring Countries: Proceedings of the 5th Conference of the Research Group 'Textiles from the Nile Valley', Antwerp, 6–7 October 2007*, Tielt

De Moor, Fluck 2011: A. De Moor, C. Fluck (eds), *Proceedings of the 6th Conference of the Research Group 'Textiles from the Nile Valley', Antwerp, 1–3 October 2009*, Tielt

Dix 1984: B. Dix, 'Ashton Roman town: archaeological rescue excavation', *Durobrivae: A Review of Nene Valley Archaeology* 9, 26–27

Dreyspring 2002: B. Dreyspring, 'Textiltechnische Untersuchungen an einer frühchristlichen Sarkophagbestattung aus St Maximin in Trier', in S. Martius, S. Russ (eds), *Historische Textilien: Beiträge zur Erhaltung und Erforschung*, Nürnberg, 9–24

Dreyspring, Schrenk 2007: B. Dreyspring, S. Schrenk, 'Seidenfragment mit Spuren einer Stickerei aus dem Paulinusgrab', in A. Demandt, J. Engemann (eds), *Konstantin der Grosse*, Mainz, 416–417, CD 11.4.34

Frere 1984: S. S. Frere, 'Roman Britain in 1983', *Britannia* XV, 266–322

Frere 1985: S. S. Frere, 'Roman Britain in 1984', *Britannia* XVI, 252–332

Fujii *et al.* 1989: H. Fujii, K. Sakamoto, M. Ichihashi, 'Textiles from At-Tar caves Part 1: Cave 12, Hill C', *Al-Rāfidān* X, 109–166

Gleba 2008: M. Gleba, *Textile Production in Pre-Roman Italy*, Ancient Textiles Series 4, Oxford

Heinzelmann *et al.* 2001: M. Heinzelmann, J. Ortalli, P. Fasold, M. Witteyer, *Römischer Bestattungsbrauch und Beigabensitten in Rom, Norditalien und den Nordwestprovinzen von der späten Republik bis in die Kaiserzeit*, Wiesbaden

Henshall 1962: A. S. Henshall, 'Cloths in burials with gypsum', in Royal Commission on Historical Monuments, *An Inventory of the Historical Monuments in the City of York I: Eburacum, Roman York*, London, 108–109

Huber 2006: B. Huber, 'Al-Kom al-Ahmar/Sharūna: different archaeological contexts – different textiles?', in Schrenk 2006, 57–68

Joy 2009: J. Joy, *Lindow Man*, London

Koster 2010: A. Koster, *Het Grafveld van Noviomagus en de rijke Graven van de stedelijke Elite*, Nijmegen

Le Bohec 1991: Y. Le Bohec, *Le Testament du Lingon*, Collection du Centre d'Études Romaines et Gallo-romaines NS 9, Lyon

Le Bohec 2003: Y. Le Bohec, *Inscriptions de la Cité des Lingons*, Paris

Migne 1864: J.-P. Migne, *Patrologiae Cursus Completus. Series Graeca* XLIII, Paris

Montserrat 1997: D. Montserrat, 'Deaths and funerals in the Roman Fayum', in M. L. Bierbrier (ed.), *Portraits and Masks: Burial Customs in Roman Egypt*, London, 33–44

Nauerth 2006: C. Nauerth, 'Opportunities and limits of post-evaluation: Qarārah and al-Hibe', in S. Schrenk 2006, 43–55

Niblett 2004: R. Niblett, 'The native elite and their funerary practices', in M. Todd (ed.), *A Companion to Roman Britain*, Oxford, 30–41

Nicolai *et al.* 1999: V. Fiocchi Nicolai, F. Bisconti, D. Mazzoleni, *Les Catacombes chrètiennes de Rome: Origine, Développement, Décor, Inscriptions*, Turnhout

Ogawa, Naruse 1976: Y. Ogawa, N. Naruse, 'Textiles and allied materials', in H. Fujii (ed.), *At-Tar I: Excavations in Iraq, 1971–1974*, Tokyo, 120–201

Pearce 1998: J. Pearce, 'From death to deposition: the sequence of ritual in cremation burials of the Roman period', in C. Forcey, J. Hawthorne, R. Witcher (eds), *TRAC 97. Proceedings of the 7th Annual Theoretical Roman Archaeology Conference*, Oxford, 99–111

Philpott 1991: R. Philpott, *Burial Practices in Roman Britain: A Survey of Grave Treatment and Furnishing AD 43 – 410*, British Archaeological Report 219, Oxford

Reifarth 2005: N. Reifarth, *Die spätantiken Sarkophagbestattungen aus St Maximin in Trier: Denkmalpflegerische Problematik – exemplarische Konzepte zur wissenschaftlichen Auswertung – Überlegungen zum künftigen Umgang*, MA dissertation, Bamberg

Reifarth 2007: N. Reifarth, 'Late antique sarcophagus burials from St Maximin in Trier: current examination', *Archaeological Textiles Newsletter* 45, 15–20

Reifarth *et al.* 2006: N. Reifarth, W.-R. Teegen, N. Boenke, J. Wiethold, 'Das spätantike Grab 279 aus St Maximin in Trier', *Funde und Ausgrabungen im Bezirk Trier* 38, 58–70

Romeuf 2001: A.-M. Romeuf, *Les Martes-de-Veyre (Puy-de-Dôme): le Quartier Artisanal gallo-romain*, Deuxième Cahier du Centre Archéologique de Lezoux, Lezoux

Schaaffhausen 1884: H. Schaaffhausen, 'Der Sarg des heil. Paulinus in Trier', *Jahrbuch des Vereins von Alterthumsfreunden im Rheinland* 77, 238–242

Schieck 2009: A. Schieck, 'Late Roman cushions and the principles of their decoration', in De Moor, Fluck 2011, 115–132

Schmidt-Colinet *et al.* 2000: A. Schmidt-Colinet, A. Stauffer, K. al-Asᶜad, *Die Textilien aus Palmyra: Neue und Alte Funde*, Mainz

Schneider 1884: F. Schneider, 'Die Krypta von St Paulin zu Trier', *Jahrbuch des Vereins von Alterthumsfreunden im Rheinland* 78, 167–198

Schrenk 2004: S. Schrenk, *Textilien des Mittelmeerraumes aus spätantiker bis frühislamischer Zeit*, Riggisberg

Schrenk 2006: S. Schrenk (ed.), *Textiles in situ: Their Find Spots in Egypt and Neighbouring Countries in the First Millennium CE*, Riggisberger Bericht 13, Riggisberg

Stead *et al.* 1986: I. M. Stead, J. B. Bourke, D. R. Brothwell (eds), *Lindow Man: The Body in the Bog*, London

Stutz 2003: L. Nillson Stutz, *Embodied Rituals and Ritualized Bodies: Tracing Ritual Practices in Late Mesolithic Burials*, Lund

Thomas 1999: C. Thomas, 'Laid to rest on a pillow of bay leaves', *British Archaeology* 50, 8–11

Turner, Scaife 1995: R. C. Turner, R. G. Scaife (eds), *Bog Bodies: New Discoveries and New Perspectives*, London

Upex 2008; S. G. Upex, *The Romans in the East of England: Settlement and Landscape in the Lower Nene Valley*, Stroud

Van Driel-Murray 1999: C. Van Driel-Murray, 'A set of Roman clothing from Les Martres-de-Veyre, France', *Archaeological Textiles Newsletter* 28, 11–15

Van Strydonck *et al.* 2011: M. Van Strydonck, M. Bondin, I. Vanden Berghe, K. Cuintelier, 'The so-called embroideress Euphemia', in A. De Moor, C. Fluck 2011, forthcoming

Walker, Bierbrier 1997; S. Walker, M. Bierbrier, *Ancient Faces: Mummy Portraits from Roman Egypt*, London

Walton Rogers 2007; P. Walton Rogers, *Cloth and Clothing in Early Anglo-Saxon England AD 450–700*, Council for British Archaeology Research Report 145, York

Wessely 1922: C. Wessely (ed.), *Studien zur Paläographie und Papyrusurkunde* XXII, Leipzig

Wheeler 1929: R. E. M. Wheeler, 'A Roman pipe burial from Caerleon, Monmouthshire', *Antiquaries Journal* IX, 1–7

Wild, Wild 2001: F. C. Wild, J. P. Wild, 'Sails from the Roman port at Berenike, Egypt', *The International Journal of Nautical Archaeology* 30 (2), 211–220

Wild 2007: J. P. Wild, 'Textiles', in Crummy *et al.* 2007, 347–350

Wild 2010: J. P. Wild, 'The gold thread', in Koster 2010, 192–194

Wild, forthcoming: J. P. Wild, 'The textiles', in C. Thomas, *Report on Excavation of a Cemetery at Spitalfields, London*, forthcoming

Eleusinian adornment?
Demeter and the Bolshaia Bliznitsa burials

Jane Rempel

When the Bolshaia Bliznitsa burial mound, located on the Taman peninsula in southern Russia, was excavated in the 1860s, archaeologists uncovered several stone-built chambers containing lavish burials, all dating to the second half of the fourth century BC. In one of the chambers, the corbelled ceiling was decorated with a painting of a wreathed woman (Fig. 1) – a discovery which led the chief investigator, Stefani, to connect the burials with the worship of the Greek goddess Demeter and more specifically with Demeter as she was worshipped by the mystery cult of Eleusis in Attica.

Stefani (1865) and subsequent scholars (e.g. Minns 1913, 423, 619; Artamonov 1969, 74; Jacobson 1995, 180) have argued for a connection between the Bolshaia Bliznitsa burials and Eleusinian Demeter, based on the funerary adornment of the deceased as well as the painting described above. More recently however, scholarly opinion has accepted that – given that the nature of some of the grave goods, including horse harnesses and clothing plaques – the people buried there were more likely to have been members of a non-Greek community, and that the goddess worshipped there was connected with the Great Goddess of the Steppe, who had been syncretised with a Greek goddess in some way (see Ustinova 1999, 57 for a summary of opinion). One of the most recent discussions of these burials suggests that they are most likely connected with Aphrodite Ourania, whose cult was very popular in the Bosporan state and who was most often syncretised with the Great Goddess of the Steppe (Ustinova 1999, 57).

While these more recent investigations are certainly right to stress the local, non-Greek features of burial and ritual in the Bolshaia Bliznitsa burials, the Eleusinian connection that was originally proposed demands more detailed consideration. There is little evidence for the syncretisation of Demeter with the Great Goddess in the fourth century BC, and aspects of the funerary adornment of the deceased in the Bolshaia Bliznitsa mound seem to reflect specifically Eleusinian imagery. While the Eleusinian mysteries were intimately connected to Eleusis in Attica, by the fourth century BC its influence was beginning to spread more widely throughout the Greek world and some new Eleusinian-type cults were set up in Asia Minor, Egypt and, as will be discussed below, in the Bosporan kingdom. After introducing the Bolshaia Bliznitsa burials, this paper examines the nature of the Eleusinian mysteries and their dissemination throughout the Greek world. It then considers in detail the potentially Eleusinian imagery in the burials and seeks to understand the nature of these images in a wider Bosporan context.

Fig. 1. Image of the goddess depicted on the ceiling of chamber that contained the first female burial (after Artamonov 1969, plate XVI).

Bolshaia Bliznitsa and the Bosporan kingdom

Bolshaia Bliznitsa is one of approximately fifteen monumental burial mounds that were constructed in the fourth and early third centuries BC in order to house the burials of elite members of society, in a state known as the Bosporan kingdom (Fig. 2). The Bosporan state was formed in the second half of the fifth century BC, and included not only the Greek colonies on either side of the mouth of the Sea of Azov but also the local populations living in the area – most notably, the Sindians and Maeotians in the eastern part of the kingdom, who were incorporated into the state by the late fifth/early fourth century BC (Fig. 3). The Bosporan kingdom was ruled by the Spartokid dynasty until the end of the second century BC. It was these Spartokid rulers and their court who established the fashion for commemorating their dead with monumental burial mounds covering stone-built corbelled chambers; these mounds were located in the vicinity of Pantikapaion, the capital city of the state. The Bolshaia Bliznitsa mound, located on the other side of the Strait of Kerch, approximately eight kilometres to the south-southwest of Phanagoria (the second most important city) represents a particular iteration of this tradition. While it conforms to the construction and size of the Spartokid 'royal' burials, it also contains elements of burial ritual that connect it to local Sindian traditions, such as the inclusion of horse-harnesses and clothing plaques in the grave goods.

Bolshaia Bliznitsa was one of the few monumental burial mounds in the Bosporan kingdom that had not been looted before archaeologists investigated, and for that reason alone it is an important archaeological document. But in addition to the constellation of burials within the mound and the wealth of grave goods associated with them, the prominence of women in the burials and their seeming connection with a goddess cult mark them out. The mound probably originally contained six individual burials: three in stone vaulted chambers, two in stone chests, and a cremation burial. All burials date to the second half of the fourth century BC, with the cremation the latest (dated by a coin of Alexander the Great). The middle stone chamber was looted in antiquity, but most famously this chamber was decorated with a portrait of a goddess on

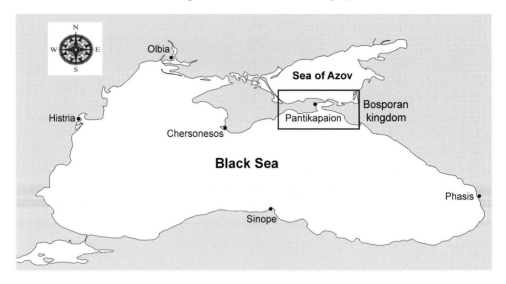

Fig. 2. Map of the Black Sea and the Sea of Azov, with key Greek colonies and the territory of the Bosporan kingdom indicated (map by J. Rempel).

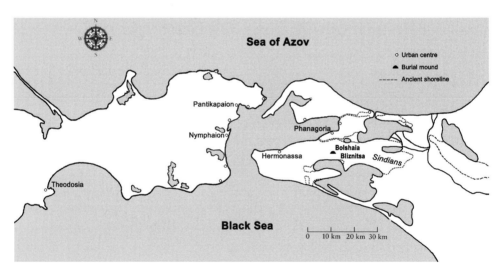

Fig 3. Map of the territory of the Bosporan kingdom, with the location of main cities, the Bolshaia Bliznitsa mound and Sindian territory indicated (map by J. Rempel).

the ceiling, holding yellow lilies in her hand and wearing a wreath of flowers (Fig. 1). In another of the stone chambers was the inhumation burial of a woman in a cypress-inlaid sarcophagus; her dress was ornamented with gold plaques and she was adorned with a set of intricate gold jewellery that included a *kalathos* (high headdress) with pendants (Fig. 4). This *kalathos* was decorated with a scene of barbarians battling griffins, while the highly ornamented temple pendants depicted Thetis, riding a hippocampus, bringing armour to Achilles. The rest of the jewellery set consisted of a strap and pendant necklace, a bracelet, and two rings. A second set of jewellery, this one less ornate, and with a more simple *stlengis* (a low-slung head band that replicated hair), was included in her sarcophagus. Other finds in her chamber include the harnesses of four horses, a bronze mirror case, and a red-figure vase (Minns 1913, 426; Artamonov 1969, 75). A second woman was interred in a stone chest, and although her burial was not as lavish as the first, she too was buried with two sets of jewellery, similar to those of the first woman; one including a simpler *kalathos*, and the other a *stlengis* (Fig. 5). Also notable amongst her collection of jewellery was an elaborate gold necklet, as well as miniature vessels and twenty-six terracotta figurines (Minns 1913, 428; Ustinova 1999, 56). A third woman was interred in another stone chest, and she was buried wearing a gold wreath and other jewellery. The final stone chamber held the burial of a man in an ivory-inlaid sarcophagus; he was buried with a gilded bronze helmet, other armour and weapons, a gold laurel-wreath, and two gold rings. All of the inhumation burials contained many small gold plaques, which would have decorated clothing and headdresses (Minns 1913, 429; Artamonov 1969, 75). In addition to the burials, the Bolshaia Bliznitsa mound preserved evidence of burial ritual, including traces of four funeral feasts laid out on special mud-brick platforms and in two cases, low altars (Artamonov 1969, 76; Ustinova 1999, 56).

Right: Fig. 4. Illustration of a portion of the gold *kalathos* (height 10 cm; depth 26 cm), depicting a barbarian fighting griffins, and one of the two temple pendants (height 15.5 cm), depicting Thetis on a hippocampus, from the first female burial (after Minns 1913, Figs 315, 316).

Below: Fig. 5. Gold *stlengis* (30 cm long) and attached ear pieces from the second female burial (after Minns 1913, fig. 319).

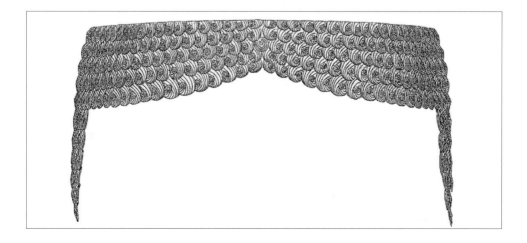

In addition to the prominent painting of a Demeter-like goddess in the central chamber, some of the gold plaques found depict Demeter and her daughter Persephone, while other connections to Demeter, and specifically her mystery cult at Eleusis, have been read in some of the other jewellery and terracotta figures. This evidence, which will be described in more detail below, combined with the 'ritual' nature of the jewellery sets buried with the women, has led to the understanding of the Bolshaia Bliznitsa burials as those of a priestly family and, originally, of their connection with the cult of Eleusinian Demeter.

Given the local, Bosporan nature of the burial mound's construction and the lavish nature of its grave goods, as well as the aspects of burial ritual that are connected to Sindian and larger Steppe traditions (e.g. the inclusion of horse harnesses, the clothing plaques), it is clear that the Bolshaia Bliznitsa burials were not referencing a primarily Greek cultural context. Nonetheless, the Demeter imagery from them is striking and in order to understand more fully its significance and the possible Eleusinian connections with the Bolshaia Bliznitsa burials, it is important first to examine the nature of the Demeter mystery cult at Eleusis and the evidence for the increasing popularity of this cult in the fourth century BC, as well as its spread into the wider Greek world.

Demeter, Eleusis and the larger Greek world

Demeter was the Greek god who governed the fruits of the earth. Although in antiquity the etymology of her name was explained as 'earth mother', it is more likely that she was actually the 'grain mother' and indeed her cult is particularly associated with grain. In depictions, Demeter often appears with a wreath of ears of grain, and more stalks in her hand (Burkert 1985, 159). Demeter had a daughter with Zeus, named Persephone, and it was the loss of her daughter that frames our understanding of the worship of Demeter at the Eleusinian mysteries in Attica. In brief outline, the story – first documented in the *Homeric Hymn to Demeter* – is as follows: Persephone, while picking flowers with her friends, was abducted by Hades, the god of the underworld. Demeter, overcome with grief at the loss of her daughter, wandered the earth trying to find her and while she was in mourning, nothing grew and the human race was brought to the brink of starvation. Consequently, Zeus compelled Hades to return his bride Persephone to Demeter, but because Persephone had tasted the pomegranate while she was in the underworld, she would be forever bound to it and compelled to return there for a third of each year. During the time that Persephone was in the underworld, the mortal world would remain infertile, as Demeter mourned the annual loss of her daughter. Since antiquity, this story has been understood as a nature allegory: Persephone is the grain that needs to 'die' so that it may germinate again (Burkert 1985, 160).

Demeter was worshipped throughout the Greek world in different guises, often connected with fertility and fecundity. She was also connected with protecting the dead; indeed the Athenians called their dead *Demetreioi* and sowed grain on their graves (Plutarch, *De faciae in orbe lunae,* 943). But the most famous aspect of Demeter worship were the mysteries – rituals connected with Demeter's search for, and eventual reunification with, her daughter Persephone. Although variants of Demeter mystery cults existed in other parts of the Greek world, the most famous of these was based at Eleusis in Attica, where Demeter had ended up after fruitlessly searching for her daughter (Burkert 1985, 161). As a gift to the Eleusinians, Demeter gave them her mysteries and the knowledge of agriculture, sending Triptolemos, an Eleusinian prince, to distribute grain to humankind. The Eleusinian mysteries, with Triptolemos as one of the first initiates, were therefore closely associated with the dissemination of agriculture and religious hope from Eleusis to the wider Greek world (Kerényi 1967, 123).

The mystery cult at Eleusis functioned for over 1000 years and, according to Diodorus Siculus (5.4.4), the great age and untouchable purity of the cult accounted for its special fame. '*Ta mysteria*', as the cult was known to the Athenians, was centred around a festival that took place annually in the autumn, involving a procession from the Eleusinion in the Athenian Agora along the Sacred Way to Eleusis and a series of events for initiates: the *drōmena* (things done); the *legomena* (things said); and the *deiknumena* (things shown or displayed) (Coldstream 1985, 90). Given that it was a mystery cult, specifics about the nature of the rituals are difficult to ascertain, but later Christian sources tell us that the high point of the celebration was the cutting of an ear of grain in silence (Burkert 1985, 285).

Initiation (*myesis*) into the Eleusinian mysteries was an individual choice but most Athenian adults were initiated, as initiation guaranteed a better fate in the afterlife. The cult was open to men, women, slaves, and foreigners (the latter only from the mid-sixth century BC), although the main priest (*hierophant*) opened celebrations with an injunction that those with impure hands and those that could not speak Greek were to be excluded (Burkert 1985, 286; Coldstream 1985, 91; Sourvinou-Inwood 2003, 26). Initiation could take place at various times of year, either at Eleusis or at the Eleusinion in Athens, and new initiates had to first sacrifice a young pig and be purified with air and fire before participating in the mystery celebrations (Burkert 1985, 286). While the sacrifice of pigs was common in ritual acts of purification throughout the Greek world, the sheer number of pig bones found in connection with Eleusinian ritual is impressive and marks the pig out as having a special connection with the Mysteries (Bowden 2010, 33).

In literature and art, Attic imagery of the cult centres around Demeter and her daughter, but in Eleusis, Persephone is always called Kore, the maiden, and is not depicted as Queen of the Underworld (Bowden 2010, 48). In addition to Demeter and Kore, other gods and heroes feature in the ancient literary and artistic depictions of the Eleusinian mysteries; most notably, Plouton (Hades), Ploutos (Wealth), Iakchos (the son of Demeter or Persephone and Dionysos), Triptolemos, Eubouleus and Eumolpos (*LIMC* cv. Demeter, p. 845; although Clinton 1992 argues that Triptolemos was more closely associated with the Thesmophoria at Eleusis). The latter three figures were mortals, citizens of Eleusis who figured in the Eleusinian story. Depictions of Demeter, Kore and Triptolemos (often in his winged chariot) were most popular, in literature and art, in the sixth and especially fifth centuries BC, while in the fourth century the figure of Ploutos (Wealth) is more often found with Demeter and Kore (*LIMC* cv. Demeter, p. 845, 891–2).

The Mysteries were very closely connected with Eleusis as a place, and a key characteristic of the cult was its uniqueness (Kerényi 1967, 115–6; Clinton 1992, 29). Especially in the sixth and fifth centuries BC, the Eleusinian cult 'stands out in contrast [to other mystery cults] by having renounced any expansion beyond the local sanctuary' (Burkert 1987, 36–7). There were other mystery cults connected with Demeter throughout the Greek world, such as the Andanian mysteries in Messenia, which Pausanias (4.33.5) considered second only to those of Eleusis (Bowden 2010, 70) and various mystery cults in Arcadia and Magna Graecia. Although these cults may have shared elements of the Eleusinian mysteries, they were distinct cults with close connections to places (much like at Eleusis). The Thesmophoria was another mystery cult connected with Demeter, but it differed from the rest in being widely spread throughout the Greek world. The Thesmophoria and the Eleusinian mysteries were intimately linked, with both involving secret aspects that invoked the myth of Demeter and Persephone and metaphorically linked human and agricultural life cycles (Stehle 2007; Rigoglioso 2010, 150–1), and it is possible that the Eleusinian mysteries evolved from the Thesmophoria (Clinton 1992). The Thesmophoria, however, was primarily associated with women and unlike the relatively unique Eleusinian mysteries, was widely celebrated around the Greek world from the archaic period onwards.

Despite the uniqueness of the Eleusinian mysteries, by the fourth century BC it is clear that the cult's influence was beginning to spread throughout the Greek world, from South Italy and Egypt to the Black Sea region. Evidence suggests that, perhaps in conjunction with its attempts to rebuild its empire during this period, Athens was keen to capitalise on the fame of the Eleusinian mysteries and to promote the idea that Demeter had given grain to humankind – thus founding civilisation – at Eleusis (e.g. Isocrates, *Panegyricus* 28–9). In a fourth-century BC law, the Athenians even demanded that first fruit offerings from the whole world be sent to Eleusis (Burkert 1985, fn II.2.2 14; *LSS* 13).

Eleusinian imagery and ultimately, Eleusinian cult ritual, is found outside of Athens beginning in the fourth century BC. The so-called Kerch vases, Attic exports that were mostly found in the region around ancient Pantikapaion (the modern city of Kerch, Ukraine) and which were often decorated with images of Demeter, Persephone and the other Eleusinian figures, are one example of the wider influence the Eleusinian mysteries were beginning to exert in this period (Kerényi 1967, 122). In addition, by the late fourth–third centuries BC there is clear evidence for the development of new Demeter mystery cults with direct connections to Eleusis. Hellenistic rulers in Ionia and Egypt established new cults that explicitly emulated the Eleusinian mysteries in an effort to create direct connections with Athens (Kerényi 1967, 115–6, Bowden 2010, 76–77). There is also evidence that aspects of Eleusinian cult were exported to other non-Greek parts of the Mediterranean; a fourth-century BC Attic relief depicting Eleusinian deities, found in Campania, was possibly used by an Italian circle of initiates in a domestic shrine, and Attic vases with Eleusinian iconography were often incorporated into burials in the region (Leventi 2007).

Demeter and the Bosporan kingdom

Much like in other parts of the Greek world, in the Bosporan kingdom there is clear evidence for the worship of Demeter in various guises, particularly in the fourth and third centuries BC (Minns 1913, 619). The Kerch vases, mentioned above, are one clear connection, while various inscriptions from the region document individual dedications to Demeter (e.g. *IAOSPE* 2.7, 2.13, 2.20, all dating to the fourth-early third centuries BC). In addition, sanctuaries connected with the worship of Demeter have been excavated in the cities of Pantikapaion, Nymphaion and Phanagoria (Koshelenko *et al.* 1984, 221). The Nymphaion sanctuary dates from the sixth century BC and a black gloss kylix (stemmed cup) from there was inscribed with a dedication to Demeter; a fifth-century BC altar base found at the foot of the acropolis in Pantikapaion, depicting a procession of *himatia*-clad women, has been associated with

Demeter Thesmophoria (*CIRB* 18). Most importantly for the purposes of this paper, however, are the specific connections with the Eleusinian mysteries found in these sanctuaries: terracottas depicting Demeter holding her daughter to her shoulder; figurines of pigs, the key sacrificial animal for the cult; and a late fifth/early fourth-century BC relief (possibly Attic in origin) that depicts Demeter, Persephone and a procession of torch-bearers, clearly an Eleusinian motif (Koshelenko *et al.* 1984, 331, pl. 121, 1; Ustinova 1999, 55).

In addition to these sanctuaries, connections with Demeter and with the Eleusinian mysteries can also be found in other burial contexts in the Bosporan kingdom, including a fourth-century BC Attic pelike; an amphora-like vessel from the Pavlovskii burial near Pantikapaion, which depicts scenes of the Eleusinian mysteries (Beazley 230431); a fourth-century burial mound near Nymphaion, the 'Three Brothers' mound, with Demeter imagery (Treister 2008), and several later Hellenistic and early Roman tombs near Pantikapaion, which depict the abduction of Persephone and other iconography associated with the Eleusinian mysteries (Minns 1913, 619; Ustinova 1999, 55; Zinko 1999).

It is perhaps not surprising that Demeter was a popular goddess in the Bosporan kingdom; many of the Greek colonies in the region were founded by Miletus, in Ionia, where Demeter had long been an important deity. In addition, from as early as the sixth or fifth century BC, Miletus and the nearby cities of Ephesus, Erythrae and Teos worshipped Demeter Eleusinia, in an effort to reaffirm their legendary connection with Athens. There is no evidence that the Ionian cults of Demeter Eleusinia were mystery cults, or that they were similar to the Eleusinian mysteries in any way, but a connection between the Ionian worship of Demeter and Eleusis existed from at least the Classical period (Bowden 2010, 75–76; Herodotus 9, 97). In addition to its metropolis's connection to Demeter and Eleusis, the territory of the Bosporan kingdom contained very fertile agricultural land, and the state's prosperity was closely linked to its exports of grain to other Black Sea city-states and especially to Athens. Indeed the fourth century BC is notable for evidence of the intensification of agricultural land-usage and the increase in storage facilities for grain in the Bosporan kingdom, as well as textual sources documenting diplomatic relationships between the Bosporan rulers and Athens based on grain exports (e.g. *IG* II² 212, *IG* II² 653; Rempel 2004). There is ample evidence for Bosporan envoys, individual citizens and the rulers themselves visiting Athens in the fourth and third centuries BC and it is not impossible that they had contact with the Eleusinian cult directly. In theory, there would have been no impediment to initiation into the Mysteries for these Bosporan visitors, as they were Greek speakers, and there is some evidence that foreign kings desired to become initiates (Plutarch, *Demetrius* 26). Even if knowledge of the Mysteries did not travel to the Bosporan kingdom directly through initiates, the frequent contact with Athens and the not insignificant amount of Eleusinian imagery in Bosporan sanctuaries and burials suggest that, at the very least, aspects of the Eleusinian mystery cult had a strong resonance within the Bosporan kingdom by the fourth century BC.

Eleusinian adornment?

It is clear, then, that Demeter was worshipped in the Bosporan kingdom in the fourth century BC and that her worship was, in places, directly associated with the Eleusinian mysteries, perhaps centred on Pantikapaion (Ustinova 1999, 55). With this background established, it is possible to examine the evidence for Eleusinian connections in the Bolshaia Bliznitsa burials more closely.

In the context of the thousands of grave goods included in the Bolshaia Bliznitsa burials, objects with indisputable Demeter and Persephone iconography are limited but significant. The clearest iconography comes from a set of gold clothing plaques that were found with the first, most lavish, female burial. These plaques are small (no more than several centimetres wide) and thin and form a set of three, depicting Demeter, Persephone and Herakles. The egg-and-dart border that frames each depiction and the similar shape and size of each of the plaque types confirms that they were used to decorate the same item of clothing worn by the deceased woman and that the three figures on the plaques were intended to be understood as a group. The identities of the three figures are quite secure, despite the fact that Demeter imagery can be ambiguous. The Demeter plaque from Bolshaia Bliznitsa (Fig. 6) depicts the goddess from the shoulders up; no clothing is shown, but she is wearing a heavy necklace and elaborate earrings. She has a centre-parted hairstyle that is adorned with ears of grain in a quasi-wreath, over top of which is a thin veil. The grain in this depiction is one clear indication that the plaque represents Demeter, and this identification is made even more certain by the depiction of Persephone in the second plaque (Fig. 7). This image of Persephone shows her with a centre-parted *stlengis*-like hairstyle adorned with a wreath of what appear to be flowers. She is also wearing an earring and necklace set, which is similar to that shown in the Demeter plaque and, crucially, she holds a lit torch across her body, an attribute that makes it clear she is Demeter's daughter. It is possible that this mother-daughter pair are intended to reflect specifically Eleusinian imagery, for when Demeter and Kore (as Persephone is called in Eleusis) are depicted as a pair, their iconography is rarely problematic; Demeter usually holds a sceptre and grain, while Kore holds one or two torches (Clinton 1992, 38; e.g. *LIMC* cv. Demeter, no. 222, an Attic red-figure lekythos, *c.* 450 BC; no. 269, a marble relief from Eleusis, *c.* 460 BC).

This Eleusinian similarity becomes even more probable when the third plaque, depicting Herakles (Fig. 8), is considered. Here also, the imagery is unproblematic. Herakles is adorned with a leaved wreath and is holding his characteristic club over his right shoulder. According to legend, Herakles was one of the first foreign initiates to the Eleusinian mysteries (Xenophon, *Hellenica* 6.3.6; Plutarch, *Theseus* 33.1–2; e.g. *LMIC* cv. Demeter, nos. 456, 457 and the Augustan-period Lovatelli Urn, Burkert 1987, 55–7, figs 2–4). In depictions in both literature and art, the theme of Herakles's initiation was most popular in the fourth century BC, as was the inclusion of Herakles in new Eleusinian iconography, which featured a central scene of a seated Demeter with Kore beside her, flanked by various gods and Eleusinian heroes (e.g. *LMIC* cv. Demeter, p.845, 891, nos. 406, 407; Kerényi 1967, 163, fig. 50). Despite the fact that it was not common to depict Herakles alone with Demeter and Kore, it seems probable that the Bolshaia Bliznitsa plaque set was intended to reflect aspects of contemporary Eleusinian cult imagery.

Nevertheless, the Demeter, Persephone and Herakles plaques (found in multiple copies) make up just a handful of the thousands of clothing plaques found in the burials. Other plaques found with those that are potentially Eleusinian, depict Athena, Helios, dancing girls, Pegasus, griffins, sphinxes and deer, as well as some non-figural motifs (Artamonov 1969, 75); they vastly outnumber the Demeter, Persephone and Herakles plaques and clearly 'reflect beliefs different from the Eleusinian' (Ustinova 1999, 58). The clothing plaques themselves, such an important aspect of the adornment of the clothing of the dead buried in Bolshaia Bliznitsa,

Top: Fig. 6. Gold plaque, about 6 cm square, depicting Demeter with ears of grain in her hair, from the first female burial at Bolshaia Bliznitsa (drawing by J. Willmott).

Middle: Fig. 7. Gold plaque, about 6 cm square, depicting Persephone (Kore) with a torch, from the first female burial at Bolshaia Bliznitsa (drawing by J. Willmott).

Bottom: Fig. 8. Gold plaque, about 6 cm square, depicting Herakles with a club, from the first female burial at Bolshaia Bliznitsa (drawing by J. Willmott).

represent a local tradition of elite ornamentation, despite the primarily Greek images they depict. Metal plaques, mostly with zoomorphic motifs, are a common feature from Scythian burials on the Steppe and were used in Sindian burial ritual (Piotrovsky *et al.* 1987, 63), so although the Demeter and Persephone plaques from Bolshaia Bliznitsa appear to represent Eleusinian imagery, they themselves form part of a non-Greek tradition of adornment.

In addition to these three plaque types, the only other grave goods from the Bolshaia Bliznitsa burials that have been confidently connected with the Eleusinian mysteries are a terracotta pig and a bust of Persephone (Ustinova 1999, 58). There was also a terracotta figurine of a standing Herakles (Artamonov 1969, 77), which could be connected to Demeter and Eleusis via the set of clothing plaques. Like the clothing plaques, however, these three arguably Eleusinian pieces come from a selection of approximately forty terracottas, and the imagery of the rest of the assemblage is unclear; fertility themes were key (Ustinova 1999, 58) but they do not specifically relate to Demeter imagery. Artamonov (1969, 75) has also argued that a finger ring decorated with a half woman/half grasshopper intaglio is a further element of Eleusinian imagery in the burial of the first woman, citing the close association of the grasshopper, the 'Muse of the Fields', with grain and the worship of Demeter and Kore. This woman-grasshopper imagery is unique, however, and the association is tenuous.

While the clothing plaques and terracottas described above do seem to reference Eleusinian imagery, it is clear that they were a small part of a much more diverse group of adornments and grave goods. In addition, there are no depictions of the other figures (Triptolemos or Ploutos, Iakchos, Euboulleus) that are associated specifically with the Eleusis cult in Attica. The imagery in the Bolshaia Bliznitsa burials, and particularly in the burial of the first women, reference aspects of Eleusinian imagery within a specific Bosporan context but there is no reason to expect that these women were actually initiates to the Eleusinian mysteries, let alone priestesses of an Eleusinian cult.

There are, however, several other specific aspects of these burials that – given the specific imagery discussed above, and the presence of Demeter and even the Eleusinian cult in the Bosporan kingdom – could be interpreted as referencing Demeter and perhaps even the Eleusinian mysteries. The image of the woman on the ceiling of the central looted chamber is the obvious connection (Fig. 1). The first excavators immediately connected her with Demeter, but later scholars have questioned or nuanced this connection (e.g. Ustinova 1999, 57). The painting depicts the head and upper torso of a female deity, who is holding her two hands up in front of her. In her left hand, she is holding flowers – probably yellow lilies – and she is wearing a wreath of flowers on her head, with a striped veil hanging down from it. She is adorned with a necklace that appears to be made of gold medallions, but no other clothing is visible. Although the garland and her position on the ceiling of the chamber place her in the realm of the gods, there is no specific Demeter imagery here, but the flowers in her hand and in her wreath do make a connection with Persephone likely. Persephone was collecting flowers when she was abducted by Hades, and the flower attribute links her directly to the story of Demeter's search for her. In addition, the floral wreath is similar to that worn by the figure of Persephone depicted on the clothing plaque described above (Fig. 7). It must be noted, however, that the painted goddess's imagery is not specific enough to positively identify her and there is no reason to expect that she represented a primarily Greek god.

The inclusion of headdresses as grave goods in the burials is also of importance here. Demeter and Persephone are the Greek gods most associated with wearing a *polos*, a type of high crown (Higgins 1967). Demeter is often depicted wearing a *polos*, sometimes with a veil draped over it (e.g. *LIMC* cv. Demeter, no. 143, a Roman copy of a late fifth-century BC statuette; no. 148, a statuette from Sicily, *c.* 460 BC). There is also a particularly strong connection between Demeter and the *polos* in depictions of the goddess from the Bosporan kingdom (Jacobson 1995, 141). The *kalathos* headdresses (Fig. 4) found with two of the women buried in the Bolshaia Bliznitsa burials are similar in form to the *polos*, and in general, the *kalathos* was worn as a symbol of fertility by women performing fertility rites for Demeter, Dionysos and Artemis (Artamonov 1969, 73). These same two burials also included more simple headdresses, *stlengides* (Fig. 5), along with second sets of jewellery, indicating that headdresses were important elements of attire for these women. It is generally assumed that they mark these women out as priestesses, and perhaps – given the similarity in form between the *kalathoi* and Demeter's *polos* – ones connected with the worship of Demeter in some way. It should be noted, however, that high, *kalathos*-type, crowns (e.g. Chertomlyk) or high pointed headdresses (e.g. Karagodeuashkh) were also adornments found with elite women in Scythian mounded burials. Much like the clothing plaques depicting Demeter, Persephone and Herakles, the headdresses included in the Bolshaia Bliznitsa burials were multivalent, apparently connecting the deceased women to the worship of Demeter and also marking them out as elite women in a local, Steppe context.

There are also similarities between the adornments with which the women in the Bolshaia Bliznitsa mound were buried and the way in which Demeter and Persephone were depicted in the gold clothing plaques already discussed. The combination of headdress, elaborate earrings and heavy necklace are seen in the depictions of the goddesses, and echo in composition the jewellery sets found in the two most elaborate female 'priestess' burials. In particular, the earrings worn by both Demeter and Persephone on the plaques are very similar to earrings found with these two female burials, with their central rosette, suspended boat-shape and dangling pendants. This style of earring is securely dated to the middle to late fourth century BC, and other examples of this type have been found in the Black Sea region, Crete, and Magna Graecia (Higgins 1961, 125–126). In addition, the *stlengis*-like hairstyle that Persephone wears in the clothing plaque is similar in effect to the *stlengides* found with the deceased women, with their swirled linear designs (Fig. 5). Since the clothing plaques must have been produced in the Bosporan kingdom, choosing to depict Demeter and Persephone ornamented in a manner similar to the women the plaques adorned, suggests a close conceptual connection between the deceased and the goddesses.

In other parts of the Greek world, lavishly ornamented female burials have been connected with priestesses (Connelly 2007, 225–226). It is possible that the amount of bodily adornment afforded to the two 'priestess' burials in the Bolshaia Bliznitsa mound give us another hint about the cultic connections expressed there. Certainly, in the Bosporan kingdom the lavish provisioning of burials – whether they be Scythian, Sindian or Greek – was quite common, and this trend is generally thought to reflect Sindo-Scythian beliefs about the afterlife (Rempel 2010). Nonetheless, Bolshaia Bliznitsa represents an extraordinary treatment of *women* in burial, and the sheer amount of gold in the female burials is unrivalled in the area. Mystery cults, and in particular the Eleusinian mysteries, were notable for the prominence of adornment in their rituals (Gawlinski 2008, 145, 148) and the Eleusinian priestess of Demeter and Kore and other officials were lavishly dressed in order to mark them out from mere initiates (Plutarch, *Aristides* 5.7; Connelly 2007, 86–7; Gawlinski 2008, 162). Even if the headdress and jewellery sets accorded the Bolshaia Bliznitsa women were not primarily intended to mark them out as priestesses, the resonance with Greek and, in particular, Eleusinian practice would have been potent.

As was discussed above, there were other mystery cults in the ancient Greek world that celebrated Demeter and Persephone and it is possible that the images of these goddesses in the Bolshaia Bliznitsa burials might reference a different Demeter cult, like the Thesmophoria. The Thesmophoria was a festival associated with women. It celebrated agricultural and female fertility and, as was mentioned above, it was closely related to the Eleusinian mysteries. The two cults shared certain elements, including a key interest in the main agrarian gods, Demeter, Persephone and Plouton (or Zeus Eubouleus or Zeus Chthonios), and elements of religious ritual, e.g. the sacrifice of piglets in pits (Clinton 1992; Stehle 2007). Considering that cults of Demeter Thesmophoria were found throughout the ancient Greek world (including in the Bosporan kingdom, as mentioned above), it is possible that the Demeter and Persephone iconography in the Bolshaia Bliznitsa burials indicate connections to the Thesmophoria instead of (or as well as) the Eleusinian mysteries. The specific inclusion of Herakles, the famous Eleusinian initiate, in the clothing plaque imagery, however, along with the general fourth-century BC spread of Eleusinian influence and the close connection between the Bosporan kingdom and Athens in that period suggest that specific Eleusinian connections are likely. In addition, ancient sources tell us that participants in the Thesmophoria festival did not wear flower crowns, because Persephone had been gathering flowers when she was captured (scholiast on Sophocles' *Oedipus at Colonus* 681, as cited in Rigoglioso 2010, 152), so the flower crown adorning Persephone in the Bolshaia Bliznitsa depictions seems inappropriate if the Thesmophoria was the main Demeter reference for the deceased.

That is not to say, however, that Eleusinian Demeter or even Demeter more generally was the sole god of importance for the women buried in Bolshaia Bliznitsa. Depictions of Athena, Helios, Thetis and, perhaps most importantly, Aphrodite, decorated other clothing plaques, rings and mirrors in the Bolshaia Bliznitsa burials (Artamonov 1969, 75–8). Aphrodite Ourania, or 'Heavenly Aphrodite', was the most prominent god in the Bosporan kingdom and by the first century AD had become fully syncretised with the local Great Goddess of the Steppe. Within the Bosporan kingdom, there are more inscriptions and temples dedicated to Aphrodite Ourania than to any other god during the Classical and Hellenistic periods. In addition, she was the only goddess who had distinct connections with local, non-Greek, populations in the Classical period (Ustinova 1999, 27–46). Certainly, there is Aphrodite imagery in Bolshaia Bliznitsa (depictions of Aphrodite and Eros on several gold rings and a bronze mirror case, Artamonov 1969, 75), and Ustinova (1999, 57) has suggested that the goddess painted on the ceiling of the looted chamber is most likely connected with Aphrodite Ourania in some way, based on the popularity and cross-cultural nature of her cult in the Bosporan kingdom. Nonetheless, the Aphrodite imagery from the grave goods is not specific to Aphrodite Ourania nor more prevalent than the Demeter imagery and there is no need to deny the importance of the latter based on the greater popularity of the former goddess.

Current interpretations of the Bolshaia Bliznitsa goddess see her as the Great Goddess of the Steppe, who was understood to have some connection – perhaps quite ephemeral – with one of the Greek goddesses worshipped in the Bosporan kingdom. The Great Goddess had many different guises; she safeguarded fertility for humans, domestic animals and cultivated fields; she protected nature; she supported the ruling powers and she ruled the netherworld; and all of the Greek goddesses worshipped in the Bosporan kingdom resembled her in some way (Ustinova 1999, 65). For Demeter, the connections were clearly in the realms of earthly fertility and the dead, which accords well with Eleusinian beliefs, but in the fourth century BC there is little other evidence for the syncretisation of Demeter with the Great Goddess.

It is possible that the Demeter connections in the Bolshaia Bliznitsa burials simply reflect some level of syncretism of Demeter with the Great Goddess, or show the use of contemporary Greek imagery to reflect specific Sindian beliefs. But the presence of specifically *Eleusinian* imagery and the connection between the funerary adornments of the deceased women and the adornment of the goddesses depicted in the burials, suggest a more specific connection to the Demeter cult. Without implying that the women buried in the Bolshaia Bliznitsa mound were priestesses of Demeter and Kore, or necessarily even initiates of the Mysteries, it seems likely that the Eleusinian cult, or aspects of it, provided an attractive complement to their Sindian beliefs and rituals. As has been discussed above, Demeter, in her Eleusinian guise, was being worshipped in the Bosporan kingdom and the people buried there could easily have been exposed to the basic principles of the Mysteries, via word-of-mouth or even from initiates themselves. Given the fourth-century BC context of these burials, a time when grain cultivation was intensifying in the land around Bolshaia Bliznitsa, and given that the Bosporan kingdom had close trade and diplomatic connections with Athens, Demeter's mystery cult might have been particularly attractive to a wide variety of inhabitants of the area. The observance of the Mysteries at Eleusis was in part practical, designed to ensure a plentiful grain supply (Burkert 1987, 20), and there has always been a close connection between Eleusis and grain because of Triptolemos's role as distributor of Demeter's gift of agriculture. It was in the fourth century BC, however, as Eleusis's influence on the wider Greek world intensified, that the idea of Eleusis as the origin of agriculture became widely accepted (Kerényi 1967, 122). Bosporans may have wished to cement and celebrate their connections to Athens via cultic connections (as happened in other parts of the Hellenistic world), and Eleusis would have been a particularly appropriate choice, given the grain they exported to Athens.

For the women buried in the Bolshaia Bliznitsa mound in particular, the Eleusinian mysteries might have been particularly attractive and compatible with their own Sindian beliefs. The Mysteries, after all, ensured initiates a good afterlife, and would have been appropriate for a burial context. At least two of the women buried in the mound were marked out as special in a ritual sense – as 'priestesses' – and the strong female presence of Demeter and Persephone, as well as the female officials who presided over the Eleusinian mysteries and perhaps even the familial connection of mother and daughter, would have been compelling complements to their already clearly elevated status. The connection to the Demeter cult, which was popular in the cities of the Bosporan kingdom, may have even provided the Bolshaia Bliznitsa women with an avenue into Bosporan elite society. In Ptolemaic Egypt, for example, Parca (2007) has suggested that the Demeter cult enabled female worshippers to 'play a role as agents of social and cultural assimilation' in a mixed society.

Conclusion

Based on aspects of the funerary adornment in the Bolshaia Bliznitsa burials, Demeter and Persephone had some special resonance with the women buried there and, given the specific nature of some of the imagery, perhaps even the goddesses in their Eleusinian guise of Demeter and Kore. While non-Greek ritual and the Great Goddess clearly provided the overall context for the burials, there is little evidence for the syncretisation of Demeter with the Great Goddess and it seems likely that selected elements of the Eleusinian cult (the emphasis on fertility, the connection with the afterlife, and perhaps the dominant role played by women) were appropriated by the women buried in Bolshaia Bliznitsa. Knowledge of the Eleusinian mysteries may have come from one of the nearby Bosporan cities, where there is evidence for the worship of Demeter and dedications with clear Eleusinian imagery. This larger Bosporan engagement with Eleusinian Demeter can be connected with the importance of grain production in the region in the fourth century BC as well as the wider spread of Eleusinian influence in that period. Bosporan rulers celebrated their special connection with Athens via honours and inscriptions, and may have endeavoured to cement that relationship via a special cultic connection with Eleusis. Other Greek gods are referenced in the Bolshaia Bliznitsa grave goods and the Sindian burial ritual suggests the Great Goddess must have been of great importance for the deceased buried there, but it is clear that Eleusinian Demeter also had a role in their lives.

j.rempel@sheffield.ac.uk

Bibliography

Artamonov 1969: M. I. Artamonov, *The Splendor of Scythian Art: Treasures from Scythian Tombs*, New York

Beazley: Beazley Archive, http://www.beazley.ox.ac.uk/index.htm

Bowden 2010: H. Bowden, *Mystery Cults in the Ancient World*, London

Burkert 1985: W. Burkert, *Greek Religion*, Cambridge

Burkert 1987: W. Burkert, *Ancient Mystery Cults*, Cambridge, MA.

CIRB: Corpus Inscriptorum Regni Bosporani = Korpus bosporskikh nadpisei, Struve, 1965

Clinton 1992: K. Clinton, *Myth and Cult: The Iconography of the Eleusinian Mysteries*, Stockholm

Coldstream 1985: J. N. Coldstream, 'Greek temples: Why and where?', in P. E. Easterling, J. V. Muir (eds), *Greek Religion and Society*, Cambridge, 67–97

Connelly 2007: J. B. Connelly, *Portrait of a Priestess: Women and Ritual in Ancient Greece*, Princeton

Diodorus Siculus: *Diodorus of Sicily, 3, Books IV (continued) 59–VIII*, trans. C. H. Oldfather, London and Cambridge, MA., 1939

Gawlinski 2008: L. Gawlinksi, '"Fashioning" initiates: Dress at the Mysteries', in C. S. Colburn, M. K. Heyn (eds), *Reading a Dynamic Canvas: Adornment in the Ancient Mediterranean World*, Newcastle, 146–169

Herodotus: *Herodotus: in four volumes*, Vol. 4, Books VIII-IX, trans. A. D. Godley, London and New York, 1924

Higgins 1967: R. A. Higgins, *Greek Terracottas*, London

Higgins 1961: R. A. Higgins, *Greek and Roman Jewellery*, London

Homeric Hymn to Demeter: D. G. Rice, J. E. Stambaugh, *Sources for the Study of Greek Religion*, Missoula, Montana, 1979, 171–183

IAOSPE : Inscriptiones antiquae orae septentrionalis ponti Euxini graecae et latinae (Latyshev 1885–1900)

IG: *Inscriptiones graecae*

Isocrates, *Panegyricus*: *Isocrates with an English Translation in three volumes*, trans. George Norlin, Cambridge, MA. and London, 1980

Jacobson 1995: E. Jacobson, *The Art of the Scythians: The Interpenetration of Cultures at the Edge of the Hellenic World*, Leiden

Kerényi 1967: C. Kerényi, *Eleusis: Archetypal Image of Mother and Daughter*, London

Koshelenko *et al.* 1984: G. A. Koshelenko, I. T. Kruglikova, V. S. Dolgorukov, *Antichnie gosudarstva Severnogo Prichernomor'ia*, Moscow

Leventi 2007: I. Leventi, 'The Mondragone Relief revisited: Eleusinian cult iconography in Campania', *Hesperia* 76 (1), 107–141

LIMC cv. Demeter: L. Beschi, 1988, 'Demeter', *Lexicon Iconographicum Mythologiae Classicae* IV, Paris, 884–890

LSS = F. Sokolowski, 1962, *Lois sacrées des cites grecques*, Paris

Minns 1913: E. H. Minns, *Scythians and Greeks: A Survey of Ancient History and Archaeology on the North Coast of the Euxine from the Danube to the Caneasus*, Cambridge

Parca 2007: M. Parca, 'Worshipping Demeter in Ptolemaic and Roman Egypt', in M. Parca, A. Tzanetou (eds), *Finding Persephone: Women's Rituals in the Ancient Mediterranean*, Bloomington and Indianapolis, 189–208

Pausanias 1918: *Description of Greece*, trans. W. H. S. Jones, H. A. Ormerod, Cambridge, MA, and London

Piotrovsky *et al.* 1987: B. Piotrovsky, L. Galanina, N. Grach, *Scythian Art*, Oxford and Leningrad

Plutarch, *Aristides: Plutarch's Lives*, vol. 4, trans. B. Perrin. Cambridge, MA. and London, 1914

Plutarch, *De faciae in orbe lunae: Moralia*, trans. H. Cherniss and W. C. Helmbold, Cambridge, MA. and London, 1957

Plutarch, *Demetrius: Plutarch's Lives*, vol. 9, trans. B. Perrin. Cambridge, MA. and London, 1920

Plutarch, *Theseus: Plutarch's Lives*, vol. 1, trans. B. Perrin. Cambridge, MA. and London, 1914

Rempel 2011: J. Rempel, 'Burial in the Bosporan kingdom: local traditions in regional context(s)', in M. Carroll, J. Rempel (eds), *Living Through The Dead: Burial and commemoration in the Classical world*, Oxford, 21–46

Rempel 2004: J. Rempel, *Rural Settlement and Elite Representation: Social Change in the Bosporan Kingdom in the Fourth Century BC*, PhD thesis, University of Michigan, Ann Arbor

Rigoglioso 2010: M. Rigoglioso, *Virgin Mother Goddesses of Antiquity*, New York

Sourvinou-Inwood 2003: C. Sourvinou-Inwood, 'Festivals and mysteries: Aspects of the Eleusinian cult', in M. B. Cosmopoulos (ed.), *Greek Mysteries: The Archaeology and Ritual of Ancient Greek Secret Cults*, London, 25–49

Stefani 1865: L. Stefani, 'Ob'iasneniie neskol'kikh drevnostei, naidennikh v 1864 g. v Iuzhnoi Rossii', *Otcheti Arkheologicheskoi Komissii*, 3–222

Stehle 2007: E. Stehle, 'Thesmophoria and Eleusinian mysteries: The fascination of women's secret ritual', in M. Parca, A. Tzanetou (eds), *Finding Persephone: Women's Rituals in the Ancient Mediterranean*, Bloomington and Indianapolis, 165–185

Treister 2008: M. Treister (ed.), *Trekhbratnie kurgani. Kurgannaia gruppa vtoroi polovini IV-III vv. do n.e.*, Simferopol and Bonn

Ustinova 1999: Y. Ustinova, *The Supreme Gods of the Bosporan Kingdom: Celestial Aphrodite and the Most High God*, Leiden

Xenophon, *Hellenica: Xenophon in Seven Volumes*, vols 1 and 2, trans. C. L. Brownson, Cambridge, MA., and London, 1918, 1921

Zinko 1999: E. A. Zinko, *The Crypt of Demeter*, Kerch

ETERNAL COMFORT: FUNERARY TEXTILES IN LATE CLASSICAL AND HELLENISTIC GREECE

DIMITRA ANDRIANOU

Textiles were used widely in the ancient Greek world, particularly in funerary contexts, where they were draped over the deceased and served as covers, hangings, pillows and mattresses to adorn funerary furnishings. Real fabrics have not, on the whole, survived in the archaeological record, since they were made of perishable materials. However, funerary assemblages periodically bring to light a variety of preserved textiles: textiles used to wrap the bones of the deceased inside the funerary vessel or placed outside it; textiles deposited in the tomb as offerings; textiles that draped the deceased, decorated the funerary chamber, or even imitation textiles carved on funerary beds.[1] Visual representations of textiles on funerary furniture and architecture (inscribed grave *stelai* or wall paintings inside the tomb chamber) provide additional knowledge. Many of these examples have only been summarily published and remain overlooked in discussions on burial customs in late Classical and Hellenistic Greece. This gap in scholarship is detrimental to our understanding of Greek funerary practice because, whether looking at real fabrics or painted or carved imitations on funerary furniture and wall paintings, these remains offer valuable clues to decode funerary beliefs and the status of the deceased in the late Classical and Hellenistic periods in Greece.

Admiration of textiles is a well known *topos* in ancient literature, along with the admiration of statues and buildings (Rusnak 2001), as is sufficiently clear from the following three passages from three successive centuries, all extolling the artistry of woven textiles: a) the famous passage from Euripides' *Ion* (1132–1165: Potter 1938), where the attendant refers to the scenes depicted in the tapestries as 'marvellous for men to see' and then proceeds to describe them for the benefit of the audience of the play as active spectators (Zeitlin 1994, 155); b) a passage from Menander's *Cutty Locks or The Forced Bobbing* (333–348: Edmonds 1961, 1152–1154) where the characters discuss and try to identify the figures of animals in a tapestry-woven piece of cloth kept in a box and c) a passage from the fifteenth *Idyll* of Theocritus in which two women in Alexandria examine a tapestry-woven textile that hangs between pillars in the sanctuary of Adonis during a festival of the god (Theocritus, *Idyll* 15, 78–90: Edmonds 1919, 175–195).

Texts and inscriptions with an astonishingly rich list of words pertaining to furniture and furnishings further prove this admiration (Andrianou 2009). In the fifth century BC, Alcibiades' confiscated property is a good source of information, recording the words *proskephalaion* (προσκεφάλαιον) (*IG* I³ 422, line 257, restored) and *knephalon* (κνέφαλον), both meaning pillow (*IG* I³ 421, lines 190–191; 422, lines 259–260, restored). Timaeus preserves the word *tyle* (τύλη), 'mattress', in an interesting passage on the luxury of Akragas (Jacoby 1964, 3B,

566, F. 26a, 607) and the word *psiathos* (ψίαθος), rush-mat, is recorded in the *Attic Stelai* (*IG* I³ 421, line 108 and 422, line 261) and in Pollux (X, 43). *Pleroma* (πλήρωμα), 'flock of wool', used for stuffing pillows. is recorded by Pollux (X, 41).

In the second century AD, Pollux also provides us with an extensive and diverse list of adjectives for bed covers, such as *lepte* (λεπτή), 'fine, thin, delicate', *euhyphes* (εὐϋφής), 'well woven', *euetrios* (εὐήτριος), 'with good or fine thread', *stilpne* (στιλπνή), 'glittering', *stilbousa* (στίλβουσα), 'brilliant', *euchros* (εὔχρως), 'bright coloured', *polymorphos* (πολύμορφος), 'with many shapes', *porphyra* (πορφυρᾶ), 'of purple', *halourgis* (ἁλουργίς), 'of purple, sea-wrought', *haliporphyros* (ἁλιπόρφυρος), 'of purple', *praseios*, (πρασεῖος), 'light green', *hysginobaphes*, (ὑσγινοβαφής), 'dyed in a bright crimson or scarlet vegetable dye', *ioeides* (ἰοειδής), 'of violet colour', *krokoeides* (κροκοειδής), 'of saffron colour', *kokkobaphes* (κοκκοβαφής), 'of scarlet colour', *orphine* (ὀρφνίνη), 'of brownish-grey colour', *periporphyros* (περιπόρφυρος), 'with purple border', *epichrysos* (ἐπίχρυσος), 'overlaid with gold' (Pollux, X, 42). More information on words can be found in the lexicographers Hesychios, of the fifth century AD, and Suidas, of the tenth century AD.

Ancient authors also refer indirectly to renowned places of textile manufacture with phrases such as *stromata Milesia* (στρώματα Μιλήσια), Milesian bed covers (in Aristophanes, *Frogs*, 543), *Sardiane psilotapis* (Σαρδιανή ψιλοτάπις), Sardian flat-woven or tapestry-woven carpet, evidently a *kilim* (in Klearchos of Soloi, quoted by Athenaeus, *Deip.* 6, 255e),² and *aulaiai phoinikinai* (αὐλαίαι φοινικίναι), Phoenician or red curtains (in Athenaeus, *Deip.* 5, 196c). Pliny places the invention of embroidery with a needle in Phrygia and specifically mentions that gold tapestry-weaving was invented in Asia by King Attalus (Pliny, VIII, 196; Greenewalt, Majewski 1980, 133–147; Wace 1948 for the correct translation of the words *pictus*, *intexere*, *acu facere*; Seiler-Baldinger 1994), a possible attestation of the survival or revival of the Lydian gold-weaving tradition. The fabric called damask (*polymita* in the Latin text) woven with a number of threads was introduced from Alexandria, according to Pliny.

Concerning the materials used to adorn furniture, wool and linen were employed, along with silk, leather and sheepskin. These fabrics were most probably made at home, one of the main tasks assigned to women. Men were also involved in the production though, as is attested by the description of Akesas and Helikon of Cyprus as 'celebrated weavers' (ἐντέχνων γενομένων) in the fourth or third century BC (Athenaeus, *Deip.* 2, 48b; for the Latin equivalent, *textor*, see Martial, *Ep.* 12, 59, 6 and Juvenal, *Sat.* 9, 30; for the weavers of Athena's *peplos*, Mansfield 1985, 54–55 and 283–289; for male weavers, Thompson 1982). Michael Vickers makes an interesting point regarding the names 'Akesas' and 'Helikon': they are not random, in fact, their roots are the words for needle, *akis* (ἀκίς), and spinning thread, *helik-* (ἑλικ-), (Vickers 1999, 32).³ Both men and women worked in the production of wool on an industrial scale, as noted by Xenophon (Xen., *Mem.* 2, 7, 6) and possibly implied by Aristophanes (Aristophanes, *Frogs*, 1331–1365); but whether free citizens or slaves formed the majority of workers in this occupation is currently debated. *Talasiourgoi* (ταλασιουργοί), wool-workers, however, were clearly comprised of both female (Tod 1950, 10–11, for female slaves who became free or were freed in fifth and fourth century BC Attica) and male workers (Lewis 1959, 208–238; 1968, 369–374). Male workers are noted as professionals with a high degree of specialisation (for example, Aristophanes, *Thesmophoriazusae* 935: *histiorhaphos* (ἱστιορράφος); Pollux, VII, 28: *nakotiltes* (νακοτίλτης); Plato, *Politicus* 281, 8: *xantes* (ξάντης); Aeschylus, *Libation-Bearers* 760: *gnapheus* (γναφεύς).

In the funerary sector, and according to the existing excavated material, late Classical and Hellenistic textiles were used to dress the dead when inhumed; to wrap the bones of the deceased when cremated, before being placed in the funerary container, *larnax* (λάρναξ); to wrap the vessel that contained the bones of the deceased; to serve as decorative hangings from the walls and ceiling of the tomb (not without symbolic connotations); and to serve as offerings to the dead. Indirect evidence of textiles can be gleaned from imitation textiles carved on funerary beds (e.g. mattresses and pillows), painted or mosaic imitations on the walls and floors of certain tombs, and textiles depicted in funerary iconography (wall paintings and *stelai*, for example). Here we will limit our examples to the excavated textiles and their imitations, excluding the numerous decorative remains (such as gold discs), which are thought to have once adorned funerary textiles, and are often found among the funerary remains. Each of these categories will be visited in detail below.

Textiles from funerary dress

Two examples of gold thread from a textile item were found lying over the remains of the deceased in Patras and Nea Orestias (Evros). More specifically, in a cist-grave of the third quarter of the second century BC in Patras, a group of gold threads was found on the chest and the legs of a woman (Papapostolou 1982, 323, no. 14, pl. 112). In Evros, the remains of the deceased's clothing were found in a pit, along with his sword and his shoes; the body of the deceased had been burnt in another pit nearby (primary cremation). The latter find is dated to the first century AD (Pantos 1980, 823).

Two further examples can be added with some degree of certainty. They were found attached to the grave-offerings rather than the remains of the deceased, but are nevertheless thought to be part of the funerary dress. The first example, a mineralised piece of a fine textile, was attached to a bronze mirror inside a tomb from Salamis, dated to the fifth century BC (Moulhérat, Spantidaki 2009, 8–9, fig. 9.) The second example, also from Salamis, was found in tomb 21 in Abelakia, attached to an iron *stlegis*, dated to the second century BC (Moulhérat, Spantidaki 2009, 13–14, fig. 20). The latter find consists of two textile pieces, one directly touching the *stlegis* on one side only (thus not wrapping the funerary offering), and the other found directly over this piece.

Literary references offer a measure of information regarding the material used in the textiles worn by the dead. Herodotus, in the second book of his *Histories*, talks about the Egyptian use of linen garments, and adds that for anyone initiated into Orphic and Bacchic rites, it is forbidden to be buried in wool (Herodotus, 2, 81), a detail that is not to be interpreted as a special burial rite, but as an indication of initiation (Graf, Johnston 2007, 160). According to literary references, white is the colour of textiles *worn* by the dead (*IG* XII 5, 593, 2 of the fifth century BC); according to visual evidence, red is the colour of textiles *offered* to the dead.[4]

Textiles as funerary offerings

One example, only briefly noted, comes from the fourth-century BC cemetery of Trachones, in Attica, where among the offerings a piece of cloth with a border design was found

(Kalogeropoulou 1971, 224–225, note 61; Zissis 1954 for the scientific analysis). The scientific analysis proved that it is actually two pieces, one of hemp and one of cotton. More information regarding the conditions of the recovery of the textile is required before drawing any further conclusions.

Textiles found inside the funerary vessel

One of the oldest extant examples of textiles is that from Koropi, where ten fragments of fine linen cloth were found under unknown circumstances (Beckwith 1954, 114–115). The piece, acquired by the Victoria and Albert Museum, was discovered in a bronze *kalpis* together with bones and fragments of other textiles. The *kalpis* is said to have been disposed of privately and its whereabouts is unknown. The sample consists of ten fragments of fine linen cloth dyed in a delicate shade of green with occasional patches of brown, the result of impregnation of copper from the urn. Five of the fragments were originally tapestry-woven and five were plain. Three fragments bear the impression of the tapestry-woven pattern and one has a selvedge (overall measurements: 54 cm by 18 cm to 5 cm by 9 cm). The design is an all-over diaper, each lozenge containing a lion walking with its tail lifted in the air and one forepaw raised in salutation. Spectroscopic analysis indicated the presence of silver and gold, which may have originally surrounded a fibre core of silk or linen.[5] This would make it the oldest precious-metal thread in the Greek world known to us so far. The piece is dated by ceramic evidence to the end of the fifth or fourth century BC.

The second example comes from the Athenian Kerameikos (tomb 35, HTR 73). It is a piece of textile found in a copper *lebes*, inside a sarcophagus (Kübler 1936, 188–190, fig. 16; Knigge 1988, 109–110, no. 17; Hundt 1969, 65–71; Margariti *et al.* 2011). The *lebes* was wrapped in straw and bound with wide, purple ribbons. The *lebes* was probably placed originally inside a wooden chest; it contained the remains of a fine fabric, decorated around its four corners with purple dye. It is not clear whether the fragments currently kept in storage by the Hellenic Ministry of Culture originate from the ribbons around the *lebes*, from the remains of the fabric inside it, or from both (Margariti *et al.* 2011, 523). The reliability of the past analyses that identified the fabric as silk is also now disputed, since recent analyses showed no proteinaceous fibres (Margariti *et al.* 2011, 526). The find is dated to between 430 and 400 BC.

A mineralised piece of linen found inside a bronze caldron from Marathon that housed the remains of a cremated child, also belongs to the fifth century BC. It was cursorily published as part of a rescue excavation (Spantidaki, Moulhérat 2004, 5–6, figs 1–5). The same holds true for three mineralised textile fragments found inside a bronze caldron from Marousi, dated to the fifth century BC (Spantidaki, Moulhérat 2004, 8, figs 11–14). Mineralised fragments of a textile (10 cm by 60 cm as preserved) were also found in a bronze *kalpis* of the fifth century BC in the Kamateros cemetery on Salamis (Moulhérat, Spantidaki 2009, 9, figs 12, 13, 14). Fragments of bone found between the threads of the cloth confirm that the bones had been placed inside the material. Scientific analysis has proved that the threads are wool, a material that is harder to work with than linen. This indicates that the cloth that wrapped the bones in this particular tomb was not simple, either in technique or, possibly, value. Working with wool was considered 'art' (τέχνη) and was not confined to the domestic sphere, as it comprised different degrees of specialisation (Spantidaki 2009, 72–75).

Yet another example is known from Eleusis, where a piece of cloth was found inside a bronze *kalpis*, which was placed inside a marble sarcophagus dated to the middle of the fifth century BC. The *kalpis* contained bones and ashes wrapped in a piece of linen cloth (Mylonas 1956, 81, fig. 9; Zissis 1954 scientific analysis) with preserved dimensions of 2.20 m by 0.50 m.

The well-known textile from Vergina is a good example from the fourth century BC (Andronikos 1984, 191–192; Drougou 1987; Flury-Lemberg 1988) (pl. 3). Found folded in several layers inside the golden *larnax* from the antechamber of the so-called Tomb of Philip II, it had tapestry-woven decoration with gold and blue-violet purple thread, possibly on a piece of woollen fabric not trapezoidal in shape, as originally thought by the excavator, but oblong, like a shawl, with estimated dimensions of 1 m by 0.60 m (Flury-Lemberg 1988, 235–236). It is woven using a tapestry technique, and the gold consists of cut strips with no indication that they were spun around a core. The running motif on the border is a meander, and the central design is a vivid, naturalistic synthesis of floral patterns (such as leaves and flowers) and two doves. The wool used for the warp and weft was dyed with genuine mollusc purple, which aided its preservation, since the stable protein structure of this dyestuff is slower to decay than wool fibre. The specific type of scroll decoration is associated with Apulian vase-painting by Asher Ovadiah (1980, 174; Valeva 2006); but the Vergina example securely places the pattern in the repertoire of textile design as well.

A purple fabric in animal fibre also covered the remains inside the *larnax* of the chamber of the so-called Tomb of Philip II (Andronikos 1984, 170). This fabric has disintegrated completely, except for a few traces of purple (Flury-Lemberg 1988). From the scientific analysis, it is evident that the chest was lined with the purple fabric before the bones and ashes were put in; the four corners of the material were then folded over them. It is assumed that this fabric was also of wool, because the alkaline ash of the cremated remains destroyed it.

A purple and gold piece of cloth dating to the same century was found in the chamber-tomb at Agios Athanasios, inside a silver-sheathed box (Tsimbidou-Avloniti 2000, 549) (Fig. 1). The textile is described as purple-gilded and a meander design is said to be just visible.

Fig. 1. Chamber-tomb of Agios Athanasios, textile (photo Archaeological Museum of Thessaloniki).

A group of gold threads was uncovered in the early second-century BC Macedonian tomb B at Pella inside a wooden *larnax*, which had been placed in a marble sarcophagus (Chrysostomou 1998, 31, no. 6, fig. 15). It may have originally covered the remains of a woman.

At Tzayesi (Amphipolis) 'silver-gilded' threads are mentioned among the remains of the Macedonian tomb and 'gold-gilded' threads from a textile decorated with a large number of small gold beads (at least 190) are mentioned from a cist-tomb (Makaronas 1940). Both tombs are dated by the excavator to the end of the fourth or the beginning of the third century BC.

Finally, a later-dated mineralised fragment, briefly published, was found inside the ceramic cover of a Roman inhumation burial at Glyphada. It has been dated to the third or fourth century AD (Spantidaki, Moulhérat 2004, 8–10, figs 16–17).

Textiles found outside the funerary vessel

Textile fragments were found outside a ceramic urn that contained the remains of three people (a woman, a man and a child) in a fifth-century BC tomb in Phoinikia, at Kalyvia (Attica) (Spantidaki, Moulhérat 2003, 2–4, fig. 1; Moulhérat, Spantidaki 2007, 163–166). The ceramic urn was placed inside a marble *kalpis* and the textile covered the lid and the sides of the urn. A flower wreath rested on top of the bone remains. The analysis of the fabric indicated linen fibres, while the extreme delicacy and the lack of twist suggest silk and the chromatographic analysis indicates the presence of true purple dye. As one can see from the starting border, the piece was woven on a vertical loom. Moulhérat and Spantidaki have concluded that it is a rare vestige of the *arachnaia* clothes worn by classical statues (Moulhérat, Spantidaki 2007, 165).

Another example was found on the exterior of a bronze *hydria*, placed in a stone *kalpis*, which was uncovered in the fourth-century BC cemetery at Elliniko (Spantidaki, Moulhérat 2004, 6, figs 7–10). The mineralised fragments were found under the shoulders of the *hydria* and the scientific analysis proved that the cloth was linen, with twenty-four threads per centimetre. The cloth wrapped the central section of the *hydria* only, and no remains of cloth were found inside the vessel.

The custom of wrapping the funerary vessel in cloth, instead of the remains *inside* the vessel, is quite interesting. It is used with both clay and metal vessels (once wrapped in straw, in an example from the Kerameikos, mentioned above) and, although arguably less frequent than examples where the textile was placed inside the vase, it might indicate a different symbolic gesture than that intended by wrapping the remains directly in the cloth. It reminds us of the painted red ribbons (*tainiai*) that wrap the funerary *stelai* at Vergina, (Saatsoglou-Paliadeli 1984, cat. nos 26–31, 191–197, pls 50–51) dated to the second half of the fourth century BC, and Demetrias (Volos),[6] dated to the third century BC (Fig. 2). On vase paintings, *tainiai* are often shown being offered to the dead by the living, or are carried in baskets to be offered.[7] They are painted in bright blue, green, vermilion, black, purple or brown. One example in the corpus of *stelai* from Demetrias shows a man offering a ribbon to Hermes Chthonios on the Menophilos *Stele*, dated to the third quarter of the third century BC (Arvanitopoulos 1909, 180, no. 26), while in other cases the ribbon is shown around the head of Hermes Chthonios.[8] Such *tainiai* appear particularly in the work of the Achilles Painter – the painter of funerary *lekythoi par excellence* – where a round, tubular fillet can be seen, laid at the foot of the funerary *stele* or wound into a wreath and placed upright against the base of the *stele* (Kurtz 1975, 50–51).

Fig. 2. *Stele* of Iason Antipatros, Demetrias (photo by D. Andrianou).

Although the textile that contains the ashes of the deceased is easily explained as a gesture of care, so that the remains would not touch the vessel, the textile on the exterior of the funerary urn is clearly visible and consequently has a more decorative connotation. Concerning the use of ribbons (*tainiai*), Robert Garland has noted that 'various explanations have been proposed to explain their meaning – that they possessed the power to ward off evil, elevated the object they adorned to a higher plane, or were a mark of homage – and it is probable that their durability and popularity owed something to each' (Garland 1985, 116). Apostolos Arvanitopoulos, in describing the *stelai* from Demetrias, asserts that the ribbon might actually be a substitute for Hermes Chthonios, who is also often decorated with ribbons.[9] Whatever the case, the *tainia* indicates the care afforded the *stele*, the funerary *sema* (marker). It has general cult significance by setting apart the object it adorned and in its placement around the *stele*, as with the textile around the funerary vessel, symbolically 'embraces' the beloved dead.

Textiles as decoration for the tomb

In the case of tomb Γ at Sedes (Thessalonica), dated to the late fourth century BC, it appears that a textile decorated with stars adorned the wooden ceiling of the tomb (Kotzias 1956, 869–875). The wooden roof of the tomb was probably entirely covered with a multicoloured piece of cloth (traces of yellow, deep blue and red still remain) consisting of cotton and silk threads (the same use of a textile is hypothesized in Bulgaria: Filow 1934, 103). Since the example from Sedes had either a purely decorative or symbolic function, if we interpret it as the remains of a baldachino, *kamara* (καμάρα) or *ouraniskos* (οὐρανίσκος) (Weber 1990, 36–39), albeit not one erected directly over the couch (*kline*),[10] it is especially intriguing. Painted imitations of textiles on the ceilings of tombs are known in literature in Greece (see below), Etruria (for instance, Holloway 1965), south Russia (Blisnitza), and Egypt (for instance, Adriani 1952,

112; Venit 2002). In Egypt in particular, the painted tapestry on the ceiling of Anfushy II, room 2, is supposed to be shown under a painted imitation of a trellis (Adriani 1952, 72–76). The find from Sedes is consequently of great importance, because it provides evidence for real textile decoration inside tombs in Greece (and thus dismisses any reservations raised by Tomlinson 1984) and, by extension, houses (see Alabe 2002 on the unique painted ceiling decoration of the House of the Seals and the House of the Sword, Delos). On the other hand, the combination of a wooden roof and a real textile is noteworthy, since this is often presumed only to be in paint.

Indirect evidence of textiles provided by the presence of nails – which could have been used to fix the suspended pieces of cloth in place – is equally valuable. A fortunate, yet questionable, example of such a case exists in the antechamber of the tomb of Eurydice at Vergina. Here, according to the excavator's report, iron nails were found set at regular intervals in the shape of the letter Π over the entire surface of the vault (Ginouvès 1993, 156). In addition to these, the remains of gold discs that once decorated a textile were found among the disintegrated organic material in the antechamber of the so-called Tomb of Philip II and, according to the excavator, might have belonged to a large piece of cloth that was originally hung 'high up', possibly on the wall or on the vault (Andronikos 1984, 179, note on the caption of figs 143–144).

Funerary wall- and floor-decoration alluding to textiles

Wall-paintings in tombs depict the use of fabrics and certainly allude to their use in house interiors as well. One of the best examples is the wall-painting found in a chamber tomb at Dion (Soteriades 1932, 43–44; Boardman 1970, 143–144). The painting takes the form of a narrow frieze on the back wall above the funerary couch, on the base of the vault, and depicts an animal, possibly a lion. Only the lower part of the lion's feet is preserved, with two decorative bands – one above and one below its body. The size of the preserved frieze is not recorded in the original publication, but the date of the tomb is placed, on architectural grounds, in the second half of the third century BC. While the publication of the tomb is not yet complete and no published photographs of the wall-painting exist, it has been compared with textiles found in Pazyryk Mound 5 (Altai) (Boardman 1970, 143, figs 2–3), and its subject matter is comparable to the lion motif found at Koropi. In the same tomb at Dion, remains of nails are recorded over the *kline* on the frieze of the base of the vault (Soteriades 1932, 43). The nails were supposed by the excavator to have once fixed textiles or (less likely) vessels.

Another notable example is the ceiling decoration from the tomb of Lyson and Kallikles at Lefkadia (ancient Mieza), dated to the second century BC (Miller 1993) (pl. 4). The ceiling of the burial-chamber is painted in imitation of a woven fabric with a turreted motif (Miller 1993, 45). This particular motif is studied in the context of the *symposion* tent of Ptolemy II by Kallixenos of Rhodes (Athenaeus, *Deip.* 5, 196–197c), where the tent is described as having a roof draped with a red-and-white canopy, *ouraniskos* (οὐρανίσκος), patterned in a turreted motif, *pyrgaton* (πυργωτόν). (For a suggested visualisation of Ptolemy's tent see Pfrommer 1999, 69–75, fig. 102.)[11]

A second tomb from Lefkadia presents a very different decorative pattern for our corpus (pl. 5, pl. 6). Here, on the ceiling of the antechamber in the Tomb of the Palmettes, we see a distinctive floral motif as the main theme (Rhomiopoulou 1973, 91; Rhomiopoulou, Schmidt-

Dounas 2010, 76–77). Huge polychrome *anthemia*, aquatic flowers and plant motifs, possibly designed with the aid of a template and a compass, are depicted on a faded, water-like, blue background seemingly meant to recall water (on scroll decoration see Valeva 2006). The tomb is now dated to 320 to 300 BC. This kind of decoration might allude to textiles, but the floral theme is quite common in other arts as well.

The painted remains on the ceilings of two third-century BC tombs might indicate that they were decorated in imitation of simple canopies. The first comes from the one-room tomb at Malathria-Dion, dated by the excavator to the second half of the third century BC (Makaronas 1961, 135–137; Miller 1993, 45, footnote 57). The second belongs to the antechamber of the tomb at Drama, where remains of multicoloured *tainiai* and triangular designs in the corners are visible (Koukouli-Chrysanthaki 1984; Miller 1993, 45, footnote 57). The Drama tomb is dated to the third century BC, with continuous usage until the first century BC. If this imitation was indeed common in Macedonian tombs, then the monochrome ceilings in various other tombs might allude to the existence of simple, monochrome canopies as well (for examples of burial-chambers with painted ceilings outside Macedonia, see Miller 1993, 46, footnote 58).

It might be of some further significance that, in instances where the funerary monuments under discussion here consisted of two rooms (chamber and antechamber), the ceiling bearing the colourful imitation belongs to the antechamber (the entrance to the funerary environment). The only exception to this is in the tomb of Lyson and Kallikles, possibly because the main chamber was used for successive burials. This correspondence might not be entirely coincidental, but its implications are not easily explained by the evidence at hand. One might propose that the transition from the antechamber (the entrance) to the main chamber (the burial place) was underlined by the different styles of painted decoration, a method similar to what has been proposed for Pompeian houses, for example, where the decoration of the *fauces* 'leads' the visitor into the main house and makes the transition from exterior to interior significant (Downey-Verfenstein 1994). In such a way, the painted imitations of textiles play a transitional role, possibly from life (antechamber) to death (main chamber). Since the ancient beliefs about death considered the dead body polluted (Parker 1983), the antechamber was probably as far as any of the relatives and attendants would like to be. Moreover, the antechamber might have been the area associated with pre-burial ceremonies, such as the ritual cleansing of both the dead and the living upon entrance (see for instance the paintings in the antechamber of the Tomb of Lyson and Kallikles in Miller 1993, 38–39).

What dictates the use of a real textile versus a painted imitation of it in the tomb? As much as one would like to know the cost of both media, evidence at hand prevents any secure and straightforward answer, since our knowledge about the artists involved and the way they divided their work (i.e. masters and pupils), the cost of the materials used (paints versus metallic and dyed threads) and the structure of the textile workshops that produced expensive tapestry-woven pieces like those found in funerary environments, is still limited. Maria Nowicka, based on the information provided in the mid-third-century BC Zenon papyri, has argued for the use of '*cahiers de modèles*' for the painted decoration proposed to clients (Nowicka 1984, 257). If this were widely the case, the cost of the painted decoration might have been significantly reduced. On the other hand, not all designs could have easily been reproduced in both paint and tapestry: we still know very little about the possibilities of weaving in Hellenistic Greece.

In addition to the ceilings, there are two examples from tombs of floor-mosaics decorated with lozenges, creating the effect of carpeting (what Rostovtzeff has called 'stone carpets'). At Langada, the main chamber's floor is painted with a rectangle in the middle filled with lozenges in black, yellow and red (Macridy 1911, 211, pl. 2; Sismanidis 1985, fig. 6, dated to the beginning of the fourth century BC); but the deterioration of the stucco in the *prothalamos* chamber does not allow the identification of any decorative motif. At Kastas-Amphipolis, both the main chamber and the antechamber are decorated with non-figural mosaics composed of coloured pebbles (Lazaridis 1966, 68–69, pl. 52a (mosaic); Salzmann 1982, 31 and 83, no. 10, dated to the last quarter of the fourth century BC). Pebble mosaics that allude to carpeting are rather rare in the Greek world, so the Kastas-Amphipolis tomb floor represents a trend little seen elsewhere in Greece. It is also possible that some of the *stelai* from Demetrias depict carpets in painting.[12]

Textiles carved on funerary furniture

Apart from the remains of actual textiles, Hellenistic tombs of the Macedonian type provide us with sculpted furnishings on funerary beds and thrones (Andrianou 2009). Such beds in Macedonian tombs were used for the placement of the body of the deceased or, in a few cases, the weapons of the deceased, when his body was cremated and placed in an urn. Sculpted versions of pillows are known from three Macedonian tombs in Eretria: a) the fourth- or third-century BC Macedonian tomb at Kotroni (Karapaschalidou 1989, 20), where the remains of a man were discovered on a stuccoed, stone-built bed with carved representations of two pillows; b) the third-century BC Macedonian tomb of Erotes (Vollmoeller 1901, 333–376; Huguenot 2008, 97–104), in which there are two limestone beds inscribed with male names and decorated with carved imitations of a mattress and pillows, and two marble throne-receptacles decorated with a carved cushion and inscribed with female names (Fig. 3); c) the third-century BC Macedonian tomb at Amarynthos, which contains two stone beds adorned with sculpted bedding that preserves painted stripes in pink, red, orange, yellow and blue (Huguenot 2008, 207–225) (Fig. 4). In addition to the Eretrian examples there are the sculpted furnishings from the fourth-century BC chamber tomb at Tekirdağ (Naip tumulus) on Ganos Mountain (Delemen 2006, 256–257; *idem*, 2004, 27–35), where carved pillows adorn the headrests of the bed.

The catalogue of furnished funerary interiors from Hellenistic Macedonia is quite rich (Andrianou 2009) and it may be assumed with a good degree of certainty that funerary furniture was also adorned with *real* bed covers and pillows. The only trace of furnishing directly associated with beds in Greece is 'the presence of a substance that gives an impression of wool or feathers' on the ground of the antechamber of the so-called Tomb of Philip II at Vergina, now stored at the Museum in Vergina (Andronikos 1977, 24–25). If they are really feathers, they might be the sole extant remains of a type of mattress mentioned by Pollux (6, 9–11; 10, 36–43). The same writer refers to the mattresses and headrests as *pterides* (πτερίδες), talks about the process of filling them (πτίλοις τά κνέφαλα ἀνεπλήρουν), and finally names them *proskephalaia ptilota* (προσκεφάλαια πτιλωτά). These, then, are probably the remains of a mattress such as that described by Pollux (VI, 9–11; X, 36–43) or a feather pillow, a *proskephalaion ptiloton* (προσκεφάλαιον πτιλωτόν) (VI, 10; X, 38).

Above left: Fig. 3. Tomb of Erotes, Eretria (photo by Andreas F. Voegelin (AMB/ESAG)).

Above right: Fig. 4. Tomb of Amarynthos, Eretria (photo by Andreas F. Voegelin (AMB/ESAG)).

Textiles on tombstones

Textiles depicted on painted *stelai* are quite informative and aid in the reconstruction of both funerary and domestic interiors. Here, the *stelai* from Demetrias (Volos) come into play; for they are a treasure-house for various types of textile on furniture and on the floor. A major drawback, however, is that the *stelai* were only briefly published in 1909, without photographs, and they are currently inaccessible to researchers. As a result, an accurate description is not yet possible. Nevertheless, a number of *stelai* depicting textile furnishings can be singled out from the corpus and presented here.

The *stele* of Stratonikos, for example, depicts a young man seated on a wooden *klismos* furnished with a thick pillow, which is covered with a decorated cloth or has stitching applied directly to it. This decoration is picked out in blue and rose paint, a common method of portraying pillows in the area (Arvanitopoulos 1909, 124, no. 9, dated to the second half of the third century BC). The *stele* of Onesimos depicts the deceased on a *kline* adorned with rose-tinted bedding and pillows, whereas the deceased is dressed in white and covered by what is possibly a white sheet.[13] The *stele* of Kleon and Artemesia shows a blue-green mattress on the *kline*, in this example adorned with red and rose bedding (Arvanitopoulos 1909, 185, 223 addendum, no. 27, dated to around 250 BC). The *stele* of Asklepiades may have belonged to a merchant from Sidon. It depicts an equally interesting type of bedding that appears to have been decorated with stitching (Arvanitopoulos 1909, 165, no. 21, dated around 200 BC). This *stele* might also suggest a red carpet covering the floor of the scene. The *stele* of Dionysius provides a different sort of information for here, on the *kline* of the *stele*, the reclining Dionysius rests his feet on a pillow, possibly a custom of Thrace, the deceased's place of origin (Arvanitopoulos 1909, 235, no. 47, dated to around 225 BC). Another single pillow, this time on a *klismos*, is depicted on the *stele* of Peneis and Herodotos (Arvanitopoulos 1909, no. 29, 196, dated to the last quarter of the third century BC), whereas two pillows seem to be rendered on the *klismos* of the *stele* of Choirile (Arvanitopoulos 1909, 258, no. 55, dated to the last quarter of the third century BC). Finally, the *stele* of Aphrodeisia is described by Arvanitopoulos as a *stele* with a unique depiction of a throne with a baldachino, formed by the two vertical beams of the throne attached to two horizontal beams, thus forming a ceiling over the seat, covered with a piece of yellow cloth (Fig. 5, pl. 7).[14]

Baldachinos (*ouraniskoi*) erected over funerary thrones (and beds)[15] are not unknown in Greek vase-painting[16] and in funerary interiors outside Greece.[17] In Macedonia their existence has been supposed in the tomb at Sedes (albeit not directly over the *kline*), the Soteriades tomb at Dion (see above) and over the well-known throne of Eurydice at Vergina. In the last case, spots of a dark-red colour in several places on the arms of the throne and in the main scene depicted on the throne (Hades and Persephone in the chariot) have been interpreted as stains from the deterioration of a purple piece of cloth that hung over the throne. If this postulation is true, the depiction of the baldachino over the throne on the Aphrodeisia *stele* becomes stronger. Further details on the *stele* show other uses of textiles: three red ribbons spill out of a box, placed on the table next to the figure. Aphrodeisia is seated on a pillow and rests her back on another pillow that projects over the top of the throne.

Textiles being offered to the dead are identified on three sculpted *stelai* where a standing female offers a wrapped piece of cloth to the seated dead: a *stele* from Palaio Phaleron dated to 360–350 BC, a *stele* from Porto Rafti dated after 330 BC (Kalogeropoulou 1971) and a *stele* from Pallene (*stele* no. 32 in the Museum of Marathon) also dated around 330 BC (Kalogeropoulou 1977) (Fig. 6). A fourth example has been mentioned by Kalogeropoulou but is not yet securely placed in this category (Kalogeropoulou 1971, 222, note 40). It is possible that a

Fig. 5. *Stele* of Aphrodeisia, Demetrias (photo by D. Andrianou).

painted version of this iconography appears on a *stele* from Pagasai (Arvanitopoulos 1909, 323, no. 104, *stele* of three figures) dated possibly to the third century BC, but the *stele* is not fully published. Five additional *stelai* depict wrapped pieces of cloth carved on their pediments; the *stele* of Kallisto; the *stele* 983 from the National Museum; the *stele* of Pythodoros from Boeotia (Kalogeropoulou 1971, 227); the *stele* of Diphilos and the Ephebic Oath from Acharnai (Kalogeropoulou 1977, 213, note 59a) and three more examples are found on painted *stelai*; the *stele* of Euferos; the *stele* of Paramythion from the Munich Glyptothek; and the *stele* of Myttion from J. P. Getty (Kalogeropoulou 1971, 227).

The textiles depicted on these tombstones are symbols of offerings to the dead and were possibly meant to be burnt, if we trust the literary sources that support this custom (Kalogeropoulou 1971). Athena Kalogeropoulou, who has investigated the subject in depth, concludes that the offering of cloth in the tomb might be connected to the hope for *eugenism* and salvation in a greater sense, and is comparable to other similar symbols, such as eggs, wreaths, flowers, grapes, pomegranates, pigeons, etc. (Kalogeropoulou 1977, 224–225).

The frieze on the façade of the Agios Athanasios III tomb, which depicts a *symposion*, is an exceptional representation of colourful bedclothes and pillows (Tsimbidou-Avloniti 2005), and ending with it is the best way to wrap up a discussion on funerary bedding (pl. 8). The colour of the bedclothes in this frieze seems to match the colour of the pillows: purple, blue and red are the main hues chosen for this specific scene. They are strikingly vivid and allude to Homer's image of smooth white bedclothes beneath the body and 'fair robes of purple colour' over the body (*Odyssey* I, 130; X, 35.2, quoted in Athenaeus, 2, 48c).

Fig. 6. *Stele* of Pallene, Museum of Marathon no. 32 (photo by D. Andrianou).

Conclusions

The wide variety of uses for textiles in tombs makes us yet again regret the fact that climatic conditions do not allow for the preservation of textiles in Greece. One factor that is not completely understood, helps to slow down the deterioration of fabrics, and this is the presence of metal (Margariti *et al.* 2011). One can only imagine the colourful interiors of funerary chambers and houses in late Classical and Hellenistic Greece. There are actually only two excavated examples of domestic painted ceilings in Greece so far that evoke carpets spread out, and that are comparable to funerary ceilings: in the House of the Seals and the House of the Sword on Delos, dated to the first decades of the first century BC (Alabe 2002). Admiration of an interior domestic space is attested in literature: Bdelikleon, in Aristophanes' *Wasps*, orders his father Philokleon to admire the woven hangings of the court, part of his 'education' on how to behave in the sophisticated society (Aristophanes, *Wasps*, 1215)! Thus, even fleeting admiration of the funerary space might have been one of the factors that dictated the setting of a tomb. Comfort that alludes to a 'homely environment' might have been another, based on funerary beliefs that are not entirely comprehensible to us through archaeological finds. Late Classical and Hellenistic tomb-interiors were not meant to be revisited: they were sealed and opened only in a few cases for secondary burials. Funerary rites were performed over the tomb or the tumulus, around its *sema*.

As Zeitlin rightly notes, the scenes of discourse about images in ancient literature are an indication that images function as a cue for memory and a means of instruction (Zeitlin 1994, 153). This is especially true and important for funerary interiors, which encrypt certain beliefs and Orphic or Dionysiac initiation rites for the afterlife, and at the same time signify the personality and status of the owner of the tomb, sometimes a member of a secret cult. Visual imagery on the walls or on the textiles of the tomb, in addition to providing eternal comfort, may have played the same role as the Bacchic tablets; to answer questions about identity, give passwords and recall or repeat formulas (Cole 2003). Textiles in the antechamber of certain tombs might have played a symbolic, transitional role from life (antechamber) to death (chamber). Furthermore, light colours and especially white, might have stood out in the gloom of the underworld and alluded to ritual purity (Graf, Johnston 2007, 109). The fact that textiles help our understanding of funerary rites is also evident through the information we gather from the materials used: although one would think that only the best and most expensive offerings, such as gold textiles (Gleba 2008), accompanied the dead in the afterlife, this is not always true. An early example, from the end of the seventh or the beginning of the sixth century BC, provides evidence for a re-used piece of cloth being placed inside a bronze *kalpis* in an archaic tomb on Corfu (Metallinou *et al.* 2009, 34).

Care, comfort and symbolism through the use of textiles in tombs worked together and were mobilised in order to aid, give sense to, and diminish fear of the incomprehensible Otherworld and the trip thereto, since 'nothing is so welcome in death as the imitation and recollection of life' (Graf, Johnston, 2007, 120). A comprehensive statistical analysis of each cemetery from the period in question, combined with a study of the relevance of the funerary finds, will in the future assist us in understanding the hopes of the deceased and his or her relatives in a better way.

dandr@eie.gr

Notes

1. On one occasion textiles were found in a foundation deposit, possibly as part of the ritual accompanying the construction of a building. The example comes from a fifth-century BC pyre deposit of miniature cooking pots underneath a building in the Agora of Athens (Unruh 2007, 170–171).

2. Sardian carpets were used in Persia (by the Persian king exclusively) according to the *Persika* of a Greek ethnohistorian who lived in the fourth century BC (Greenewalt, Majewski 1980, 134).

3. An *akestria* is mentioned in *IG* II² 1556, line 28.

4. See, for instance, the painted *stele* (no. 119) from Demetrias depicting a *symposion*, where the sheet covering the body of the reclining man, who is dressed in a white *chiton*, is painted red (Arvanitopoulos 1909, 348). For the use of red in Greek tombs in general, see Kalogeropoulou 1977, 215–216, notes 74–75. For the interpretation of red as the colour of blood and consequently of the living, see Johansen 1951, 116. However, exceptions do occur: red is the colour of the *chiton*, interpreted as a shroud, worn on the Lyseas *stele* from the end of the sixth century BC (Johansen 1951, fig. 53).

5. A recent unpublished study of the cloth has shown no linen in the X-ray analysis. Another woollen fabric with a gold tapestry-woven vine leaf and ivy design was found in a woman's grave at Kertch, dated to the third century BC (Beckwith 1954, 114).

6. Arvanitopoulos 1928, 135, fig. 162; *idem*, 1909, no. 6 (*stele* of Diodotos), dated to the second quarter of the third century BC, depicts a *tainia* with colours that mimic the texture of the textile, and small threads are visible on the edges of the textile (see Kurtz 1975, pl. 33, 2); no. 24 (*stele* of Antimachos), dated to the last quarter of the third century BC; no. 57 (*stele* of Aristoboule), dated around 200 BC; no. 70 (*stele* of Leon), dated around 225 BC; no. 72 (*stele* of Xenarchos), dated a little before 300 BC; no. 81 (*stele* of Glaphyra), dated to 250 BC; no. 101 (*stele* of Dionysodoros), dated to the first quarter of the third century BC; no. 170 (*stele* of Rodon), dated around 250 BC.

7. See for example Kurtz 1975 for several fifth-century BC examples which show different uses of the *tainiai*: pl. 19, 3 (*tainiai* around the shaft of the *stele*); pl. 33, 2 (suspended from the *stele*); pl. 26, 2 (*stele* with several *tainiai*); pls 20, 1, 2, and 25, 2 (woman with basket full of *tainiai* to be placed on the *stele*); pl. 33, 2 (*tainiai* with loose threads along their edges); pl. 29, 1 (dead adorned with *tainiai*); pl. 51, 3 (youth sitting on a funerary mound draped with *tainiai*). Another use of these *tainiai* has to do with what may be rolled scrolls, tied together with ribbons (*ARV* 1337, no. 12; *ARV* 1378, no. 44; *ARV* 1380, no. 80). See also Kurtz 1975, 61–62 for discussion of the Reed workshop. On Red Figure painting see, for example, *RVAp* I, p.195, 8/6.

8. Arvanitopoulos 1909, no. 84, p. 298, *stele* of Artemidoros, dated around 250 BC. On the *stele* the *tainia* is shown below the inscription, and Hermes, usually absent from the space below the *tainia*, is here depicted with a second *tainia* on his head. Hermes with a ribbon around his head also appears on nos 85, 100.

9. Arvanitopoulos 1909, 115. On the *stelai* from Demetrias, Hermes is often depicted below the main scene, except on the *stelai* with *tainiai*. In one case this Hermes is dressed with a red ribbon around his neck (Arvanitopoulos 1909, no. 15, p. 144, *stele* of Charmides, dated to the first quarter of the third century BC) or around his head (see earlier note).

For depiction of Hermes below a *tainia* see earlier note. For a *tainia* with a painted scene on the same *stele* see the unique example no, 98, pp. 313–314, a *stele* with a *symposion* (?) scene.

10. Kotzias 1956, 874. According to Guimier-Sorbets 2001, the funerary chamber is the setting of an eternal *prothesis* for the heroicised deceased. Baldachinos became common in Egypt in the third millennium BC, and have been grouped into three types by Marga Weber 1900. In Egypt they are found in the cults of the gods as well as in funerary practice. Later, in Assyria, Babylonia, and Persia, they acquire significance as a sign of wealth and become a status symbol, but are not found in funerary practice. In Archaemenid art in particular, baldachinos are often found set up over thrones. In Greek art they are found in the sacred space for the commemoration of the deities, and with the emergence of temple architecture we find them inside monumental temples, in hypaethral areas. Later, baldachinos are more likely to be found in processions (*Prozessionsschrein*) or in other cultic areas in ephemeral structures. In Rome they are associated, from the very beginning of Imperial times, with the divination of rulers.

11. For a *chitonis* and a *chitoniskos pyrgatos* see also *IG* II² 1514, lines 26 and 46 respectively, from Brauron.

12. Arvanitopoulos 1909: the *stele* of Peneis and Herodotos (no. 29, p. 197); the *stele* of Hedeste (no. 1, addendum, p. 218), dated to the second half of the third century BC; the *stele* of two figures (no. 54, p. 256), dated to around 200 BC; the *stele* of a *symposion* (no. 144, p. 340). I have been able to see the *stele* of Hedeste myself: the carpet is just visible with the naked eye.

13. Arvanitopoulos 1909, no. 19, p. 153, *stele* of Onesimos, dated around 300 BC. This *stele* is particularly important, since it is said to depict a table covered by a piece of cloth of unknown colour; the floor of the scene is also said to be covered by a piece of cloth or carpet.

14. Arvanitopoulos 1909, no. 28, p. 190, *stele* of Aphrodeisia, dated around 225 BC. The *stele* is depicted in Arvanitopoulos 1908, pl. 4, 2, but in black and white, which does not render the details clearly. Personal observation of the *stele* at the Museum of Volos and the painted rendering of its iconography (by E. Zilliéron) at the Archaeological Society of Athens were not conclusive and showed no trace of horizontal beams. A semicircular line over the throne, however, might indicate the presence of a piece of cloth, but it is not clear whether the cloth is hanging from vertical posts, as described by Avanitopoulos. Whatever the case, the *stele* should be investigated in greater detail under different lights.

15. Weber 1990, 38–39 for the proper use of the word; Guimier-Sorbets 2001 for a thorough study of baldachinos on funerary beds in Macedonian tombs.

16. For iconographic examples in vase-painting see also *CVA Geneva, Musée d'Art et d'Histoire* 2, pl. 74, 9 (a seated Dionysius on an *okladias diphros* under a baldachino supported by two beams, dated around 490 BC or later, from Selinunt); *CVA Musei Comunali Umbri* 1, pl. 15, 4 (three young males under a baldachino or tent, with no traces of supports, only part of the cloth (?) that would have formed the baldachino); Alfieri, Arias 1960, pl.34 (volute krater with Dionysos Sabazios and Cybele under a baldachino supported by two Doric columns, with no trace of a cloth ceiling, dated to 440 BC, from Valle Trebba); Reho-Bumbalova 1990, pl. 13, 146 (four reclining figures under a baldachino, with no

trace of supports, only the cloth that covered the baldachino, from Sozopol (Apollonia), dated to 360–340 BC). Textile remains of a baldachino have been supposed over the dead in a burial pit on a Sarmatian site in Yuzhny Bug, Sokolova Mohyla (Ukraine), dated to the first century AD (mentioned in Gleba 2008, 67).

17. For instance Nowicka 1984, 259, note 25 for imitations of baldachinos in Alexandrian tombs and Weber 1990, for a thorough treatment of the subject.

Bibliography

Adriani 1952: A. Adriani, 'Nécropoles de l'île de Pharos. B) Section d'Anfouchy', *Annuaire* 3 (1940–1950), 55–128

Alabe 2002: F. Alabe, 'Décors peints au plafond dans les maisons hellénistiques à Délos', *Bulletin de Correspondance Hellénique* 126, 231–263

Alfieri, Arias 1960: N. Alfieri, P. E. Arias, *Spina : Guida al Museo Archeologico in Ferrara*, Firenze

Andrianou 2009: D. Andrianou, *The Furniture and Furnishings of Ancient Greek Houses and Tombs*, Cambridge

Andronikos 1977: M. Andronikos, 'Βεργίνα. Οι βασιλικοί τάφοι της Μεγάλης Τούμπας', *Athens Annals of Archaeology* 10, 1–40

Andronikos 1984: M. Andronikos, *Vergina. The Royal Tombs and the Ancient City*, Athens

ARV: J. D. Beazley, *Attic Red-Figure Vase-Painters*, Oxford, 1963

Arvanitopoulos 1908: A. Arvanitopoulos, A. "Η σημασία τῶν γραπτῶν στηλῶν τῶν Παγασῶν', *Archaiologike Ephemeris* 1908, 1–60

Arvanitopoulos 1909: A. Arvanitopoulos, Θεσσαλικά Μνημεία, Ἀθανασάκειον Μουσεῖον ἐν Βόλῳ, Athens

Arvanitopoulos 1928: A. Arvanitopoulos, Γραπταί Στῆλαι Δημητριάδος-Παγασῶν, Athens

Beckwith 1954: J. Beckwith, 'Textile fragments from classical antiquity: an important find at Koropi, near Athens', *Illustrated London News* 1954, 114–115

Boardman 1970: J. Boardman, 'Travelling rugs', *Antiquity* 44, 143–144

Bonacasa, Di Vita 1984: N. Bonacasa, A. Di Vita (eds), *Alessandria e il Mondo ellenistico-romano: Studi in Onore de Achille Adriani* 2, Roma

Chrysostomou 1998: P. Chrysostomou, Μακεδονικοί Τάφοι Πέλλας, Ι. Τάφος Β', ο ασύλητος, Thessaloniki

Cole 2003: S. G. Cole, 'Landscape of Dionysos and Elysian Fields', in M. B. Cosmopoulos (ed.), *Greek Mysteries, the Archaeology and Ritual of Ancient Greek Secret Cults*, London, 193–217

CVA: *Corpus Vasorum Antiquorum*, 1925–

Delemen 2004: I. Delemen, *Tekirdağ Naip Tümülüsü*, Istanbul

Delmen 2006: I. Delemen, 'An unplundered chamber tomb on Ganos Mountain in southeastern Thrace', *American Journal of Archaeology* 110, 251–273

Downey-Verfenstein 1994: C. Downey-Verfenstein, *Fauces Decoration*, unpublished paper

Drougou 1987: S. Drougou, 'Τό ὕφασμα της Βεργίνας. Πρῶτες παρατηρήσεις', in M. Tiverios, S. Drougou, C. Saatsoglou-Paliadeli (eds), Ἀμητός: Τιμητικός τόμος για τον καθηγητή Μανόλη Ἀνδρόνικο 1, Thessaloniki, 303–316

Edmonds 1961: J. M. Edmonds, *The Fragments of Attic Comedy* 3b, Leiden

Edmonds 1919: J. M. Edmonds (ed.), *The Greek Bucolic Poets*, London and New York

Filow 1934: B. D. Filow, *Die Grabhügelnekropole bei Duvanlij in Südbulgarien*, Sofia

Flury-Lemberg 1988: M. Flury-Lemberg, 'The fabrics from the royal tomb in Vergina,' in M. Flury-Lemberg (ed.), *Textile Conservation and Research*, Bern

Garland 1985: R. Garland, *The Greek Way of Death*, Ithaca

Gilles, Nosch 2007: C. Gilles, M.-L. B. Nosch (eds), *Ancient Textiles, Production, Craft and Society: Proceedings of the First International Conference on Ancient Textiles, held at Lund, Sweden, and Copenhagen, Denmark, on March 19–23, 2003*, Oxford

Ginouvès 1993: R. Ginouvès (ed.), *Macedonia. From Philip II to the Roman Conquest*, Athens

Gleba 2008: M. Gleba, '*Auratae vestes*: gold textiles in the ancient Mediterranean', in C. Alfaro, L. Karali (eds), Purpureae Vestes II: *Vestidos, Textiles y Tintes: Estudios sobre la Producción de Bienes de Consumo en la Antigüedad*, Valencia, 61–69

Graf, Johnston 2007: F. Graf, S. I. Johnston, *Ritual Texts for the Afterlife: Orpheus and the Bacchic Gold Tablets*, London

Greenewalt, Majewski 1980: C. H. Greenewalt Jr, L. J. Majewski, 'IX. Lydian textiles', in K. De Vries (ed.), *From Athens to Gordion: The Papers of a Memorial Symposium for Rodney S. Young*, Philadelphia, 133–147

Guimier-Sorbets 2001: A.-M. Guimier-Sorbets, 'Mobilier et décor de tombes macédoniennes', in R. Frei-Stolba, K. Gex (eds), *Recherches Récentes sur le Monde hellénistique. Actes du Colloque International Organisé à l'Occasion du 60e Anniversaire de Pierre Ducrey (Lausanne, 20–21 novembre 1998)*, Bern, 217–229

Holloway 1965: R. R. Holloway, 'Conventions of Etruscan painting in the Tomb of Hunting and Fishing at Tarquinii,' *American Journal of Archaeology* 69, 341–347

Huguenot 2008: C. Huguenot, *Eretria XIX. La tombe aux Érotes et la Tombe d'Amarynthos. Architecture funéraire et Présence macédonienne en Grèce centrale*, Lausanne

Hundt 1969: H.-J. Hundt, 'Über vorgeschichtliche Seidenfunde', *Jahrbuch des Römisch-Germanischen Zentralmuseums* 16, 65–71

IG: Inscriptiones Graecae, Berlin, 1873–

Jacoby 1964: F. Jacoby, *Die Fragmente der Griechischen Historiker*, Leiden.

Johansen 1951: F. J. Johansen, *The Attic Grave-Reliefs of the Classical Period: An Essay in Interpretation*, Copenhagen

Kalogeropoulou 1971: A. Kalogeropoulou, 'Δύο αττικά επιτύμβια ανάγλυφα', *Archaiologikon Deltion* 24A (1969), 211–229

Kalogeropoulou 1977: A. Kalogeropoulou, 'Νέα Αττική επιτύμβια στήλη', *Archaiologikon Deltion* 29A (1974), 194–225

Karapaschalidou 1989: A. Karapaschalidou, *Μακεδονικός Τάφος στο Κοτρώνι Ερέτριας*, Athens

Knigge 1988: U. Knigge, *Der Kerameikos von Athen. Führung durch Ausgrabungen und Geschichte*, Athens

Kotzias 1956: N. Kotzias, 'Ο παρά το αεροδρόμιον της Θεσσαλονίκης (Σέδες) Γ' τάφος', *Archaiologike Ephemeris* 1937 (1956), 866–895

Koukouli-Chrysanthaki 1984: C. Koukouli-Chrysanthaki, 'Μακεδονία, Νομός Δράμας', *Archaiologikon Deltion* 31 B2 (1976), 303–304

Kübler 1936: K. Kübler, 'Ausgrabungen im Kerameikos', *Archäologischer Anzeiger* 1936, 182–208

Kurtz 1975: D. C. Kurtz, *Athenian White Lekythoi. Patterns and Painters*, Oxford

Lazaridis 1966: D. Lazaridis, Ἀνασκαφαί καὶ ἔρευναι Ἀμφιπόλεως, *Praktika tes en Athenais Archaiologikes Hetaireias* 1960, 67–73

Lewis 1959: D. M. Lewis, 'Attic manumissions', *Hesperia* 28, 208–238

Lewis 1968: D. M. Lewis, 'Dedications of Phialai at Athens', *Hesperia* 37, 368–380

Macridy 1911: T. Macridy, 'Un tumulus macédonien à Langaza', *Jahrbuch des deutschen archäologischen Instituts* 26, 193–215

Makaronas 1940: C. Makaronas, Ἀνασκαφαὶ καὶ ἔρευναι ἐν Μακεδονίᾳ κατὰ τὸ ἔτος 1939, *Makedonika* 1, 495–496

Makaronas 1961: C. Makaronas, Ἀνασκαφικὴ ἔρευνα "μακεδονικοῦ τάφου" ἐν Δίῳ Πιερίας, *Praktika tes en Athenais Archaiologikes Hetaireias* 1956, 131–138

Mansfield 1985: J. M. Mansfield, *The Robe of Athena and the Panathenaic 'Peplos'*, dissertation, University of California, Berkeley

Margariti *et al.* 2011: C. Margariti, S. Protopapas, V. Orphanou, 'Recent analyses of the excavated textile find from grave 35 HTR73, Kerameikos cemetery, Athens, Greece', *Journal of Archaeological Science* 38, 522–527

Metallinou *et al.* 2009: G. Metallinou, C. Moulhérat, Y. Spantidaki, Ἀρχαιολογικά υφάσματα από την Κέρκυρα, *Arachne* 3, 22–43

Miller 1993: S. Miller, *The Tomb of Lyson and Kallikles*, Mainz

Moulhérat, Spantidaki 2007: C. Moulhérat, Y. Spantidaki, 'A study of textile remains from the 5th century BC discovered in Kalyvia, Attica', in Gillis, Nosch 2007, 163–166

Moulhérat, Spantidaki 2009: C. Moulhérat, Y. Spantidaki, Ἀρχαιολογικά υφάσματα από τη Σαλαμίνα: προκαταρκτική παρουσίαση, *Arachne* 3, 8–21

Mylonas 1956: G. Mylonas, Ἀνασκαφή νεκροταφείου Ἐλευσῖνος, *Praktika tes en Athenais Archaiologikes Hetaireias* 1953, 77–87

Nowicka 1984: M. Nowicka, 'Theophilos, peintre Alexandrin, et son activité', in Bonacasa, Di Vita 1984, 256–259

Ovadiah 1980: A. Ovadiah, *Geometric and Floral Patterns in Ancient Mosaic*, Roma

Pantermalis *et al.* 2000: D. Pantermalis, A. Despoini, C. Koukouli-Chrysanthaki, A. Adam-Veleni (eds), *Μύρτος: Μνήμη Ιουλίας Βοκοτοπούλου*, Thessaloniki

Pantos 1980: P. Pantos, Θράκη, Νομός Ἕβρου, *Archaiologikon Deltion* 29 (1973–1974), 823–827

Papapostolou 1982: I. Papapostolou, Ἑλληνιστικοί τάφοι τῆς Πάτρας, Ι, *Archaiologikon Deltion* 32A, 1977, 281–343

Parker 1983: R. Parker, *Miasma: Pollution and Purification in Early Greek Religion*, Oxford

Pfrommer 1999: M. Pfrommer, *Alexandria im Schatten der Pyramiden*, Mainz-am-Rhein

Potter 1938: R. Potter, *Euripides. The Complete Greek Drama* 1, New York

Reho-Bumbalova 1990 : M. Reho-Bumbalova, *La Ceramica Attica a Figure nere e rosse nella Tracia bulgara*, Rome

Rhomiopoulou 1973: K. Rhomiopoulou, 'A new monumental chamber tomb with paintings of the Hellenistic period near Lefkadia (West Macedonia)', *Athens Annals of Archaeology* 6 (1), 87–92

Rhomiopoulou, Schmidt-Dounas 2010: K. Rhomiopoulou, B. Schmidt-Dounas, *Das Palmettengrab in Lefkadia*, Mitteilungen des deutschen archäologischen Instituts Beiheft 21, Mainz

RVAp: A. Trendall, A. Cambitoglou, *Red-Figured Vases of Apulia* I, Oxford, 1978

Saatsoglou-Paliadeli 1984: C. Saatsoglou-Paliadeli, Τα επιτάφια Μνημεία από τη μεγάλη Τούμπα της Βεργίνας, Thessaloniki

Salzmann 1982: D. Salzmann, *Untersuchungen zu den antiken Kieselmosaiken*, Berlin

Seiler-Baldinger 1994: A. Seiler-Baldinger, *Textiles: A Classification of Techniques*, Bathurst

Sismanidis 1985: K. Sismanidis, 'Οι μακεδονικοί τάφοι στην πόλη της Θεσσαλονίκης', *Η Θεσσαλονίκη*, 35–70

Soteriades 1932: G. Soteriades, Ἀνασκαφαὶ Δίου Μακεδονίας', *Praktika tes en Athenais archaiologikes Hetaireias* 1930, 36–51

Spantidaki 2009: Y. Spantidaki, Ἡ εξειδίκευση στον χώρο του υφάσματος στην κλασική Αθήνα', *Arachne* 3, 72–75

Spantidaki, Moulhérat 2003: Y. Spantidaki, C. Moulhérat, 'Μελέτη τμημάτων υφάσματος του 5ου αιώνα π.Χ. από τα Καλύβια Αττικής', *Arachne* 1, 2–4

Spantidaki, Moulhérat 2004: Y. Spantidaki, C. Moulhérat, 'Υφάσματα Αττικής', *Arachne* 2, 5–13

Thompson 1982: W. Thompson, 'Weaving: a man's work', *Classical World* 75, 217–222

Tod 1950: M. N. Tod, 'Epigraphical notes on freedmen's professions', *Epigraphica* 12, 10–11

Tomlinson 1984: R. A. Tomlinson, 'The ceiling of Anfushy II.2', in Bonacasa, Di Vita 1984, 260–264

Tsimbidou-Avloniti 2000: M. Tsimbidou-Avloniti, 'Λάρνακα ἐς ἀργυρέην... (Ἰλ. Σ, 413)', in Pantermalis *et al.* 2000, 543–575

Tsimbidou-Avloniti 2005: M. Tsimbidou-Avloniti, *Μακεδονικοί Τάφοι στον Φοίνικα και στον Αγιο Αθανάσιο Θεσσαλονίκης*, Athens

Unruh 2007: J. Unruh, 'Ancient textile evidence in soil structures at the Agora excavations in Athens, Greece', in Gilles, Nosch 2007, 167–172

Valeva 2006: J. Valeva, 'Late Classical and Early Hellenistic scroll ornament', in *ΚΑΛΑΘΟΣ. Studies in Honour of Asher Ovadiah*, Tel-Aviv University, Tel Aviv, 451–482

Venit 2002: M. S. Venit, *Monumental Tombs of Ancient Alexandria: The Theater of the Dead*, Cambridge

Vickers 1999: M. Vickers, *Images on Textiles: The Weave of Fifth-Century Athenian Art and Society*, Xenia 42, Konstanz

Vollmoeller 1901: K. Vollmoeller, 'Über zwei euböische Kammergräber mit Totenbetten', *Mitteilungen des deutschen archäologischen Instituts, Athenische Abteilung* 36, 333–376

Wace 1948: A. J. B. Wace, 'Weaving or embroidery?', *American Journal of Archaeology* 52, 51–55

Weber 1990: M. Weber, *Baldachine und Statuenschreine*, Rome

Zeitlin 1994: F. I. Zeitlin, 'The artful eye: vision, ecphrasis and spectacle in Euripidean theatre', in S. Goldhill, R. Osborne (eds), *Art and the Text in Ancient Greek Culture*, Cambridge and New York, 138–196

Zissis 1954: B. G. Zissis, 'Βαμβακερά, καννάβινα καὶ λινᾶ ὑφάσματα τοῦ 5ου π.Χ. αἰῶνος. Ἀποδίπλωσις καὶ συντήρησις αὐτῶν', *Praktika Akademias Athenon* 29, 587–593

Minor burial textiles and religious affiliation: an archaeological case study from Roman Egypt

Kristin H. South

To the west of the Nile in Middle Egypt, the large depression known as the Fayum has been occupied since earliest times, but most famously during the Graeco-Roman period, when the burials containing the 'Fayum Portraits' were deposited. These portrait mummies have attracted much interest, and deservedly, have been studied in great detail for over 100 years. Beyond these famous instances, however, there are many other preserved burials that have emerged from the Graeco-Roman period in the Fayum. A large Ptolemaic to late Byzantine cemetery brackets the eastern edge of the Fayum, about 100 km south of Cairo. Known as Fag el-Gamus, it lies just past the modern limits of irrigation and extends eastward into the desert. Fag el-Gamus has been systematically excavated by Brigham Young University since 1981. Because of the dry desert conditions, many fragile artifacts have been well preserved, including an abundance of textiles associated with the burials.

The burials of Fag el-Gamus are packed into shafts dug directly into the hard, sandy substratum, often with five to six burials within the same shaft. These shafts consistently lie on an east-west axis, varying slightly in keeping with expected seasonal variations in solar alignment. The oldest burials have a westward-facing orientation, but after one or at most, two layers of such burials, the higher (later) burials switch instead to an eastward-facing ('head-west') orientation. The project director, Wilfred Griggs, has suggested from his earliest seasons on site that these burials belong to a Christian population (Griggs 1988). Small crosses appear intermittently, either on necklaces, as stand-alone finds, or woven into the textiles. We estimate the dates for the 'head-west' portion of this cemetery to fall within the range of AD 100–600.

The dates for this cemetery overlap with the portrait mummies, but it is striking and potentially significant that our burials, although deriving from the same time period and the same place, differ in some important ways from their more famous contemporaries: the Fag el-Gamus burials have a built-up structure over the face area (a 'face-bundle') that is created using layers of cloth, but they do not include portraits, art, or inscriptions on the linen and there is no use of cartonnage. The portrait mummies have either a flat area over the face to allow the inclusion of a portrait or they are covered with plaster for a mask. The Fag el-Gamus burials include many held together with ribbons instead of torn strips of linen; the cordage simply stretches around the body instead of having intensely decorative patterns of rhomboid-wrapping (although some of this type have emerged from Fag el-Gamus, they derive from an earlier period than those studied here).

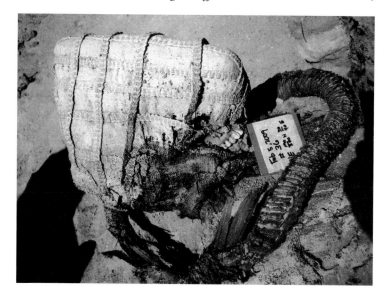

Fig. 1. 'Face-bundle' on a typical burial (2009-NE-36). Note also the red and white ribbons holding the wrappings in place (photo courtesy of BYU Fayum Excavation).

In general, the burials employ only textile wrappings to protect the bodies. There are no wooden or stone sarcophagi, although some burials employ slabs of rock or toob (mud brick) placed strategically over or to the side of the body as an added measure of protection and recognition. Despite the relative simplicity of the burials, however, there are some striking elements that occur consistently and that differ from earlier Pharaonic burial practices (and from the Fayum portrait mummies, as noted above). One of these elements pertains to the wrappings that cover the area of the face (Fig. 1). The second of these elements pertains to the use of brightly coloured purpose-woven 'ribbons' to hold the wrappings in place (pl. 9).

These two elements of the Fag el-Gamus burials are worthy of study in several ways: 1) they represent a clear departure from earlier Egyptian burial practices; 2) they are ubiquitous at our site; and 3) they have not been the formal object of study until now. 'Face-bundles' and ribbons are innovations that first appear in the earliest Christian centuries. The aim of this analysis is to seek a more nuanced picture of late Roman burial practices in Egypt and to examine the idea that these innovations signal Christian affiliation. The data for this study come specifically from the 2000, 2006, 2007, and 2009 excavation seasons, but they are representative of the finds from other years of excavation as well.

Face-bundles

Through the use of extra padding material at the head and foot areas, the burials often mimic the shape of earlier Egyptian sarcophagi, which also had an exaggerated height at the head and foot areas. The head area is often built up using rectangles of linen folded into strips and supported in place directly down the centre of the face by smaller folds or wads of linen. These face-bundles occur on almost every head-west burial that is well-preserved enough to display it. This includes burials of men and women, adults and children (South *et al.* 2009).

Face-bundles at Fag el-Gamus show some variation, but several aspects are consistent. They always employ linen strips, folded and laid in a single vertical line over the area of the mouth,

Fig. 2. The contents of a typical face-bundle (from burial 2005-SW-26), in order as found. The twist is the outermost layer, furthest from the face (photo courtesy of BYU Fayum Excavation).

nose, and eyes. The most common weaves are 1/2 and 2/2 basket weave. The strips are folded 3–6 cm wide and doubled lengthwise to make the strips 13–20 cm long. They are made of torn strips of linen (no wool and very rarely any colour), even on burials that otherwise include brightly coloured textiles. In many of the burials, a twist of linen follows as the final layer, furthest from the face (Fig. 2). The twist is tight and secure, often with visible stitching to hold it in place. The number of layers below the twist (i.e. between the twist and the face) can vary, but usually amounts to a depth of around 10 cm.

To date, after nearly thirty years of excavation at this site, face-bundles appear to be nearly universal among the well-preserved head-west burials at Fag el-Gamus, and burials that do not have them usually have scanty enough textile remains that poor preservation can be the reason for their absence. The few exceptions are the subject of ongoing study to determine the reasons for their exclusion. Notably, none of the 'head-east' burials have been found to include face-bundles, but it is also important to note that virtually all of them are so poorly preserved that few, if any, textile finds remain in those burials. Nonetheless, face-bundles are completely unknown in earlier periods of Egyptian history, prior to the Roman period. In burials from slightly later periods, variations on the face-bundle have shown up at a few sites, including Kom el-Ahmar and el-Hibeh (see 'Parallels' below).

Ribbons

A second aspect of the Fag el-Gamus burials signals another innovation. Through all of the stages of Egyptian mummification, wrapping the body in linen comes as one of the last steps.

In order to hold the linen wrappings in place, thin strips of linen were bound around the body. Usually these were made by tearing, folding lengthwise, and pressing long strips of plain-weave or basket-weave linen to create narrow tapes with the frayed edges tucked underneath. On rare occasions, including the burial of King Tutankhamun, the binding tapes were woven to shape instead of torn (Metropolitan Museum 2011). The modes of binding changed over time, but torn strips of linen were the common thread. By contrast, the burials of Fag el-Gamus employ a mixture of different binding materials. In all, they include torn strips of linen, ropes (small and fine or coarse and large), and purpose-woven 'ribbons' or tapes.

A word on terminology is in order here: when talking of the binding materials for mummies, scholars have variously referred to cordage, tapes, bands and ribbons. Cordage is a general term that can take in the whole spectrum of binding materials, but is most often used to refer to rope. Tapes, bands and ribbons all mean roughly the same thing, but scholars have used tapes and bands to talk about the binding materials used in Pharaonic Egypt, which differ in specific ways from our binding materials. At Fag el-Gamus, ribbon is preferred as a more specific descriptive term that implies that the binding materials found there, as opposed to ropes and torn strips of linen, are flat, narrow and woven to shape with two selvedges.

The ribbons are made of plant materials, the majority being linen. Most employ plain, un-dyed linen in combination with red-dyed linen. Darker brown threads also appear, generally among the later burials. The red threads are stained on the outside with red ochre (ferrous oxide), as confirmed by chemical analysis. The red is not colour-fast, suggesting its specific preparation for this mortuary use without an intention of reuse or washing. Even in these post-Pharaonic times when brightly-coloured clothing was allowed in burial, rather than only linen shrouds, the ribbons nearly always remain limited in their colour variety to red and naturally occurring shades of plant fibres. The extremely rare exceptions (limited thus far to only two burials in close proximity to each other) include single-colour ribbons of blue linen and of yellow linen (South 1998, 10).

Once ribbons entered the funerary vocabulary, they themselves evolved over time. The earliest ribbons are of the 'typical' kind: six warps of un-dyed linen in one shed and four warps of red linen bracketed by two warps of un-dyed linen in the other shed (pl. 10). As the ribbons continue in use, however, several variations arise: sometimes the red-and-white ribbons have paired warps for a total of twenty-four threads; other times the red warps occur in unexpected orders and numbers. Occasionally the positions of the red-and-white are reversed. Altogether, though, red-and-white ribbons occur in 77 per cent of all ribbon burials. Later ribbons are made of un-dyed linen alone, or only of red, and others of brown alone or brown and white. In one unusual case (2007–SW-1) we found a single ribbon of brown, white, and red. The ribbons tend to change in quality as well as in colour: the weft is hidden in the earlier examples under a strongly warp-faced weave that creates horizontal lines, but later ribbons include balanced weave patterns where the weft is equally visible, creating more of a checkerboard effect.

Although there may have been an ideal ribbon technique, they varied widely in reality: combinations of each element occur often in ways that appear random, and weaving mistakes abound. These observations suggest that ribbon construction occurred at a local level and was practiced by weavers of varying understanding and ability. At some of the latest levels, we find ribbons that can only be characterised as sloppy: the distance between weft returns is as great as 20 mm, they include fewer warp threads (as few as four), and they are all of one colour rather than attempting any kind of pattern. These sloppy monochrome ribbons tend to be used in groupings of several colours in a single burial. A burial of this type at Kom el-Ahmar dates to the fifth century or later (Huber, 2007).

The relative abundance and the levels at which each type of binding occurs, display some interesting trends. The following analysis is based on a study of 132 burials with respect to age at death, burial depth (as a gross estimate of date or at least of relative chronology), and types of binding material used in wrapping them. Very few of the burials can be dated with certainty, although pottery finds place them within the first to sixth centuries AD. In most instances it is clear that the lower burials were undisturbed as later burials were placed on top of them. In those few instances where a burial clearly disturbs earlier strata, it was omitted from the calculations to prevent confusion.

Working upward from the deepest burials, torn strips of linen first appear in abundance, but red-and-white ribbon also occurs sporadically (Fig. 3). Over a 150 cm depth, burials move from only employing torn strips (two burials at depths 225 cm, 200 cm) to torn strips in combination with ribbon (nine of the burials between 185 and 80 cm, or 20 per cent of the total torn-strips burials) to exclusive use of ribbons. The last use of torn strips not in conjunction with ribbon occurs at 95 cm below the surface, and at 80 cm below the surface, the torn strips completely stop appearing in burials, although another forty-two burials were found above this level. The trajectory, while not perfectly even, is nonetheless very clear: the ancient, Pharaonic practice of binding mummies with torn strips of linen was entirely replaced within this community by the use of purpose-woven ribbons after about 70 per cent of the burials at this site had been deposited. Based on the scanty datable evidence, this may correspond to about the end of the third century.

With respect to age at death, torn strips are used in almost equal measure in adult and child burials. This is not surprising, given that torn strips of linen were the usual method of wrapping mummies of all ages throughout Egyptian history prior to this time. The percentage of child burials with torn strips is slightly higher (30 per cent as opposed to 26 per cent), and this is accounted for by the later date at which ribbons were adopted for children's use: during a transition period, ribbons are used in adult burials, but not children's. At 124 cm the first child burial has ribbons: there had been eighteen adult burials with ribbons before this depth (25 per cent of the ribbon burials) and already thirteen child burials without ribbons. Around this level, there are two cluster burials in which the adults have ribbon but the children instead have torn strips or rope (Fig. 4). Then at 110 cm, a child has torn strips and ribbon. After four more child burials with torn strips, these strips disappear from the record and child burials use ribbons in the majority of burials (59 per cent) from this time forward. When ribbon is not present, it is rope that is used (41 per cent), rather than linen strips.

Rope was arguably the cheapest and most readily available material. It is used over three times as often in child burials as in adult ones when measured by percentage of total burials by age (Table 1). When an adult burial does include rope, 75 per cent of the time it is paired with torn strips or with ribbon; only twice does it stand alone as the only type of binding material on an adult burial. In contrast, child burials use rope alone 84 per cent of the time that rope occurs. If rope truly were the inexpensive default, this pattern might suggest less importance attached to burying children with a certain protocol, or simply that child burials were often unexpected and more hastily performed. Ribbon, if mortuary use was its only function, might not have been readily available in the case of an untimely death. We do find children buried in reused household textiles more often than adults, who usually have previously unused

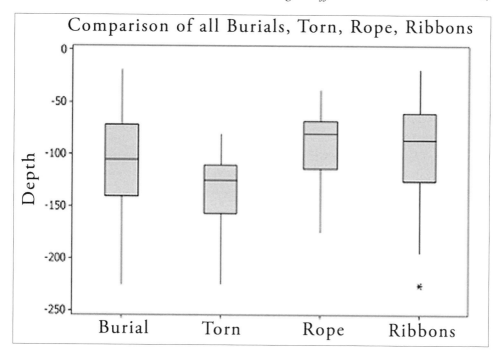

Fig. 3. Considering all of the burials together and then separating out those with torn strips vs. rope vs. ribbons, we see that torn strips abruptly vanish at 80 cm from the surface, while ribbons are used at all depths, but more frequently at higher levels. Rope starts later but continues in parallel with torn strips (drawing by K. South).

Fig. 4. A cluster burial showing an adult with ribbons and a child with torn strips (2007-SW-11 and 12, depth 120 cm) (photo courtesy of BYU Fayum Excavation).

	Adult	Child/Infant	All
Torn Strips	29 (26%)	17 (30%)	46 (27%)
Rope	10 (9%)	19 (33%)	29 (17%)
Ribbon	72 (65%)	21 (37%)	93 (56%)
All	111 (100%)	57 (100%)	168 (100%)

Table 1. Occurrence of types of cordage as percent of total, separated by age at burial. If more than one type of binding occurs in a single burial, each is counted separately, causing the total number to exceed the actual number of burials studied (graph by K. South).

rectangular sheets of linen for their burying cloths (see, for instance, South *et al.* 2011). Perhaps this is another indication that speed or lack of uniform protocols come into play with child burials.

In summary, these results suggest that the patrons of this necropolis who used torn strips of linen did so without regard to age at death, but that torn strips of linen gradually passed out of use, first among adults and later among children, at a level that corresponds to datable finds from about the third century AD. Once ribbons made their way into child burials, they appeared in the majority (59 per cent) of child burials, with the others using rope. Rope occurred in child burials at a much higher rate than in adult burials, and continued to be used contemporaneously with ribbons throughout all levels, suggesting that their use was due more to economic factors than to any deeper conviction.

Parallels

If face-bundle and ribbon inclusions seem so unusual, were they actually unique to the community at Fag el-Gamus? The short answer is: no. Of more interest, however, is the question of the geographic spread and the self-identification of the other people who used them. Fanning outward from Fag el-Gamus, and excluding any other Fayum burials, to which we will return later, similar burial inclusions have emerged from Saqqara, Dahshur, and Lisht to the north, and from el-Hibeh, Qarara, Kom el-Ahmar/Sharuna, Antinoopolis, and Thebes to the south.

At North Saqqara, Dahshur, and Lisht, the burials surround Old and Middle Kingdom pyramids, as at Fag el-Gamus, but the burials themselves derive from a much later time. The publication of the 'Coptic' cemetery at North Saqqara contains this description:

> Originally there were at least seventy graves. The interments so far opened show that without exception the bodies, wrapped in coarse linen shrouds bound in criss-cross fashion with striped red-and-white cords, are laid with head to the west, feet to the east, and with the arms straight down by the sides. (Martin 1974, 21)

The site was originally described as a Christian community that had built a village over the remains of the temple of Nectanebo II in the late fourth and early fifth centuries AD (Martin 1974, 19), but a second report moves the occupation of the village connected to the cemetery to sometime from the beginning of the fifth to the middle of the sixth century (Jeffreys, Strouhal 1980, 33). The identification of this site as Christian depends on an inscribed *stele* found in situ and from Coptic-inscribed storage vessels and surface debris (Martin 1974, 20). Although the description of the burials is brief, the reference to 'striped red-and-white cords' in the context of head-west burials does provide an important parallel to the burials of Fag el-Gamus. Nothing similar to face-bundles is mentioned in the reports from North Saqqara.

Lisht was excavated in the 1930s by the Metropolitan Museum of New York, and although the later burials were not their primary focus, finds from that site confirm the presence of multicoloured ribbons and face-bundles. In the words of the excavators:

> ... the site lay unused for centuries--until after the beginning of the Christian era. At that time, though the date cannot be fixed with certainty, another community began using it for the burial of their dead. The Copts (the one inscription found, a grave stela, was in Coptic) were apparently also of the poorer class. The graves were shallow and the linen used was poor, but *the bandaging was in most cases quite elaborate*. The outstanding characteristic of the burials was the small amount of linen used on the bodies and the *astonishingly high padding over the faces*. (Lansing, Hayes 1933, 25 (with emphasis added))

Although this description would be enough for a positive identification, figures 36 and 37 included with the text (Lansing, Hayes 1933, 29–30) confirm beyond doubt that face-bundles and ribbons of familiar type were present here. A particularly fine example of the ribbons, accession number 34.1.121, was kept by the Metropolitan Museum as part of their share of the finds. It is exactly the width of the classic ribbon of Fag el-Gamus, but has alternating brown and white warps with deeply-dyed red warps on either side. The museum speculatively dates it to the first century AD, but given the many similarities with well-documented finds from Kom el-Ahmar/Sharuna (see below), it is likely that these burials are a few centuries later.

Ongoing excavations by the Metropolitan Museum of New York in the necropolis around Dahshur have revealed ribbons similar to those at Fag el-Gamus but the presence or absence of face-bundles has not been established (Emilia Cortes, personal communication). This cemetery is dated to the third to seventh centuries AD and is considered to hold a Christian population. North Saqqara, Dahshur, and Lisht are all within 100 km to the north of Fag el-Gamus and provide probably the closest similarities of any sites, given that all three are later Christian necropoleis in the vicinity of Pharaonic pyramids.

Proceeding southward, el-Hibeh, Qarara, and Kom el-Ahmar are all clustered in Middle Egypt, starting about 180 km south of Fag el-Gamus. Excavations at el-Hibeh have been ongoing since 2001 under the direction of the University of California at Berkeley; Robert J. Wenke led a previous season of work in 1980. Wenke's preliminary report indicated the presence of a 'narrow [brown and un-dyed] linen band with both side selvages present' (Wenke 1984, pl. IX), but its finding out of context made further analysis difficult (*ibid.* 82). More recent excavations have produced both ribbons and face-bundles in situ on Coptic burials dated to the same centuries as the burials of Fag el-Gamus (Deanna Heikkinen, personal communication). The face-bundles of el-Hibeh, however, have not thus far produced any linen twists or strips of linen. The cordage of el-Hibeh includes brown and white ribbons, red alone, white alone, rope, and torn strips of linen (Heikkinen, personal communication).

Ludwig Borchardt explored Qarara in the early twentieth century and reported on finding a great Coptic cemetery, most of which had been plundered. Some tombs remained intact, including a number richly decorated with Christian imagery (Borchardt 1915). The complete description of the cemetery at Qarara was given by H. Ranke (1926), and a recent article by Ulrike Horak (1995, 65–66) provides a good summary. The cemetery was in use from the fifth to the seventh centuries AD. The burials are oriented with their heads to the west and are usually found at a depth of .05–1 m, and rarely up to 2 m deep. Unlike the burials at Fag el-Gamus, many were wrapped in mats or laid on wooden boards or in wooden sarcophagi (Horak 1995, 65; Gomaa, Farid 1995, 64). Face-bundles occur here, as is strikingly apparent from the photographs of the uncovered burials (Horak 1995, 65; Ranke 1926, pls 2, 10). The area over the face was elevated with palm-leaf ribs or pieces of wood and stuffed with old cloth and palm fibre. The whole thing was covered in linen and then tied with red, black, and white ribbons, which also continued down the body in a criss-cross pattern (Horak 1995, 65). The use of both ribbons and face-bundles at Qarara makes this an important parallel site for Fag el-Gamus.

At Kom el-Ahmar/Sharuna, the burials of interest lie next to a Christian church and near a monastery. The church was built no earlier than the end of the third century and the entire site was abandoned in the seventh or eighth century (Huber 2007, 37). The burial area, although mostly looted, originally contained at least thirty burials of men, women, children, and infants, oriented east-west (Huber 2007, 39). The single unlooted burial, dated by ^{14}C analysis to the late fourth to mid-sixth century, included elaborate ribbon patterns over a face-bundle described in the publication as 'a kind of superstructure that was slipped on like a mask ... in the form of a parabola' (Huber 2007, 41–42). The internal portion contained 'a compact bundle composed of different padding elements [including palm ribs, textile scraps, and palm fibres] that ultimately made up the triangular shape of the head superstructure' (p. 44). The ribbon colours in this burial included a brown and white ribbon, red alone, and brown alone. Rope was also used.

Another important city of late Antique Egypt lay at Antinoe, 220 km south of Fag el-Gamus. Antinoe (Antinoopolis, Ansina, Sheikh Ibada) was founded in the early second century AD and existed as a thriving city into Islamic times. Antinoe was a prominent centre of Christian martyrdom in the Diocletianic persecutions of the early fourth century, and was known for its many monastic enclaves as well. Ribbons found at Antinoe include red-and-white ribbons, brown and white, and red alone. The technique, look, and size of these ribbons correspond exactly to those from Fag el-Gamus. The ribbons themselves cannot be dated accurately: they were found in the 'peristyle court' but do derive from the mummies that were found in the area, the remains of which have since been scattered (Cäcilia Fluck, personal communication). From an image of Albert Gayet's work at Antinoe at the turn of the twentieth century (Gayet 1904, 34), it is apparent that face-bundles covered with wide linen strips were also once present at this site.

A final witness, furthest distant both in place and time, exists at the monastery of Epiphanius at Thebes. Dating from the sixth and seventh centuries (Winlock, Crum 1926, 3), the site consists of individual cells, communal areas, and a small cemetery that was apparently exclusively used by the monks themselves. Of the original eleven graves, six were totally empty, three partially plundered, and two intact; the bodies were laid out with heads to the southwest and covered in multiple layers of linen wrappings secured by sets of binding tapes (Winlock, Crum 1926, 45, 48–49). Plates XI and XII of this publication show that these 'binding tapes' were ribbons of the brown and white type, similar in width and technique to those we have seen at other sites (one is shown in detail on Plate XXII,C). While the existence of a face-bundle cannot be definitely shown at this site, it seems a plausible explanation for the protrusion over the face seen in the first to third stages of unwrapping the mummy (shown in Plate XII); the fourth stage shows a piece of linen twisted over from the crown of the head and tucked into a rope at the neck. Whether this was an intentional reference to an earlier face-bundle practice or simply a practical means of wrapping the end of the cloth (as Winlock suggests on p. 48) is unclear.

The evidence from the excavations at the monastery of Epiphanius is enhanced by the addition of written material that discusses the use and importance of the objects found there (Crum, White 1926). Among the letters found at the monastery is one (p. 351) in which a monk mentions 'bandages mounted upon the loom' and requests more linen in order to finish them. Other letters comment on 'pairs of bandages' in company with burial clothing (p. 532). The term used for these 'bandages' is the same used in the New Testament account of Lazarus to describe how his (now living) corpse is bound (Crum, White 1926, 245 n. 2). It seems likely, then, that these bandages/ribbons were specifically made for funerary purposes and were locally produced and sold to outsiders as a means of supporting the inhabitants of the monastery. This clear connection between funerary ribbons and a Christian monastery, although somewhat late, provides useful potential for analysis.

In summary, ribbons and/or face-bundles like those at Fag el-Gamus have been found at several sites up and down the Nile, all dated within a few centuries of each other and among populations that included, or were exclusively made up of, those who identified themselves as Christian. Of the few sites in Egypt where face-bundles have been found, they co-occur in every instance with ribbons. On the individual level at Fag el-Gamus, we have seen that earlier burials might employ either torn strips of linen or ribbons in company with face-bundles, but at the later sites like Kom el-Ahmar and Hibeh, multicoloured ribbons and/or rope are the rule. Observing the changes over time from tidy and uniform red-and-white ribbon to less carefully crafted monochrome ribbons, it is not a surprise to learn that a similar degeneration occurred among the face-bundles: those found at these later sites, while having a similar appearance on the outside, do not exhibit the careful internal contents of the earliest of the face-bundles found at Fag el-Gamus.

Discussion

Face-bundles present such a different appearance from earlier Egyptian burial practices that their presence raises the question of what purpose they served. Although protection of the face area could make sense of the size of the bundle, such an explanation cannot account for the carefully prepared twist of linen and stacks of cloth that are often found in the earliest face-bundles. Likewise, the presence of ribbons is easily explained by the need to hold the burial wrappings in place; less clear, however, is the reason for switching from the millennia-long tradition of using torn strips of linen to multicoloured, purpose-woven ribbon. Do they somehow represent a new set of beliefs, or can they be traced back to another starting point? It would be easy to speculate about some of the symbolism of red-and-white, for instance, but at this point it would only be speculation. What we do know is that face-bundles have never been found on Pharaonic or Hellenistic burials. Narrow, purpose-woven ribbons, either of plain linen or with other colours, are extremely rare among Pharaonic and Hellenistic burials (however, see below). Both of these burial innovations are ubiquitous at our site and can also be found in several other sites along the Nile Valley, mostly in Middle Egypt from Saqqara to Antinoopolis. Each of the sites where these textile accessories occur have been independently identified, through literary, monumental, and burial accessory evidence, as including a Christian population at the time from which these finds originate.

The question of Christian identity in late Roman and Byzantine Egypt is problematic and complicated by many factors. We do not assume that entire populations would have self-identified as Christian or that religious affiliation was necessarily the most important factor leading to decisions about what to include in burial, but thus far ribbons and face-bundles have not been found on identified non-Christian burials; where ribbons and face-bundles have been found, Christianity is unquestionably present in the community by the time to which these finds correspond. It seems, then, that ribbons and face-bundles are not only post-Pharaonic innovations, but that they might also have carried a religious connotation or served as markers of a Christian community.

Another more prosaic but no less plausible explanation focuses on the locations where these innovations occur. If ribbon and face-bundle use is limited to one geographic area, perhaps this indicates a simple fashion or preference that took hold in one area and spread from there. This would help explain why ribbons and face-bundles have not been found in necropoleis of Christian populations in other parts of Egypt, and indeed other parts of the ancient world: the western oases, for example, experienced a similar transition from the ancient Egyptian religious beliefs and tradition of mummification to the new ideas of Christianity, but did not develop these innovations (Bowen 2003, Hauser 1932). Are there other sources, closer to home, to which we might look for parallels?

The one visible link between earlier burials and these innovations comes, fittingly, from the Fayum and occurs on one of the portrait mummies. The mummy in question, named Artemidorus, has been dated, based on the appearance of the portrait and the hairstyle, to AD 110 to 160. Artemidorus was excavated by Sir Williams Flinders Petrie at Hawara, which is less than 20 km from Fag el-Gamus; the mummy now resides at the museum of the University of Manchester (Manchester). Although most of the mummy is covered with red painted cartonnage, the bottom end has become exposed, showing the bindings used to hold the mummy together: they are purpose-woven ribbons of 2.5 cm width, made of white linen with a single red thread at either edge (Susan Martin, personal communication).

This burial, therefore, hints at the transition that is otherwise lacking, at least with regard to the ribbons: it does come from the Fayum, but it is not Christian. It does have red-and-white binding materials, but they do not follow the later pattern (the red threads are near the edges and there are only two of them). The ribbons are purpose-woven to shape and used as a burial tape, but they are not as narrow or complex as those from Fag el-Gamus. In other words, this burial is a perfect candidate to demonstrate the existence of a link between the traditional Pharaonic torn strips of linen and the full-blown, varied, and expertly crafted ribbons of Fag el-Gamus and similar burials. We end, then, where we started, with a comparison of the famous

Fayum portrait mummies to the humbler, anonymous burials of Fag el-Gamus. Although to all appearances they represent two separate traditions, the correspondence with the mummy of Artemidorus shows this separation to be less than complete.

The finds at Fag el-Gamus provide an important witness to late Antique burial practices in Egypt, because they are numerous, span several centuries, and display a generally straightforward progression from earliest (deepest) to latest (highest). We continue to work toward a greater ability to provide tight and accurate dates for the burials, and present our data here as preliminary observations only. Given that the present study has not included an exhaustive look at all Egyptian burials from this period or all Christian burials in the Mediterranean world, perhaps further links will yet emerge to provide a certain explanation for these seemingly radical innovations to one of the world's oldest and most conservative set of practices for dressing the dead.

Acknowledgements

Excavation in Egypt is a privilege. I am grateful for the opportunity to join the Brigham Young University 2009 team. Special thanks to Dr Zahi Hawass, Former Minister of State for Antiquities Affairs, to Mr Magdy El Ghandour, General Director of Foreign Missions and Permanent Committees, and to Mr Ahmed Abdel Al, Director of Antiquities in the Fayum, as well as to the inspectors who ably supervise and facilitate the work each year. Thanks, too, to the generous scholars who have shared unpublished information and guided me to useful sources, particularly Hero Granger-Taylor, John Peter Wild, Emilia Cortes, Deanna Heikkinen, Susan O. Martin, John Taylor, and Cäcilia Fluck. A portion of the expenses for attendance at the 'Dressing the Dead' conference were borne by a grant from Ancient Near Eastern Studies at Brigham Young University.

kristinsouth@gmail.com

Bibliography

Borchardt 1915: L. Borchardt, 'Die deutschen Ausgrabungen in Ägypten (1912/1913)', *Klio* 14, 116–124

Bowen 2003: G. Bowen, 'Some observations on Christian burial practices at Kellis', in G. E. Bowen, C. A. Hope (eds), *The Oasis Papers 3*, Oxford, 167–182

Crum, White 1926: W. E. Crum, H. G. E. White, *The Monastery of Epiphanius at Thebes. Part 2: Coptic Ostraca and Papyri and Greek Ostraca and Papyri*. Metropolitan Museum of Art Egyptian Expedition, New York

Gayet 1904: A. Gayet, *Fantomes d'Antinoe: Les Sepultures de Leukyone et Myrithis*, Paris

Gomaa, Farid 1995: F. Gomaa, S. Farid, 'Bericht über die im Jahr 1983 durchgeführte Ausgrabung in Qarara', *Göttinger Miszellen* 144, 63–74

Griggs 1988: C. W. Griggs, 'Excavating a Christian cemetery near Seila, in the Fayum region of Egypt', in C. W. Griggs (ed.), *Excavations at Seila, Egypt*, Brigham Young University, Provo, Utah, 74–84

Griggs *et al.* 2001: C. W. Griggs, R. P. Evans, K. H. South, G. Homsey, A. Ellington, N. Iskander, '2001 Brigham Young University Seila Pyramid/Fag el-Gamous Cemetery Project – Report of the 2000 Season', *Bulletin of the Australian Centre for Egyptology*, 12, 34–53

Hauser, 1932: W. Hauser, 'The Christian necropolis in Khargeh Oasis', *Metropolitan Museum of Art Bulletin 27:3 Part 2: The Egyptian Expedition 1930–1931*, Metropolitan Museum of Art, New York, 38–50

Horak, 1995: U. Horak, 'Koptische Mumien: Der koptische Tote in Grabungsberichten, Funden und literarischen Nachrichten', *Biblos* 44, 39–71

Huber 2006: B. Huber, 'Al-Kom al-Ahmar / Sharuna: different archaeological contexts – different textiles?', in S. Schrenk (ed.), *Textiles in situ: Their Find Spots in Egypt and Neighbouring Countries in the First Millennium CE*, Abegg-Stiftung, Riggisberg, 57–68

Huber 2007: B. Huber, 'The textiles of an Early Christian burial from el-Kom el-Ahmar/ Sharuna (Middle Egypt)', in A. De Moor, C. Fluck (eds), *Methods of Dating Ancient Textiles of the 1st Millennium from Egypt and Neighbouring countries*, Tielt, 36–69

Jeffreys, Strouhal, 1980: D. G. Jeffreys, E. Strouhal, 'North Saqqara 1978–9: The Coptic cemetery site at the sacred animal necropolis: preliminary report', *Journal of Egyptian Archaeology* 66, 28–35

Lansing, Hayes 1933: A. Lansing, W. C. Hayes, Jr, 'The Egyptian expedition: the excavations at Lisht', *The Metropolitan Museum of Art Bulletin* 28, 11 (Part 2), 4–38

Manchester: Manchester Museum. n.d. [1775] Human mummy, object, registered, Africa, Egypt, Faiyum, Hawara. http://emu.man.ac.uk/mmcustom/Display.php?irn=197825&QueryPage=%2Fmmcustom%2FEgyptQuery.php accessed 24 January 2011

Martin 1974: G. T. Martin, 'Excavations in the sacred animal necropolis at North Saqqara, 1972–3: preliminary report', *Journal of Egyptian Archaeology* 60, 15–29

Metropolitan Museum 2011: Metropolitan Museum of Art, Works of Art Collection Database, Accession Number 09.184.797, accessed online

Ranke 1926: H. Ranke, *Die Koptischen Friedhöfe bei Karara und der Amontempel Scheschonks I bei El Hibe*, Berlin

South 1998: K. H. South, 'Preliminary report of the textile finds, 1998 season, at Fag-el-Gamous', *Archaeological Textiles Newsletter* 27, 9–11

South *et al.* 2009: K. H. South, J. Y. Smith, G. Tata, C. W. Griggs, '"Face-bundles" in Early Christian burials from the Fayum', *Archaeological Textiles Newsletter* 48, 2–5

South *et al.* 2011: , K. H. South, J. Y. Smith, G. Tata, and C. W. Griggs, 'Textile finds from a typical Early Christian burial at Fag el-Gamus (Fayum), Egypt', in C. Alfaro *et al.* (eds), *Purpureae Vestes: III Symposium Internacional sobre Textiles y Tintes del Mediterráneo en el Mundo antiguo*, 111–119

Wenke 1984: R. J. Wenke, Archaeological Investigations at El-Hibeh 1980: Preliminary Report, American Research Center in *Egypt Reports* 9, Malibu, Undena

Winlock, Crum 1926: H. E. Winlock, W. E. Crum, *The Monastery of Epiphanius at Thebes. Part 1: the Archaeological Material.* Metropolitan Museum of Art Egyptian Expedition, New York

RECOVERING CONTEXTS: THE ROMAN MUMMIES EXCAVATED BY THE METROPOLITAN MUSEUM OF ART AT DAHSHUR, EGYPT

EMILIA CORTES

The field experience reflected in this paper is an example of collaboration between archaeologists, physical anthropologists, curators, object conservators, textile conservators, and skilled excavation workers who perform textile conservation work associated with human remains in excavations.

The work focuses on mummies created from flat textiles wrapped around a body. The textiles and the body they enshroud should be studied and treated as a unit. The challenge for everyone working on the site lies in understanding the textiles in conjunction with the human remains they serve. As Mike Parker Pearson said:

> As archaeologists, we should be wary of how we separate the material culture on the body (clothes) from the material culture of the body (posture and body modification) from the material culture off the body (weapons, furniture and other items). We need to be aware of how easily we impose our own categories on to the past, dividing up 'clothing', 'furniture', 'weaponry' and 'jewellry' out of assemblages whose totality relates to the entire representation of the deceased appearance or 'dress'. The clothing of the dead thus constitutes a hall of mirrors, representations of representations, in which things may not be entirely what they seem at first glance. (Parker Pearson 2005, 9)

After excavation, it is up to the conservators working with curators, scientists, and designers in the museum to preserve the context in the long term.

The Metropolitan Museum of Art (MMA) Egyptian expedition

The MMA Egyptian Expedition began excavations in 1906 at Lisht and in Upper Egypt at Western Thebes, in Deir El-Bahri and in the Kharga Oasis. The excavations ceased in 1936. In 1984 Dorothea and Dieter Arnold resumed the museum excavation in Lisht at the Middle Kingdom pyramids of Senwosret I and Amenemhat I, and they continued until 1991.

In 1990, Dieter Arnold, Director of the MMA Egyptian Expedition, began excavating the Middle Kingdom pyramid of Senwosret III (c. 1981–1952 BC) at Dahshur. The excavation's aim was to gain an understanding of, and to reconstruct the architecture and decoration of, the pyramid complex. Finding architectural evidence, such as stone reliefs, is one of the main purposes of the annually conducted excavation. A cemetery was found on top of these structural remains and it had to be dug through. Well-preserved burials were exposed in the 1998 season, and in the following season a full-scale excavation of the newly discovered cemetery began.

It was not until 2000, however, that a considerable number of burials in fairly good condition were unearthed. With the sudden increase in the number of textiles from the burials in the 2000 season, the excavators realized that it was essential to have a textile conservator working at the site. I have been part of the expedition team to the excavation, responsible for the textiles and mummies from the Roman to late Antique cemetery, since 2001. As of 2010, 848 burials have been excavated, of which we have been able to exhume more than thirty as complete mummies.

The wrapped mummies from this Dahshur cemetery can be considered as one of the few Egyptian collections of textiles scientifically excavated and documented, making them an important reference and source of cultural information on funerary traditions from the early Roman period to the end of the late Antique era, that is from around 30 BC to the sixth or beginning of the seventh century AD.

Textiles can tell us about manufacture, iconography and trade. They add many clues to the discussion of dating, such as the changes and evolution of the shrouds, the different types of woven tapes and ropes that hold the mummy wrappings, the use of colour and materials, the different shapes of the mummies, and the funerary biers made of palm brier or wood supports.

Preparation for fieldwork

This paper focuses on my experience with archaeological textiles at the MMA and at the MMA excavation. The following remarks could be applied equally well to other textiles and mummies from different periods and cultural provenance in other museum collections for the long-term preservation of both (Cortes 2009, 219–238).

On an excavation site where mummies and textiles are unearthed, ideally a textile conservator should be part of the permanent excavation team with a budget for conservation expenses: equipment and materials should be allocated, as well as a budget for an appropriate storage space and furniture relevant to the type of find. For every season, the archaeologist, the physical anthropologist, and the textile conservator should be working together. The initial approach by the conservator at a site requires preparation work including the following:

ONE: A review of the seasonal environmental records of the excavation area. A major problem at Dahshur was the fluctuation in temperature and humidity during the winter months in the desert between day (82 °F/30 per cent RH) and night/early morning (65 °F/100 per cent RH).

TWO: A preliminary survey and review of the artefacts and documentation of what has been excavated in the past, to find out if there are objects from the same sites or nearby sites, in museums or private collections. Museum collections and archives from past archaeological expeditions are crucial reference sources and should be taken into account when excavating.

THREE: Team work by archaeologists, curators, and conservators as members of an excavation team. This improves planning and understanding, which is critical when dealing with fragile human remains and textiles.

Conservators working with relevant museum collections such as the MMA Egyptian art collection are in a position to use the museum collection and archives as a reference tool to compare and contrast the site finds for the benefit of both. The importance of this research allows the potential for having several specimens for comparison, which may provide the additional information needed to solve a difficult puzzle in the field. The following examples illustrate points two and three.

Persea leaves and twigs are found from the period of Dynasty 12. In the MMA Egyptian art collection, persea leaves are present as early as in the New Kingdom Dynasty 18 in two of Tutankhamun's floral collars (MMA 09.184. 214 and .216). In Dynasty 21 thay are found in the floral garlands of Nany (MMA 30.3.33) and in the Third Intermediate Period Dynasty 27–30 in the garlands from the Mummy of Prince Amenemhat (MMA 25.3.146a). In Dynasty 21, persea leaves were used as decorative elements on a Ptolemaic period mummy-wrapping (Fig. 1). The leaves were folded in exactly the same way as the ones found in the Dahshur mummy and were placed in a similar manner over the body, the main difference being that the museum mummy (MMA 12.182.48A-C) from Assiut has few strings of persea leaves, while the Dahshur mummy is completely enveloped in them.

Furthermore, in the Dahshur cemetery a great quantity of wrapping shrouds have dimensions and technical characteristics such as the weaving structure, make-up, texture and visual appearance, that are very similar to, if not the same as, the shrouds from al-Bagawāt, a cemetery dated to the fourth century AD and located in the Kharga Oasis in the Egyptian Western Desert. Al-Bagawāt was excavated by the MMA Egyptian Expedition in the early twentieth century and the textiles from that excavation are in the MMA collection and in the Textile Museum in Cairo.

Fig. 1. Dahshur, Burial B-792 mummy *in situ*, a) and b), completely wrapped with strings of a plant leaf identified as persea leaves, folded in exactly the same way as those on the body c) and d), of a Ptolemaic mummy (MMA 12.182.48A-C) from Assiut. Photos by Christine Marshal (MMA Egyptian Art Excavation to Dahshur) and Gustavo Camps (MMA Egyptian Art Department). © The Metropolitan Museum of Art.

One of the characteristics of the 'Kharga type' shrouds are the width-to-width spaces without wefts in several areas of the woven textile, creating a stripe of exposed warps up to approximately fifteen centimetres in several areas of the shrouds. A number of the wrapping shrouds of the Dahshur burials are associated with the 'Kharga type' mummy-wrapping shroud.

Comparisons were done using the archaeologist's drawings found in the excavation records, the textile conservator's notes, analysis, photos and documentation of Dahshur B-146 and the MMA files from the Kharga textile collection in the museum, where all the analysis, documentation, photography and photomicrography was done by myself, years before, under Nobuko Kajitani (Fig. 2). By consistently having the same textile conservator at the site it was possible to identify that the wrapping shroud of the Dahshur burial B-146 has the same weaving design and construction as four complete shrouds (MMA 33.10.27, .28, .31, .32); and five fragmentary Kharga shrouds (MMA 33.10.4, .5, .14, .29, and .45) in the MMA collection. Nobuko Kajitani, in her article on the al-Bagawāt textiles (Kajitani 2006, 95–112), identified all the above mentioned MMA shrouds as 'Early Kharga'. She also documented a 'Kharga Type' shroud of the same type as the Dahshur shroud in the Egyptian Museum in Cairo (ac. no. 65796).

FOUR: A study of the finds from the same site, or nearby locations, to have an idea of the types of artefacts and the deterioration expected.

The following examples illustrate this last point. The archival photographs and documentation from the MMA Egyptian Expedition 1906–1936, at the archaeological sites of Kharga, Lisht and Deir el Bahri, are a great source for understanding the context of some Dahshur burials, such as the mummy with slightly enlarged head and padded feet. The shape is held by woven

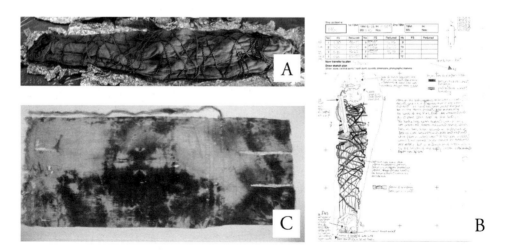

Fig. 2. The archaeologist's drawings (G. MacKinnon) from the 2000 season Dahshur excavation records of burial B-146 and the textile conservator's notes of the same burial, a) and b). It was recognised that this wrapping shroud had the same weaving design and construction as four MMA complete shrouds, c), excavated much earlier at al-Bagawāt in the Kharga Oasis (MMA 33.10.28). Photos by MMA Egyptian Art Excavation to Dahshur 2000 and Sheldon Collins. © The Metropolitan Museum of Art.

tapes made of red and un-dyed colour yarns called 'red/un-dyed woven type tapes', and may be compared to similar woven tapes in the MMA collection from Lisht excavated in 1933–1934 (MMA 34.1.121), as well as a mummy in a photograph from the excavations at Lisht (Fig. 3). Another photograph from the archives, also from a Lisht mummy, helps to recover the context of a Dahshur dislocated head (B-208) with a large triangular shape and voluminous feet; the mid-section of this mummy collapsed when lifted. The archival photo is a good reference to visualize the shape of the mummy that collapsed and helps the conservator, as well as the archaeologist, to understand the original appearance.

FIVE: An examination of conservation literature, to assist with a preliminary conservation plan to be prepared for any possible contingencies.

SIX: A comparison of conservation treatments done in the past.

SEVEN: A plan for *in situ* treatments, preventive conservation measures, written, graphic, and photographic documentation, and storage for the short and long term.

Points five, six, and seven are illustrated by the following examples. Archaeologists and textile conservators have to work as a team; their approaches are complementary. The daily work scenario

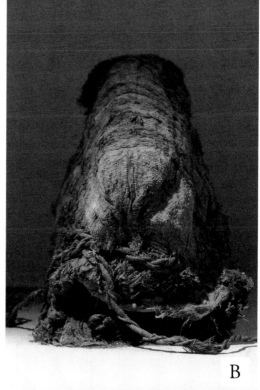

Fig. 3. Archive photo of Burials 24 and 25 from Lisht, a). These helped recover the context of a dislocated head (B-208) from Dahshur, b). Photos MMA Egyptian Expedition to Egypt 1932–1933 (L 32-33)71 and MMA Egyptian Art Excavation to Dahshur. © The Metropolitan Museum of Art.

is in permanent evolution, sometimes under extreme circumstances. Space and time restrictions are always an issue. The condition of a burial begins to change as soon as it is exposed to air. Problems vary from burial to burial, and changes are caused by a number of variables, including the high relative humidity during the night and the occasional rain in the winter months. Both of these can cause *in situ* deterioration of the textile wrappings. Often the evidence of details associated with ancient textiles is so fragile it can only be seen *in situ*. This is preserved in photographs, as this evidence vanishes when the burial is lifted. Many of the mummies were not eviscerated in antiquity, causing the body to decay more rapidly and resulting in damage to the textile wrappings.

Because movement stresses these bodies, a protocol involving material, support and storage changes and improvements, was devised between archaeologists and the conservator to keep handling to a minimum, enhancing the long term preservation of the finds. Custom-made wood supports were provided, properly buffered, labeled, and each mummy secured to its support with cotton tapes. The mummies excavated prior to 2005 had to be re-housed with conservation materials, and were thus moved several times for this purpose. Unnecessary manipulation has to be avoided at all costs when dealing with archaeological collections, and if handling has to be done, it should be carefully planned ahead.

In order to reduce handling during the excavation, a 'Mummy Kit' was developed in 2005 and improved in 2008 (pl. 12). This kit allows the archaeologist, with or without the conservator, to wrap the mummy *in situ* with the final storage material, thus eliminating the need for changing packing materials between excavation and storage. This important methodology reduces handling of the mummy. How to construct the 'Mummy Kit' and handle the mummy has been previously described in detail (Cortes 2009, 224–225).

EIGHT: Develop plans ahead of time to avoid drastic irreversible treatments, such as washing textiles on the site without the appropriate equipment and supplies (at Dahshur we do not wash textiles). Irreversible treatments should be totally eliminated unless there is no other way in which to preserve the find.

The latter point is illustrated as follows. In the 2007 excavation season, the only evidence of painted cartonnage ever found at Dahshur (burial B-768) was discovered and had to be rescued. Only the painted layer a few millimeters thick was left from the cartonnage, and it was lying on the sand. Consolidating the sand into a brick around and underneath the painting layer was the only option for the survival of the painting, so it was decided to apply Paraloid B-72, a copolymer of ethyl methacrylate and methyl acrylate, which is chemically stable and non-reactive at 3 to 5 per cent. After five days of work *in situ*, the painting on the sand brick was successfully removed and placed in storage. At the time, Paraloid B-72 was the only option available at the site, but this product affected the original colour of the pigments in the painting, turning it slightly darker, due to the refractive index.

Back at the MMA, a series of tests were conducted in search of another option to consolidate the sand and the painting without altering the colour. Aquazol, a non-ionic polymer, very successfully used on painted surfaces in the museum world, and the best alternative to B-72, was tested. However, when the test brick of consolidated and painted sand with Aquazol was placed in the humidity chamber at 100 per cent RH, recreating the overnight environment during the winter months at Dahshur, the sand brick collapsed due to the high humidity since Aquazol can be dissolved either in water or in alcohol. Thus, Aquazol was eliminated as a possibility, leaving B-72 as the only alternative.

In order to be prepared for a similar situation, and to improve the outcome, a kit for the use of Cyclododecane *in situ* was developed. Its application on textiles is a matter of on-going research and experimentation. Cyclododecane is a solid white, waxy cyclic alkane that slowly sublimes at room temperature without leaving residues, making it completely reversible. It is chemically stable, inert, and can be used as a temporary fixative, consolidant, blocking, masking agent and adhesive. In the future at Dahshur, the use of Cyclododecane *in situ* will allow the consolidation of finds in a short time, allowing them to be moved to the storeroom to complete the conservation treatment later, in a more comfortable context, and without the time restrictions and pressure of an on-going excavation.

NINE: Establish in advance a preliminary methodology for the analysis of the textile material, as well as the use of the appropriate textile terminology according to the nature of textile material to be studied.

TEN: Carry out a review and evaluation of conservation materials and equipment before each excavation season.

A textile conservator working in an excavation has to be creative, and resourceful, able to improvise quickly and develop alternative technologies for preservation and conservation treatments, maximizing the use of whatever is available and accepting that preservation has to be done in stages; some of these stages follow from one year to the next. Thus, the conservator must address finds that require temporary stabilization with patience and good organisational skills in order to keep track of what work must be continued and has the potential to be improved the following year.

The care of human remains requires a certain disposition and mindset. One should feel at ease, perhaps, with a kind of tacit, intrinsic connection of regard in handling the dead. There are occasions when one may spend day after day alone in a storeroom, surrounded by over eight hundred excavated mummies and human remains. This kind of situation has made me aware that though alone, I am not by myself, and, for a fleeting moment in time, I, as a visitor, acknowledge and respect their presence and intersect their space and their world. Taking care of the dead is an exceptional experience, in its own way a privilege, to be honoured and performed with deep respect. The experience a textile conservator acquires in working with human remains in a museum setting is very helpful in attending to the needs of the dead in the field.

The Dahshur storeroom for organic material and human remains

In Dahshur, the excavated materials remain at the site. The storeroom for organic material and human remains is constructed below the desert surface, located on the north side of the pyramid, on top of the queen's shaft. This is the place where the human remains and textile objects are stored. In 2004, the storeroom was enlarged and the human remains made up of only bones were separated from those associated with textiles, and stored in a different room. In 2009, a new storeroom for these human bones was built on the south side of the pyramid.

The MMA excavation season runs each year from mid-September to early December. A textile conservator is at the site for three weeks each season during different excavation periods. Every season has brought improvements in the storage of the collection: cardboard boxes were replaced with plastic ones; plastic and wooden trays were provided as supports; and wooden supports became standard for all mummies.

Environmental assessment began in 2001 under the textile conservator's supervision, in order to keep organic materials from being exposed to dramatic temperature and humidity fluctuations and the falling of unwanted sand. The air shafts on the door and on the storeroom roof at desert floor level were permanently sealed in 2002.

Registration documents and classification of the finds

The registration process has two components: information provided by the excavator, and information supplied by the textile conservator. The archaeologist assigns a registration number, and does the burial documentation *in situ*, using recording forms created by the Museum of London. The piece of metal foil on which the original registration information of the find was written by the archaeologist is kept with the find at all times; all registration information is also documented elsewhere.

Once the textiles have been brought to the storeroom, the textile conservator processes the find. The find is verified with a brief archaeological description accompanying the object.

Initial analysis of the textile is carried out with close observation. At this stage, material and weaving techniques can be identified, and a tentative assessment of the possible dye source can be conducted. Written documentation is done and sometimes a diagram is rendered. Dimensions of the find are taken.

When possible, visual fibre identification of the material and make-up is done and weaving characteristics such as warp and weft, headings, finishes, selvages, and weaving structure are recorded, if visible. A photographic record is made in addition to that done by the archaeologist. Relevant close-ups are taken from different angles and positions, if the find can be handled without being disturbed. An assessment of the preservation condition is conducted with remarks written in red so they cannot be missed. When necessary, labels with handling instructions are written and placed on each object; not only on the outside, but in strategic places inside the packing. Conservation remarks and handling instructions or restrictions appear mostly in red on the outside of the packed find. Sometimes all the above information is placed on a separate label with the object.

After a preliminary study is completed, a standard documentation sheet is created and all preliminary information is transferred. In 2005 each find excavated in prior seasons (2001 through 2004) was assessed and classified, and all information was added to the database.

Classification of human remains having textiles at Dahshur is as follows:

1. Complete human remains with textiles;
2. Mummies;
3. Incomplete or fragmented human remains with textiles, usually legs;
4. Dislocated human remains with textiles, often skulls with hair;
5. Organic materials associated with human remains and textiles (for example, a funerary bier made of palm brier).

Preliminary classification of the textile material at Dahshur is described here:

I. Shrouds (pl. 13):

1. Late Dynastic / early Roman shrouds: These are associated with woven fabric tapes. The shroud weaving quality is finer compared to the 'Kharga Type' shrouds.

2. 'Kharga or Roman Type' shrouds ('Early Kharga': Kajitani): These are associated with the 'red/un-dyed woven type tape' and the similar 'brown/un-dyed woven type tapes' woven with the same un-dyed linen yarn as the 'red/un-dyed woven type tape' and a less common brown color instead of the red. A characteristic is the width-to-width spaces without wefts in several areas of the woven shroud, creating a stripe of exposed warps up to approximately fifteen centimetres in several areas of the shroud. In several of the MMA Kharga shrouds, designs with supplementary wefts in blue and red wool are present. At Dahshur, small fragments with similar designs have been found.

3. Shrouds with complete wefts: These are associated with woven tapes in a solid red color and totally un-dyed yarn. These shrouds are similar in weaving structure and quality to the 'Kharga Type' shrouds and are totally woven.

4. Shrouds with tapestry weaving designs: These are associated with the 'red/un-dyed woven type tape'. Tapestry weaving of different designs are found located on diverse places in the mummy, inside and outside wrapping shrouds; on the chest, the legs, and at the base of the feet.

II. Woven Tapes (pl. 11)

A. Wrapped around the shrouds of the mummies:

1. Crisscross in a pattern;

   1.1.   Woven fabric tapes, made of strips of previously woven fabric;

   1.2.   'Red/un-dyed woven type tapes', rare at Dahshur and associated with 'Kharga or Roman type' wrapping shrouds, and with wrapping shrouds that have tapestry designs

2. Crisscross in no pattern:

   2.1.   'Red/un-dyed woven type tapes' and 'brown/un-dyed woven type tapes', most common at Dahshur, associated with 'Kharga or Roman type' wrapping shrouds, and shrouds with tapestry designs.

   2.2.   One solid colour woven tapes, totally un-dyed or dyed.

   2.3.   Ropes, made of linen and palm tree fibres of varying thickness.

B. Woven tapes placed on top and on the sides of the mummy shroud 'apron type':

1. Woven tapes in a square cross pattern;

   1.1.   One colour, un-dyed and red. 'Red/un-dyed woven type tapes' are the more common types in most of the Dahshur burials, and have been found in several nearby cemeteries. From the MMA excavations at Lisht, there is a sample now in the MMA collection, MMA 34.1.121. In the Fayum, 'red/un-dyed woven type tapes' have been reported by Kristin South from Brigham Young University, excavating at Fag el-Gamus Necropolis (South 2009, 2–5; see also this volume); also, similar tapes have been recorded by Natalia Sinitsyna (pers. comm.) at the Del El Banat; and in middle Egypt at Al-Kom al-Ahmar, they have been described by Beatrice Huber (Huber 2006, 57–68).

It can be concluded that tapes of crisscross type without a pattern, are thinner in Dahshur and that they do not have an organized, repetitive, definite pattern that could be identified, as is the case of the finds reported from the Fag el-Gamus Necropolis in the Fayum.

Fig. 4. Dahshur mummy B-132 *in situ* with the feet heavily padded to form a large bulbous shape. The detail photo b) shows that, unusually, a design in purple tapestry weaving is woven into the shroud at the bottom of the feet (I.4). Photos by MMA Egyptian Art Excavation to Dahshur. © The Metropolitan Museum of Art.

Most of the burials in Dahshur follow the human body's shape. In some burials, the feet are heavily padded and have a large bulbous shape. The mummies of unusual shape at Dahshur were created at times by folding up fabric, the accumulation of fabric layers, or by the use of date palm fibre stuffing. These methods are verified through the study of dislocated burials from the same site, assisting the archaeologists and textile specialists in understanding how the unusual shapes were accomplished.

In burial B-132, the un-dyed linen shroud held by 'red/un-dyed woven type tapes' follows the body shape; however at the feet, the mummy's shape balloons into a large round form encompassing the feet, the soles of which are decorated with a tapestry design in purple colour (Fig. 4). The shape around the feet as well as the location of the tapestry is unusual, and unique to the site.

Preserving the collection

The archaeologists are the first to have contact with the burials, and therefore must make immediate decisions about handling the human remains, focusing on the state of preservation of each find. This work, however, is more successful when the textile conservator is involved.

The textile conservator on this excavation works with the archaeologists to lift, document, analyse, and take care of mummies, and dislocated human remains associated with textiles, as well as textiles and objects related to textiles. This experience enables the textile conservator to contribute to the discussion about the cemetery, using information from the textiles to assess how funerary customs and social attitudes to death have changed through time.

After the conservator has opened the initial packing that was done in the field, verified the documentation of the find, and concluded the assessment of its condition, whatever measure is necessary to improve or stabilise the object is immediately adopted. This includes creating conservation-standard supports to improve long-term storage for bulky or three-dimensional finds, or finding containers for a body part. The aim is always to improve the packing, to stabilise the find, and to facilitate its handling without damage. Special pieces, such as skulls wrapped with textiles and textiles with parts of human remains, are manipulated and packed with the assistance of the archaeologist or physical anthropologist. Over-size and three-dimensional textiles, as well as those that are in fragile condition, require special handling. All the finds are then properly documented, stabilised, wrapped, and labeled for long-term storage.

By 2005, the conservation methodology for long-term storage of the human remains at the MMA excavation was established. Custom made wooden supports were provided and labeled for each mummy. Wooden supports were not sealed. To avoid direct contact between the textile and the wood, a barrier was installed between the modern wood and the finds.

The Dahshur excavation keeps several 'Mummy Kits' of different sizes in the storeroom ready to be used by the archaeologist, with or without the conservator, to wrap the mummy *in situ* with the final storage material, thus eliminating the need for changing packing materials between excavation and storage. The kit consists of packing materials, and instructions on how to put the kit together, and a temporary board, made either from wood or a thick metal sheet, that is easily introduced underneath the mummy into the soil (Cortes 2009, 224–225).

The 'Mummy Kit' is designed to lift a mummy in a single block to help keep the mummy intact, since the mummy has to be lifted and carried horizontally. The storeroom door as well as the storage shelves should be designed for facilitating the horizontal carrying position at all times. In the storeroom, the mummy is then transferred from the temporary board to the long-term custom made wooden support.

Why we do not unwrap mummies

According to John Taylor, Assistant Keeper of Ancient Egypt at the British Museum, in his lecture 'Transforming the living and the dead: wrapping, shrouding and binding in Ancient Egypt', given at University College London in 2010:

> The wrapping of the corpse was a crucial element of the formal disposal of the body in ancient Egypt, a key part of the complex rituals which were to bring about renewal of life and the transformation of the dead person into a being of higher status in the hierarchy of the cosmos.
>
> The role of the wrappings in this process included confirming the restoration of the body's physical unity and its reconstitution as a divine image, and providing the 'cocoon' in which the renewal of life-force and powers took place. This temporary phase was characterized by concealment and physical inertia or restraint. The former supported the sacred character of the transformation that was taking place beneath the wrappings, while the latter reflected the deprivation of the faculties which came with death and which would be reversed by ritual acts. (Taylor, 2010)

The Dahshur mummies and their grave goods present an unusual opportunity to study not only human remains, but the manner of preparation for eternity that was practised near the ancient Egyptian capital during the early Roman-late Antique era. The finds from each burial are kept intact so that everything can be studied as a unit. At Dahshur, we do not unwrap mummies for the following reasons. The Dahshur intact burials are a unique group; they belong to the few untouched burials corresponding to the time-span of the Dahshur cemetery, and they illustrate a variety of ways in which wrapping was carried out, from date to date. Furthermore, in the collection of finds, there are many dislocated body parts with textile fragments, where information may be gathered on the wrapping process and the contents of the wrappings. Finally, the information from these mummies may be used as solid comparative material for the numerous undocumented fragments from these periods in worldwide collections.

Today, because there was a tradition of unwrapping excavated mummies, we know a great deal about the methods, materials, and objects used during the funerary ritual. But that invasive process, while adding to our knowledge, also contributed to a loss of an enormous amount of information. Mummies unwrapped in earlier fieldwork and in museums have lost data that today, with our advanced medical technology, we could have used to better understand the period and culture in which they were created.

Non-invasive technologies, such as the ones used in the 1996–1997 MMA X-ray radiography and the three-dimensional computerized tomography, the CT project on all the pre-Dynastic and Dynastic mummies in the museum, are technologies currently used on mummies by several museums. The three-dimensional visualisation, used by the British Museum in the exhibition 'Mummy: The Inside Story' curated by John Taylor in 2004, allows us to study and interpret what is inside a mummy without any destruction to the body and its wrappings. Also, the example of The Manchester Mummy Project at Manchester University, directed by Rosalie David, should be followed.

In November 2010, a trial with terahertz radiation (THz) was organized by the MMA Department of Scientific Research and the National Institute of Information and Communications Technology in Tokyo, Japan, completing the first terahertz use on the wrapping of a human mummy. For this research the Egyptian mummy of Kharushere, Dynasty 22, *c*. 825–712 BC was chosen.

> In terahertz pulsed time domain reflection imaging (THz imaging), contrast depends on the refractive index of the materials. Thus, THz imaging can be complement to X-ray techniques. The pulsed THz waves are reflected by any discontinuity in the probed material: this gives THz imaging the potential to provide indications on the sequence of fabric layers and on eventual objects placed in-between the bandages. (Fukanaga *et al*. 2011)

The evaluation of the trial concluded that THz needs to be developed further. While both X-rays and THz do not destroy the mummies' wrappings, THz pulses are safer, since there is no exposure to radiation hazards and THz scanners are mobile and compact, and can be used in museum galleries as well as at archaeological sites.

Research using other new portable technologies such as Reflectance Transformation Imaging (RTI), should be attempted on the wrappings in order to enhance 3D information, and possibly make visible surface details that cannot be seen by the naked eye or through standard magnification or photography.

Other future development of non-invasive portable technologies may greatly enhance research at the excavation site. This is the direction future work should take for the study of human remains, and the proper use of these technologies will take place through the efforts and commitment of archaeologists, conservation scientists, curators and conservators working together.

Also, one must try to keep in mind that it is not necessary to excavate an entire cemetery. It may be better to leave a portion for a future generation who may well be able to improve on what we can now do. There are circumstances in which we preserve more when we do nothing. The challenge is to figure out 'how not to do' and this is one of the hardest challenges for the conservator and archaeologist, since it is difficult to grasp that we are doing the most when nothing is touched.

Conclusion

This paper presents a methodology developed by a textile conservator (the author) for long-term preservation of textiles associated with human remains. This methodology evolved and improved as a result of teamwork in the field over the past ten years of excavation between archaeologists, physical anthropologists, curators, object conservators, skilled excavation workers, and a textile conservator. My experience of taking care of mummies and archaeological textiles in a museum setting created a foundation of knowledge that assisted with the work at Dahshur.

It is important to spend quality time with the finds, which allows the conservator to analyse and reflect in order to benefit research. The experience in the study of textiles has taught us that much may be missed at first glimpse, since there is no way to apprehend all that an object can reveal in one viewing. The communication between artefact and researcher is a slow and meticulous process.

This paper focused on Egypt; however, unwrapping mummies, regardless of their culture, should not be considered an alternative. Their study with the development of non-invasive technologies and conservation methodologies is the alternative, so that the time previously spent in unwrapping should be invested in research with new technologies, to achieve the goal of studying human remains as well as their material culture *in situ*, making all efforts to keep both intact. When a mummy is unearthed, it is the dead who are giving a gift to the finder; this gift includes all of the material culture that surrounds them. Preservation and appropriate research is our reciprocal gift to the dead.

The aim of this paper is to continue the dialogue between conservators and curators, archaeologists, physical anthropologists, and conservation scientists. Such a dialogue allows everyone to learn from each other to develop new methods for the study and preservation of textiles associated with human remains.

This paper is dedicated to the people who were buried in the Dahshur cemetery.

'I will have more to say when I am dead' – E. A. Robinson (Pringle 2001, 11)

Acknowledgements

I am very grateful to Dorothea Arnold, Chairman of the Department of Egyptian Art at The Metropolitan Museum of Art; Dieter Arnold, Director of The Metropolitan Museum of Art Egyptian Expedition to Dahshur; the members of the Dahshur excavation team, especially Chris Marshall; the Qurna workmen, and Ali Hassan; Florica Zaharia, Conservator in-Charge of Textile Conservation; Giovanna Fiorino-Iannace, Collections Manager of the Antonio Ratti Textile Center at The Metropolitan Museum of Art. I am indebted to The Bioanthropology Foundation and The Adelaide Milton de Groot Fund for financial support. My thanks also go to Ann Heywood, Diana Craig Patch, Marco Leona, Jeff Daly, Elena Phipps, Helen Evans, Catharine Roehrig, Lawrence Becker, Christine Giuntini, Lucy Belloli, Isabelle Duvernois and Antonio Cosentino, all of The Metropolitan Museum of Art; Nan Rothschild, Director of Museum Studies Program, and Zoe Crossland of the Anthropology Department, at Columbia University; and Nobuko Kajitani, The Metropolitan Museum of Art Conservator Emerita, for her instruction on archaeological textiles.

emilia.cortes@metmuseum.org

Bibliography

Cortes 2001 to 2010: E. Cortes, *Excavation Seasons Diary, and textile Conservation Records, The Metropolitan Museum of Art Egyptian Expedition Records. Working documents*, unpublished

Cortes 2006: E. Cortes, *Textiles from Roman period Burials at Dahshur*, unpublished

Cortes 2009: E. Cortes, 'Long Term Preservation of Ptolemaic to Late Antique Period Burials at The Metropolitan Museum of Art Excavation in Dahshur, Egypt', in *7th North American Textile Conservation Conference Preprints*, 219–238

Fukanaga *et al.* 201: K. Fukanaga, I. N. Duglin, I. Stuenkel, M. Leona, M. T. Minimberg, A. Cosentino, E. Cortes, *A non-invasive research with Terahertz imaging applied on a MMA Egyptian mummy*, unpublished

Huber 2006: B. Huber, 'Al-Kom al Ahmar/ Sharūna: Different Archaeological Contexts – Different Textiles?', in *Textiles in Situ. Their Find Spots in Egypt and Neighbouring Countries in the First Millennium CE* (13 Riggisberger Berichte), Bern, 57–68

Kajitani 2006: N. Kajitani, 'Textiles and Their Context in the Third to Fourth Century CE Cemetery of al-Bagawat, Khargah Oasis, Egypt, from the 1907–1931 Excavations by The Metropolitan Museum of Art, New York', in *Textiles in Situ. Their Find Spots in Egypt and Neighbouring Countries in the First Millennium CE* (13 Riggisberger Berichte), Bern, 95–112

Manniche 1989: L. Manniche, *An Ancient Egyptian Herbal*, London

Metropolitan Museum of Art 1906–1936: MMA *Egyptian Expedition Archives from the archaeological sites of Kharga, Lisht and Deir el Bahri, Egyptian Art Department*, New York

Metropolitan Museum of Art 1999–2010: MMA *Egyptian Expedition Burial Records by Archaeologist and Textile Conservator, Egyptian Art Department*, New York, unpublished

Minimberg 2001: D. T. Minimberg, 'The Museum Mummies: an Inside View', *Neurosurgery*, 49.1, 192–199

Parker Pearson 2005: M. Parker Pearson, *The Archaeology of Death and Burial*, Austin

Pringle 2001: H. Pringle, *The Mummy Congress, Science, Obsession, and the Ever Lasting Dead*, New York

South 2009: K. South, J. Y. Smith, G. Tata, and C. W. Riggs, 'Face-bundles' in Early Christian Burials from Fayum, *Archaeological Textiles Newsletter* 48, 2–5

Taylor 2004: J. Taylor, *Mummy. The Inside Story*, London

Taylor 2010: J. Taylor, 'Transforming the living and the dead: wrapping shrouding and binding in Ancient Egypt' from the lecture delivered at *Wrapping and Unwrapping, Archaeological and Anthropological Perspectives 20–21 May 2010*, London

DRESSING THE DEAD IN PALMYRA IN THE SECOND AND THIRD CENTURIES AD

ANNEMARIE STAUFFER

The dead and their funerary monuments were an integral part of life at Palmyra. The town was surrounded by a belt of cemeteries, so that monumental tombs were the first buildings visitors to Palmyra encountered – in antiquity as well as today (Wood, Dawkins 1753). As Michal Gawlikowski recently noted, everyone first passed through the 'City of the Dead' before reaching the 'City of the Living' (Gawlikowski 2005). The importance of burials and burial ceremonies is reflected in the three types of monumental tombs known from Palmyra: tower tombs, temple tombs and *hypogea*. Each tomb belonged to a family or clan and contained hundreds of burials. All tombs were secured by a door, and, although entrance to the tombs might not have been exclusively restricted to members of the clan or the tribe of the owners, the door clearly marked the physical and symbolic separation of the interior chamber from the outside world. The internal design was more or less the same in all the tombs from the middle of the second century, the dead generally being buried in narrow slots, so called *loculi*, arranged in vertical rows (Gawlikowski 2005, 45–46). Each *loculus* was closed by a plaque of limestone, stucco or terracotta.

The tomb founders and family members of outstanding political, cultic or tribal rank, however, often were not buried in *loculi*, but in huge stone sarcophagi. Their lids were carved with reclining figures or banqueting scenes that may have included several members of the family (Schmidt-Colinet 1992, 105–106).

Considering all the wealth and the importance given to manifold markers of status and social position, it is most astonishing that the Palmyrenes did not dress their dead in clothing. There is hardly any documentation of a burial assemblage within a *loculus* or sarcophagus, but reports and descriptions by earlier travellers and scholars, my own research, and the analysis of a mummy in the Ny Carlsberg Museum in Copenhagen, clearly indicate that the bodies of the dead at Palmyra were carefully treated, using precious textiles and embalming substances, but they were not actually dressed. Clothing and other textiles, such as hangings or shrouds, played no role in this context, and hardly any jewellery was given to the dead (Pfister 1934, 8–12; Pfister 1937, 9, 15; Pfister 1940, 9–10; Schmidt-Colinet *et al.* 2000, 55–57; Nockert 1988, 15).

Corpses were wrapped for burial in three distinct layers of textile bandages soaked in bituminous substances, the final and external layer being decorated with colourful textile strips (Schmidt-Colinet *et al.* 2000, fig. 53). Extremely precious garments were used for the bandages, selected according to functional criteria. Large cloaks and tunics of Roman style provided the inner wrappings, as they did not contain any seams, whilst colourful decorative motifs taken from clothing of local and Persian type were used for the final and outer adornment of the mummy.

Although the burials and wrapped bodies do not reveal the importance of clothing in a funerary context, dress as means of non-verbal communication nevertheless was of outstanding importance in burial (Schmidt-Colinet 2009, 225). But the message was on the outside of the *loculus* or sarcophagus, thus gaining in visibility and impact. Much importance was given to being identified after death, not only as one of the many members belonging to a family, but also as an individual part of the clan (Finlayson 2002/2003). Therefore a portrait of the deceased, with the name and the relevant genealogical information, sealed the *loculus* or decorated the sarcophagus. These images and messages would be seen by those visiting the tomb and taking part in feasts and ceremonies. Inscriptions are incised into many *loculus* plates and wall niches. They are always written in the local Aramaic language to address local visitors, and occasionally there is an additional Greek inscription.

These images were designed to convey essential and personal information about individual members of the clan, and here we return to the theme of dressing the dead. The portraits of the deceased depict them dressed in all their finery, the clothing chosen for the images possibly having been determined by special dress codes that we can no longer recognise (Finlayson 2002/2003). The *loculus* reliefs, in particular, appear, at first sight, quite uniform, but closer scrutiny reveals that there was great variety in dress from the second to the middle of the third century (Stauffer 2010). The garments can be classified roughly according to cut, size and decoration into a Graeco-Roman, a local and a Parthian group (Table 1).

The Graeco-Roman group of cloaks comprises the classical voluminous *himation*, worn both by men and women (Fig. 1). From the middle of the second century it might show frilled or fringed edges (Dentzer-Feydy *et al.* 1993, cat. no.192), and from this time frilled vertical edges can be found on nearly all garments (Figs 2–3). A local variant of the *himation* was of rectangular, less voluminous shape. Figures 2 and 3 illustrate how this cloak tightly envelops the body, in contrast to the larger Graeco-Roman *himation* (Fig. 1). Local cloaks might be decorated with geometric elements (Fig. 3 and Table 1), such as forms in the shape of an H or the Greek letter gamma (Γ), or with large horizontal bars in contrasting colours. They are marks of distinction, rather than ornaments (Sadurska 1977, 77; Schmidt-Colinet *et al.* 2000, 46–47). The large Roman-style *himation* is combined exclusively with Graeco-Roman garments, in contrast to the local cloak worn with Graeco-Roman, local, or Parthian-style clothing. Good examples of the former Roman-style cloak are especially numerous on the *loculus* plaques (Tanabe 1986, Figs 281, 282, 303), whilst many images of the local, less voluminous cloak, are found in almost all tombs. Impressive examples are preserved from temple tomb 36 and 186 (Schmidt-Colinet 1992, pls. 34a, 36a, 73b) and the underground burial chamber of Alaine (Tanabe 1986, fig. 386).

Another local cloak is a short shoulder mantle, both with straight or frilled selvedges or finished edges (Fig. 4, pl. 14 and Table 1). Unlike the Roman *paludamentum* it is always decorated. It is worn with a Graeco-Roman short sleeved *chiton* (Fig. 4), the local long-sleeved shirt, and the Parthian caftan (pl. 14). Numerous *loculus* plaques and sculptures from different tombs illustrate this usually lavishly decorated cloak.

The Parthian over-garment is a coat, cut to shape, with over-long sleeves. After the middle of the second century AD, this coat is also characterized by frilled vertical edges (Table 1). This coat can be found, for example, on Maqqai's sarcophagus (Schmidt-Colinet 1992, pl. 69b). It is worn exclusively with Parthian dress and by men only.

Ladies might wear the large Graeco-Roman *himation*, but examples are extremely rare (Parlasca 1990, fig. 6). Their outer garment is usually the local *himation* (Table 1, Fig. 6 and pl.

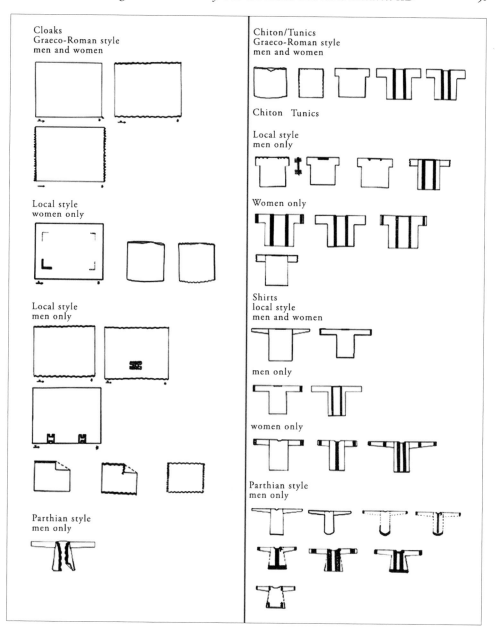

Table 1. Cloaks and shirts on *loculus* plaques and sarcophagi (by A. Stauffer).

Above left: Fig. 1. *Loculus* plaque with a man dressed in a Graeco-Roman *himation*, Palmyra Museum (photo by A. Stauffer).

Above right: Fig. 2. *Loculus* plaque with a man dressed in a local *himation*, Palmyra Museum (photo by A. Stauffer).

Fig. 3. Detail of a banquet relief showing a man in the tightly wrapped local *himation* with H-shaped decoration, Palmyra Museum (after Tanabe 1986).

Fig. 4. Banquet relief showing two men wearing the local shoulder mantle with a Roman tunic (left) and a long-sleeved shirt (right) from the burial chamber of Artaban in Palmyra (photo by A. Stauffer).

14), commonly draped in the Parthian manner, i.e. wrapped around the body and fastened at the left shoulder with a brooch (Sommer 2003, fig.29). Some scholars have suggested that this element of dress was a Greek *peplos* (Böhme-Schönberger 1997, 87), but a few sculptures of late date clearly indicate that it is indeed a cloak. Two images from Tomb 36 and near Tomb 159 depict ladies in a reclining pose on the centre of a couch, a position mainly occupied by men (Schmidt-Colinet 1992, pl. 45a, pl. 72e). They are dressed in the local tight *himation*, but it is not draped as usual around the woman's body and fastened with a brooch, but worn, like her male counterparts, over her left shoulder leaving her right arm uncovered. The local cloak is worn with a long or a short veil, and only rarely is the cloak draped in the Roman manner over the woman's head (Parlasca 1990, fig. 6; Dentzer-Feydy *et al.* 1993, cat. no.192).

Like cloaks, tunics and shirts also can be grouped according to the different clothing traditions they follow (Table 1). The Graeco-Roman tunic, woven to shape and known all over the Roman world, is characterized by voluminous sleeves forming vertical folds and by the horizontal neck slit (Figs 1, 4–5). Both ladies' and men's tunics may be decorated with pairs of monochrome stripes (Fig. 5 and Table 1). There was also a local shirt for both men and women. It is of less voluminous shape but longer than the tunic, especially when worn by women. Long narrow sleeves are sewn to the main part of the garment to form horizontal circular folds (Figs 4, 6). In contrast to the tunic, openings for the head and neck are narrow and mainly rounded (Figs 4, 6), side openings are necessary to put on the dress (Ploug 1995, 211; Schmidt-Colinet 1992, pl.36c). The local shirt was worn usually with trousers by both sexes. Men's shirts are nearly always undecorated, whereas ladies' local shirts are frequently embellished with a single stripe or vertical pairs of them (Figs 5, 6) and can have ornamented cuffs (Fig. 6) (Tanabe 1986, fig. 338, 339, 351, 361).

Parthian fashion is worn exclusively by young boys and men (pl. 14–15 and Table 1). The short Parthian caftan is tighter and shorter than the local shirt. Characteristic elements are side slits at the side of the garment and on the left shoulder. It is always combined with trousers and frequently also with breeches (pl. 14–15). In the period around AD 200 and in the third century, this garment is made of fabric with decoration woven into it or it is adorned with elements sewn on the fabric (Figs 3–4, pl. 14 and Table 1). The same luxurious decorations can be found on Parthian trousers, breeches, and boots.

A special item of clothing, rarely illustrated, are Parthian-style shirts with decoration that is quite different. The cut of the shirt corresponds to the Parthian caftan, but the decoration is restricted to geometric motifs such as arrows, triangles or rhomboids along the lower seam, on the cuffs and at both ends of the neck opening (Schmidt-Colinet 1992, pl. 73a; Stauffer 2010, fig. 7–8). This shirt is worn with narrow trousers, boots and always with a short fringed shoulder mantle. This outfit can be found on *loculus* plaques as well as on sarcophagi. It is neither purely Roman nor Parthian.

Looking at hundreds of tomb portraits from Palmyra, we might well ask whether the garments and their decoration represented in funerary sculpture reflect real garments and clothing styles of the period or whether they stem from the imagination of the artists. The textile scraps found within the tombs prove beyond doubt, however, that the clothing depicted in Palmyrene funerary art corresponds to that actually worn at the time. The gamma-shaped decoration on women's cloaks, for example, is a well known decorative motif seen on textiles

Above left: Fig. 5. *Loculus* plaque with a lady in a short-sleeved tunic, Palmyra Museum (after Tanabe 1986).

Above right: Fig. 6. *Loculus* plaque with a woman in the local long-sleeved shirt with decorative bands, Palmyra Museum (photo by A. Stauffer).

from archaeological contexts (Schmidt-Colinet *et al.* 2000, pl. IIId). More exotic motifs, such as the triangles with stepped sides shown on men's tunics, are found in the tower tomb of Elahbel, and the decoration of a boy's tunic corresponds to textile finds from the tomb of Kitot (Stauffer 2010, 211–212, 215). Many more examples could be cited.

The variety of garments and types of decoration represented in funerary portraits is very surprising, although this has found very little discussion in scholarly literature (Plough 1995, 30–31; Finlayson 2002/2003; Stauffer 2010). It appears that no one style was predominant during a particular period; Roman, Parthian and local clothing styles and traditions existed simultaneously in the same tombs. Indeed, Schmidt-Colinet concluded that Palmyrene noblemen might be represented on their sarcophagi in both Roman and Parthian dress at the same time (Schmidt-Colinet 2009). Furthermore, it seems that dress depicted in a funerary context is not a reflection of a general political orientation of the family to whom the tombs belonged. This is well illustrated by the funerary portraits in the tower tomb of Elahbel. One of four brothers who built the monument, Elahbel's full Roman name was Marcus Ulpius Elahbelus, reflecting that he had a loyal and close relationship with, and shared the same family name as, the Roman emperor Marcus Ulpius Trajanus. Nevertheless, there is no evidence here that Roman-style dress played a greater role in the self-representation of this family than in the portrayal of the owners of other Palmyrene tombs (Gawlikowski 1969; Schmidt-Colinet 2011). It appears, instead, that social status and rank were much a stronger driving force for dress choice. If we compare the garments on the *loculus* plaques, lids of sarcophagi and in wall paintings to those worn by individuals of high social rank on sarcophagus lids, significant differences are apparent. In the *loculus* slabs, sarcophagus reliefs and paintings, Graeco-Roman and local style garments can be found in more or less equal numbers, with an astonishing variety of different forms and decorative motifs for both men and women. These individuals clearly represent themselves as fashionably aware. On the sarcophagus lids, however, the elite heads of clans exhibit dramatically less variety in their clothing styles (Table 2). Graeco-Roman style clothing is extremely rare in reliefs and sculptures from almost twenty tombs, dating from the end of the first to the second half of the third century. If Graeco-Roman dress is used, it is worn only by male family members of lower rank or by small boys. Men who held priestly functions are never shown in the sculpture of sarcophagus lids wearing Roman-style garments. There is only one exception of a priest clad in a short sleeved tunic, but this is combined with the local cloak (Fig. 4). Another remarkable fact is that, in contrast to the *loculus* portraits of lower ranking individuals, the Roman-style garments of the banqueters on sarcophagus lids are not decorated. Only the plain short-sleeved tunic and the *himation* are shown. Women and girls in this context do not wear any Roman-style clothing at all, and their garments are not adorned with decorative stripes, not even when the use of decorative elements became popular at the end of the second century (Table 2). There is only one exception here, on a sarcophagus in Tomb 186, where a lady is taking part in the banquet as the symposiarch, or toast-master, reclining with her male counterpart (Schmidt-Colinet 1992, pl. 73b).

In studying the clothing of the dead in Palmyra during a time span of at least two centuries, it becomes obvious that dress styles in Palmyra are not influenced by political changes, but rather they are intimately related to the social position of the deceased within the internal structure of a clan and its representation in the context of the mausoleum. The *loculus* reliefs show individuals of average importance, including even freed slaves, nurses and teachers, as the inscriptions reveal. Their dress does not conform to any particular conventions, and even priests wear different types of clothing when they are shown 'off duty', rather than officiating in cultic rituals.

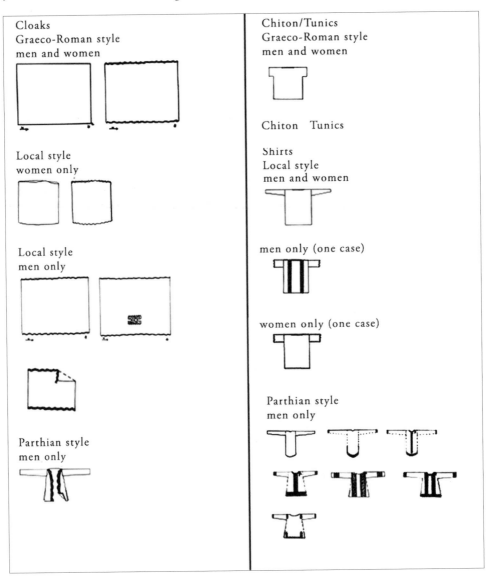

Table 2. Cloaks and shirts on sarcophagi only (by A. Stauffer).

1. Late Roman sarcophagus from Castor, Cambridgeshire, 1968, after removal of the silt (photo by J. P. Wild).

2. Metal-replaced linen cloth on copper-alloy bangle of twisted wire from a Late Roman sarcophagus at Castor, Cambridgeshire (photo by J. P. Wild).

3. Tomb of Philip II, Vergina, textile (photo after Andronikos 1984, Figs 156–157).

4. Tomb of Lyson and Kallikles, detail of ceiling in burial chamber (photo after Miller 1993, pl. Vb).

5. Tomb of the Palmettes, Lefkadia, ceiling in antechamber (photo after Rhomiopoulou, Schmidt-Dounas 2010, pl. 11).

6. Tomb of the Palmettes, Lefkadia, detail of ceiling in antechamber (photo after Rhomiopoulou, Schmidt-Dounas 2010, pl. 13).

7. *Stele* of Aphrodeisia, Demetrias, detail (photo by D. Andrianou).

8. Tomb of Agios Athanasios, façade (photo after Tsimbidou-Avloniti 2005, pl. 34).

9. Red and white ribbons, 1 cm wide, used to hold the wrappings of the burial in place. In this example (2006-SE-32), the two sheds include one with six pairs of undyed threads and one with four pairs of red threads (two now faded) with one pair of undyed threads on either side, for a total of twenty-four warps. The weft is two threads of undyed linen (photo courtesy of BYU Fayum Excavation).

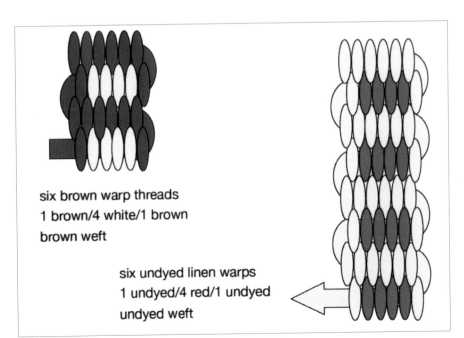

six brown warp threads
1 brown/4 white/1 brown
brown weft

six undyed linen warps
1 undyed/4 red/1 undyed
undyed weft

10. Schematic drawing of the technique used in making the most typical ribbons. These warp threads can also be paired, as seen in pl. 9 (drawing by K. South).

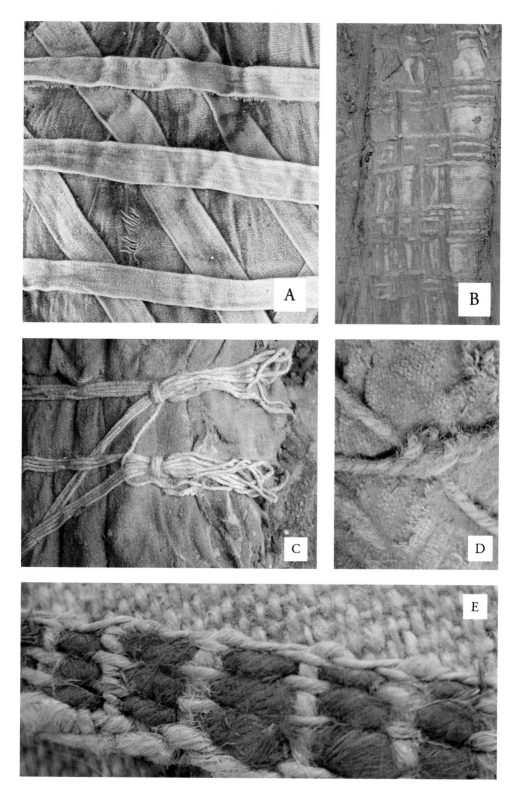

11. A selection of tapes and ropes: a) B-159 with woven fabric tapes made of strips of previously woven fabric (II.A.1.1); b) B-607 with woven tapes with cross pattern in red colour and un-dyed yarn. (II.B.1.1); c) B-200 with thin rope of linen (?) (III.A.2.3); d) B-27 ropes made of palm tree fibres (II.A.2.3); e) B-164 with 'red/un-dyed woven type tapes' (II.A.1.2 and II. A.2.1). Photos by Emilia Cortes (MMA Department of Textile Conservation). © The Metropolitan Museum of Art.

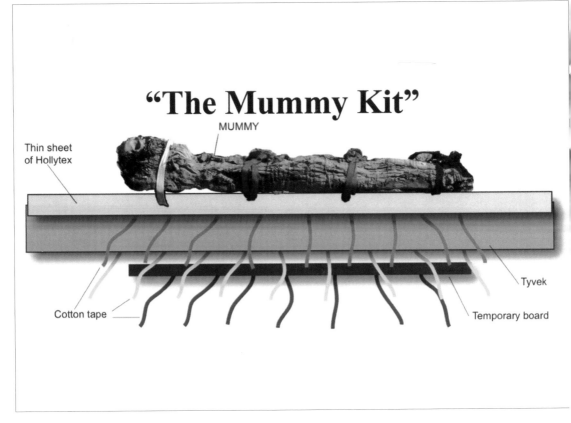

"The Mummy Kit"

MUMMY

Thin sheet
of Hollytex

Cotton tape

Tyvek

Temporary board

12. Preparation of the 'Mummy Kit' developed in 2005 and improved in 2008. This kit allows the archaeologist, with or without the conservator, to wrap the mummy *in situ* with the final storage material, reducing unnecessary manipulation of the mummy. Drawing by Jeff Daly, MMA Senior Design Advisor to the Director for Capital and Special Projects. © The Metropolitan Museum of Art.

Opposite page: 13. Dahshur Mummies: a) B-159 wrapped in a late Dynastic/early Roman shroud (I.1) associated with woven tapes made of strips of previously woven fabric wrapped around the mummy in a crisscross pattern (II.A.1.1); b) B-607 wrapped in a shroud (I.3) similar in weaving structure and quality to the 'Kharga Type' shroud and associated with woven tapes placed on the top and on the sides of the mummy shroud 'apron type', in a square cross pattern in red or un-dyed yarn (II.B.1.1); c) B-1 in a shroud with complete wefts similar in weaving structure and quality to the 'Kharga Type' shrouds and is totally woven (I.4), with a large medallion design on the front on top of the chest in tapestry weave; associated with 'red/un-dyed woven type tapes' the most type common at Dahshur (II.A.2.1). Photos MMA Egyptian Art Excavation to Dahshur 2000 and Emilia Cortes (MMA Department of Textile Conservation). © The Metropolitan Museum of Art.

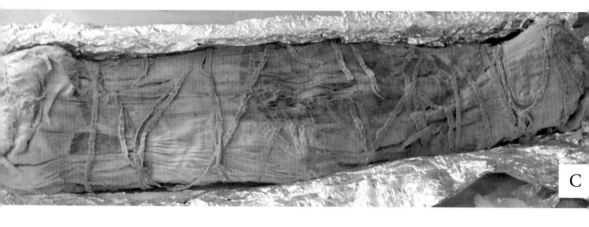

14. Fragment of a banquet relief showing a man in Parthian dress from the tower tomb of Elahbel in Palmyra (photo by A. Stauffer).

15. Detail of Parthian dress from the tomb of Elahbel, seen in pl. 14. The lavishly decorated trousers are combined with breeches (photo by A. Stauffer).

16. Figures shown wearing pointed hats, north necropolis, tomb C, Ghirza (Istanbul Archaeology Museum).

17. Figures shown wearing pointed hats, north necropolis, tomb C, Ghirza (Istanbul Archaeology Museum).

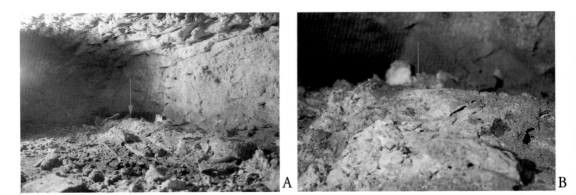

18. (a) View into *loculus* 2 in Sant'Agnese; (b) a detail of the different textile qualities present (photos by S. Mitschke).

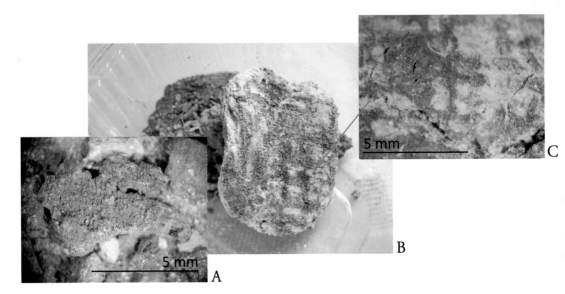

19. Lump of gypsum with calcined textile fragments: (a) sample MP 1; (b) detail of sample MP 2 (photos by S. Mitschke).

20. (a) Stockings with assembly seam; (b) detail of block-damask under the transmitted light microscope (photos by S. Mitschke).

21. The impressions of an adult and a swaddled infant are preserved in the gypsum deposit in a sarcophagus in York (photo by M. Carroll).

22. Flavia Aiulo from Aquincum holds a swaddled infant on her grave *stele* of the late first or early second century (photo by M. Carroll).

23. On this funerary monument of the second century AD, a woman from Budapest wears the ethnic dress of the Celtic Eravisci, her two-year-old daughter is clothed in a girl's version of that attire without a headdress (photo by M. Carroll).

24. Gold hair net and jewellery from the burial of a young woman from Vallerano, a suburb of Rome (photo by M. Carroll, with permission of the Museo Nazionale Palazzo Massimo).

Individuals in the group banquet scenes on sarcophagus lids, however, are of socially elevated status, as they represent the most important members of the clan. Their dress is mainly the local one. This is especially true for women and girls, but also for men with priestly functions. Prestige and position within the clan is reflected by the jewellery the women wear and, in the course of time, by the decorative appliqués and jewellery on men's garments (Fig. 3), the latter assuming the same role of status indicator as jewellery for women. It is obvious that the dress of those individuals whose identities are revealed by their personal names, as well as by paternal and maternal names, is far from a product of artistic licence. The representation of dress in a funerary context is a means of commemorating individuals and their social status, something that clearly was as important for the deceased as for the remaining members of the clan. According to Jean-Charles Balty (Balty 1996, 439) and, more recently, Jean Baptiste Yon (Yon 2003, 220), contemporary written sources indicate that noble women and priests represented a strong traditional element in a society that, due to its political and strategic importance, was significantly exposed to changes and all sorts of political and cultural influences. This claim is strongly supported by the evidence for dress and self-representation of the dead in the family tombs of Palmyra. Andreas Schmidt-Colinet, on the other hand, concluded that all the tombs in Palmyra show an eclectic mixture of Graeco-Roman, local and Parthian elements, intentionally chosen to convey important messages to visitors and viewers. The clothing in which the deceased is shown plays an important role in this eternal communication between the living and the dead.

Acknowledgements

This contribution is part of a research project on elements of dress in Palmyra. The project has benefited from the support of the European Union project 'Clothing and Identities. New Perspectives on Textiles in the Roman Empire'. First results were published in Stauffer 2010. My principal thanks are due to Andreas Schmidt-Colinet (Vienna) for fruitful discussions, to Waleed al As'ad, Director General for Antiquities in Palmyra, for permission to take photographs, and last, but not least, to the editors for help with the translation.

annemarie.stauffer@fh-koeln.de

Bibliography

Balty 1996: J.-C. Balty, 'Palmyre entre Orient et Occident: acculturation et résistances', *Annales Archéologiques Arabes Syriennes* 42, 437–444

Böhme-Schönberger 1997: A. Böhme-Schönberger, *Kleidung und Schmuck in Rom und den Provinzen*, Stuttgart

Dentzer-Feydy *et al.* 1993: J. Dentzer-Feydy, J. Teixidor, M. Pic, *Les Antiquités de Palmyre au Musée du Louvre*, Paris

Finlayson 2002/2003: C. Finlayson, 'Veil, turban and headpiece: funerary portraits and female status at Palmyra', *Annales Archéologiques Arabes Syriennes* 45/46, 221–235

Gawlikowski 1969: M. Gawlikowski, 'La famille d'Elahbel', *Studia Palmyrenskie*, 47–58

Gawlikowski 2005: M. Gawlikowski, 'The City of the Dead', in E. Cussini (ed.), *A Journey to Palmyra. Collected Essays to Remember Delbert R. Hillers*, Leiden and Boston, 44–73

Nockert 1988: M. Nockert, *Öknens Drottning*, Stockholm

Parlasca 1990: K. Parlasca, 'Palmyrenische Skulpturen in Museen an der amerikanischen Westküste', *Ancient Portraits in the J. P. Getty Museum* 1, 133–144

Pfister 1934: R. Pfister, *Textiles de Palmyre*, Paris

Pfister 1937: R. Pfister, *Nouveaux textiles de Palmyre*, Paris

Pfister 1940: R. Pfister, *Textiles de Palmyre III*, Paris

Ploug 1995: G. Ploug, *Catalogue of the Palmyrene Sculptures Ny Carlsberg Glyptothek*, Copenhagen

Sadurska-Bounni 1994: A. Sadurska, A. Bounni, 'Les sculptures funéraires de Palmyre', *Révue d'Archéologie* (Suppl. 13), Rom

Schmidt-Colinet 1992 : A. Schmidt-Colinet, *Das Tempelgrab Nr. 36 in Palmyra*, Mainz

Schmidt-Colinet *et al.* 2000 : A. Schmidt-Colinet *et al.*, *Die Textilien aus Palmyra – Alte und neue Funde*, Mainz

Schmidt-Colinet 2006: A. Schmidt-Colinet, 'L'architecture funéraire de Nabatène et de Palmyre: une biographie', in J.-C. Moretti, D. Tardy, *L'Architecture funéraire monumentale: la Gaule dans l'Empire romain*, 181–190

Schmidt-Colinet, Kh. al-As'ad 2007: 'Zwei Neufunde Palmyrenischer Sarkophage', in *Akten des Symposiums des Sarkophag-Corpus 2001, Marburg, 2.-7. Juli 2001*, Mainz, 271–278

Schmidt-Colinet 2009: A. Schmidt-Colinet, 'Nochmal zur ikonographie zweier palmyrenischer Sarkophage', in M. Blömer *et al.* (eds), *Lokale Identität im Römischen Reich*, Münster, 223–234

Schmidt-Colinet 2011: A. Schmidt-Colinet, 'Priester beim Festmahl: Etpeni, Symposiarch 130/31 n. Chr. und andere palmyrenische Tesserae', in C. Lippolis, S. de Mario (eds), *Un impaziente Desiderio di Scorrere il Mondo. Studi in Onore di Antonio Invernizzi per il suo Settantesimo Compleanno*, Florence, 161–167

Seyrig 1937: H. Seyrig, 'Armes et costumes iraniens de Palmyre', *Syria* 18, 4–31

Sommer 2003: M. Sommer, *Hatra : Geschichte und Kultur einer Karawanenstadt im römisch-parthischen Mesopotamien*, Mainz

Stauffer 2000: A. Stauffer, 'Material und Technik', in A. Schmidt-Colinet *et al.*, *Die Textilien aus Palmyra – Alte und neue Funde*, Mainz, 8–32

Stauffer 2010: A. Stauffer, 'Kleidung in Palmyra: Neue Fragen an alte Funde', in B. Bastl (ed.), *Zeitreisen. Syrien – Palmyra – Rom. Festschrift für Andreas Schmidt-Colinet zum 65. Geburtstag*, Wien, 209–218

Tanabe 1986: K. Tanabe, *Sculptures of Palmyra*, Tokyo

Yon 2002/2003: J.-B. Yon, 'Zenobie et les femmes de Palmyre', *Annales Archéologiques Arabes Syriennes* 45–46, 215–220

Wood, Dawkins 1753: R. Wood, H. Dawkins, *The Ruins of Palmyra otherwise Tedmor, in the Desert*, London

DRESSED TO IMPRESS:
THE TOMB SCULPTURE OF GHIRZA IN TRIPOLITANIA

LUCY AUDLEY-MILLER

The tombs of Ghirza, Tripolitania in North Africa are covered in sculpted relief images, which are remarkable for their vivid depiction of activities such as agricultural production, animal hunts, combat, and local ceremonies. These scenes offer important insights into the lives of people in this region; not as straightforward depictions of daily events, but as charged iconographic programmes that were invested with local social values and negotiations of status (Fontana 1997; Mattingly 1999; Mattingly 2003; Zanker 2008; Mattingly 2011). The technical style of these images is summary, but the sculptors have been relatively painstaking in depicting details of dress. Various hypotheses have been proposed to explain the artistic style of the images and the reasons behind the lack of technical finish (e.g. Mattingly 1999, 390; Johns 2003, 20), but, whatever the motive for the mode of depiction, it is significant that details of dress received comparatively close attention. This indicates that such information was important for the patron who commissioned the monument, and presumably therefore for the local audiences, which the tombs were designed to impress. The manner of representation at Ghirza makes it seem an unpromising body of evidence for an examination of dress, but as local people apparently prioritised the depiction of details of clothing, it merits our attention.

Dress at the site has not been the subject of specific investigation, but important work on these tombs has used clothing as one means of identifying the social role or status of particular individuals within the scenes (e.g. Brogan, Smith 1984; Mattingly 1999, 393; Mattingly 2003, 164–165; Zanker 2008). A range of dress styles was represented: from the standard plain or pleated short tunics worn by individuals engaged in a variety of activities (e.g. Brogan, Smith 1984, figs 52c, 82a, 82c, 111c, 123a,124a, 125a) to armed soldiers, naked victims, or those driving camel-caravans depicted with two spears and pleated kilts (e.g. Brogan, Smith 1984, figs 61, 69b, 110b). However, the dress of the wider community is generally shown in a summary way while, as Mattingly noted, elite figures are 'almost invariably depicted with more complex costumes' (Mattingly 2003, 164–165). Clothes were used to indicate relative status. In agricultural scenes, for example, subjects shown wearing long tunics or with decorated clothing rather than the normal short tunics, are depicted in overseers' roles or on a larger scale than other figures suggesting their higher rank (e.g. Zanker 2008, 217–219). The tomb images do not focus upon the self-representative concerns of the wider community; important factors in shaping identity, such as age, or gender, are differentiated only in the dress of the elite. This does not mean that dress was not used by ordinary people to negotiate a wide range of different allegiances or identities; it is simply that conveying such nuances was not the primary focus of

Ghirza's sculptors, who catered to the concerns of their elite local patrons. The way that dress is shown on the tombs is dictated by the desire of high-status patrons to convey an image that enforced their role at the top of a clearly defined social order. It is the dress of these elite figures that forms the focus of the following discussion.

Mattingly's observation that dress was used to express social importance at Ghirza is convincing, but examination of subjects shown to be of high status, through their imposing scale or individual representation as a bust or statue, reveals a differing range of elite dress forms. This paper argues that these variations in elite dress styles appear because what was considered to be 'prestigious dress' changed over time. The tombs at Ghirza span a considerable period in an era of significant social change. Although regions such as the Greek East did make striking statements of cultural continuity through their dress (Smith 1998, 66), this was far from inevitable. Recent work has emphasised that choices in what to wear are the products of individuals actively engaging with culturally approved body styles and negotiating them, to decide on how they wanted to be seen. It is through such processes of identification that changing paradigms in self-representation emerge and new identities develop (e.g. Tarlo 1996; Pratt, Rafaeli 1997; Lynch 1999). In the following discussion, dress styles at Ghirza are explored as the product of dynamic processes whereby individuals used their appearance as an important agent in the negotiation of personal status. While the dress styles of Ghirza have been observed 'to not appear to emulate Roman models' (Mattingly 2003, 165), this paper will suggest that when dressing to express their own high status, the elites of Ghirza did selectively draw upon and reinterpret personal styling models, which had been popularised by Rome. The paper traces the changing relationship with Roman styling, as local patrons shaped how they wished to be seen by local audiences within changing cultural contexts. Throughout this discussion I take 'dress' not only to include important details of clothing, but also other forms of body modification, such as jewellery or personal grooming; it is through all such aspects in styling the human body that identity is constructed (Eicher, Roach-Higgins 1992, 8–23).

The local context: Ghirza and its monumental tombs

Ghirza is situated on marginal land in the Tripolitanian pre-desert, on a southern tributary of the Wadi ZemZem, eighty miles inland from the Gulf of Sirte. It became an important settlement in the region at a late date, flourishing between the fourth and sixth centuries (Brogan, Smith 1984, 78–80; Mattingly 1995, 198). The settlement architecture relates to this period, but pottery and coins from the first and second centuries found at the site, indicate small-scale occupation of an earlier date (Brogan 1971, 123–127; Brogan, Smith 1984, 114, 227, 234–242). Ghirza came to be one of the largest urban centres in the region, boasting an important pagan temple, six *gsur* (fortified settlements), five cemeteries, and two monumental necropoleis (Brogan, Smith 1984; Mattingly 1995, 197–200; Barker *et al.* 1996b, 106–120; Sjöström 1993, 205–210). These necropoleis comprise two tomb groups, conventionally referred to as the north necropolis and the south necropolis, with the seven monuments within each group denoted by letters A–G. The tombs are referred to here by the acronyms used elsewhere, so that, for instance, NA signifies north necropolis tomb A. Each necropolis contains six tombs and one unadorned building of different architectural form (NG, SB), which Mattingly argued served specific local ritual needs (Mattingly 1999, 394–395; Mattingly 2003, 166–170).

In order to examine changes in dress choices at Ghirza, it is necessary to focus for a moment on the chronology of the tombs. The exact date for each of the monuments is uncertain, but a sequence was suggested by Brogan and Smith using internal references in the tomb inscriptions, portrait style, topographical location, and architectural analysis, which focused particularly on a typological study of the tomb capitals (Brogan, Smith 1984, 209–213). This sees the sequence of monuments run as follows: SA, NA, SE, SC, SD, NB, NC, SF, SG, ND, NE, NF (Brogan, Smith 1984, 212). Brogan and Smith suggested that the tombs began to be constructed from the mid-third through to the fifth century (Brogan, Smith 1984, 185, 212). They believed that tombs SA, NA, SE were built during the second half of the third century and that SC and SD were constructed somewhat later than these examples. Inscriptions on NB and NC put them securely in the fourth century, and SF, SG, and ND were dated to the fourth century on typological criteria. Tombs NE and NF were believed to belong to the fifth century.

Brogan and Smith's meticulous work makes for a convincing framework. It is, however, possible that the first tomb built at the site was constructed in the early third, rather than the mid-third, century because Brogan herself noted that its capitals were most comparable to pre-Severan and Severan examples (Brogan, Smith 1984, 210). It is the only 'obelisk tomb' at Ghirza, a type typically found in the pre-desert during early phases of agricultural exploitation (Brogan, Smith 1984, 185; Mattingly 1995, 162–163; Moore 2007, 75–81). The obelisk tomb is also close to the only cemetery at Ghirza to yield late first- or early second-century material (Brogan, Smith 1984, 107, 114), perhaps suggesting that it was a monumental addition to an older burial tradition in the area. Nevertheless, this is a small modification to the initial date of tomb construction at the site and does not affect the sequence that Brogan and Smith proposed. In the following discussion, choices in elite dress styles in the relief images are traced in relation to this chronological sequence. The clothing choices fall into two distinct groups, which are examined separately here. The 'early tombs' discussed below are mainly third-century, with the latest perhaps appearing in the early fourth century; the 'later tomb' group comprises the fourth-century monuments which followed these. The cultural contexts for changing elite dress preferences will be examined here in relation to their contemporary cultural context in order to explore the social significance of these personal styles.

Ghirza's earlier tombs

The earlier monuments at Ghirza (SA, NA, SE, SC, SD) are dominated by representations of the principal subjects in bust reliefs or statue format. These constitute the vehicle for elite representation at this time and provide the focus for the discussion of their self-representation here. The images usually depict two principal subjects: frequently a male and a female. The earliest tomb at the site, SA, is exceptionally rich in portrait images, which include the only statues from this site, busts in relief, and even portraits in the capitals (Brogan, Smith 1984, figs 100a-b). The images are similar, indicating that the same male and female subjects were repeatedly depicted. The elite subjects are shown in this earlier group of tombs wearing a tunic with an outer layer of cloth draped about the body like a mantle or a scarf. This personal styling preference remains broadly consistent, but there are some modifications over time, including a decrease in detailed depiction of dress, which is worth exploring.

The first tomb at the site (SA) shows the female subject in statue form, wearing a long tunic that clings to the subject's body, emphasising the breasts and then falling in vertical folds from the waist to the ankle (Brogan, Smith 1984, fig. 103). A scarf encircles the neck and the end is shown here hanging from the subject's right shoulder (Fig. 1). This scarf is also seen on the tomb's two female bust portraits where it is drawn over the left shoulder (e.g. Fig. 2). The statue and bust images show the subject's head covered by three super-imposed tiers, which could represent an elaborate coiffure or a 'turban', perhaps covered by a veil (Brogan, Smith 1984, 184–185). The same personal styling is attested at the broadly contemporary obelisk tomb at Wadi Messueggi (Bauer 1935, 69, 73–74; Merighi 1948, 169–170; Di Vita 1964, 75, pl. 38; Brogan 1971, fig. 1). It has also been tentatively identified on less detailed reliefs from the region (Fontana 1997, 153–154). A fresco image in a fourth-century tomb at Gargáresh, Tripoli, shows a high-status female wearing a full white turban and veil (Romanelli 1922, 26). It is not inconceivable that this tomb displays a dress style, which was related to that seen earlier at Ghirza, but it cannot be used as definitive evidence that a turban was being worn in the third-century pre-desert. If it was worn, it ceased to be an elite female styling preference in images at Ghirza after its first appearance on this monument.

The male subject on this tomb is also dressed in a mode that does not appear again at the site. Unfortunately only the torso and legs of the male statue survive (Fig. 3), but the fragments show the subject wearing a tunic which falls to just below the knee, with a mantle drawn diagonally over the tunic to the subject's left shoulder. A thick vertical band hangs centrally over these oblique folds. The male bust on the tomb has the same pleats of cloth drawn over the left shoulder and a right shoulder without folds of material (Fig. 2). It seems probable that the broad band represents the end of the pleated mantle, bunched up and drawn over the right shoulder, so that it hangs down the body in a thick strip. The feet appear bare and over-

Above left: Fig. 1. Female statue from south necropolis, tomb A, Ghirza (drawing by Joseph Wilkins based on photographs held in the Olwen Brogan Archive, Libyan Society Archive).

Above right: Fig. 2. Portrait images from the north frieze of south necropolis, tomb A, Ghirza, shown with possible junior elite figure and a victory (drawing by Joseph Wilkins based on photographs held in the Olwen Brogan Archive, Libyan Society Archive).

sized, but footwear may have been added in paint. The bust has neat rows of curled hair and a carefully rendered beard, personal grooming that would not be out of place in the Rome, or Lepcis, of Septimius Severus' day (e.g. Fittschen, Zanker 1985, 94–98, nos. 82–85). Elaborate artificially curled hair and a neat beard are more clearly depicted on the obelisk tomb at Wadi Messueggi, where highly styled curls have been rendered with considerable care, suggesting again parity in the personal styling embraced at these two sites.

The next group of portrait images produced at Ghirza on tomb NA represent two women (Fig. 4). Both are depicted wearing a mantle with the folds of fabric drawn across the body from the shoulders to create an x-shaped drapery, with the cloth from the left shoulder on top. The woman on the right is shown wearing a necklace and large hooped earrings. The woman on the viewer's left wears either a necklace or perhaps has decoration ornamenting the interior edge of her mantle. She does not wear other jewellery. It is clear that the women have carefully styled hair, and the woman on the right appears also to have a veil drawn over the back of her head. These bust images show the women's centrally parted hair falling in neat curls to behind the ears and then drawn back at the nape of the neck in a style which appears to be inspired by women of the imperial court, akin to those worn by Otacilia Severa (e.g. Fittschen, Zanker 1983, 34–35, no. 37) or perhaps, as Brogan suggests, Julia Mammaea (Brogan, Smith 1984, 123).

The next tombs in the series are more roughly rendered. Tomb SE shows the male and female subjects in similar dress to that in NA (Brogan, Smith 1984, fig. 115). The figures again wear their mantles drawn across the body, but the tunics are clearly visible here, and the male is shown, unusually, with the right side of the mantle over the left. Gender distinctions are

Above left: Fig. 3. Male statue from south necropolis, tomb A, Ghirza (drawing by Joseph Wilkins based on photographs held in the Olwen Brogan Archive, Libyan Society Archive).

Above right: Fig. 4. Female portrait images from north necropolis, tomb A, Ghirza (drawing by Joseph Wilkins based on photographs held in the Olwen Brogan Archive, Libyan Society Archive).

articulated through grooming: the woman is represented with long locks, while the male is shown with short curly hair and a beard (Brogan, Smith 1984, fig. 115). The later busts on tombs SC and SD are depicted in particularly abbreviated style, but they also show the subjects wearing tunics, with female gender defined through differences in hairstyling and the addition of a necklace (Brogan, Smith 1984, Figs 108, 111a). The male on tomb SD has an additional serrated 'ruff' around the top of the tunic (Fig. 5), which the sculptor has taken care to differentiate from the necklace worn by his companion, shown much higher up the throat. The mantle worn on these two later tombs is represented only as a narrow band of pleated fabric, which no longer covers the arms. As with earlier tomb NA, it has the x-shaped drape arrangement with the left side of the fabric on top. These pleated bands worn on tombs SC and SD are not radically different from the mantle worn on NA. The bands are simply thinner, indicating that the sculptors were depicting an abbreviated form for an audience familiar with the dress style, or perhaps that the mantles wrapped about the body had become narrower.

It has been suggested that this x-shaped fabric may indicate a funerary shroud (Mattingly 2003, 165). This is possible, but we do not know whether the corpse was dressed in a specific way for burial, and images, such as the full-length statues, show individuals wearing garments that could certainly serve to clothe the living. The emphasis in the tomb depictions in general is upon clothed subjects engaged in lifetime activities, and so it is perhaps more probable that this was the resonance here. This does not mean that the subjects were represented in 'daily dress', but it does suggest that the portrait form at this site showed people wearing clothes that they might wear in life, probably their most prestigious attire.

On two of these monuments the elite subjects are accompanied by other figures in the frieze. The identity of these individuals is uncertain (Brogan, Smith 1984, 184), but they are described briefly here because they may represent junior elites. They appear only on the first tomb (SA) and on the latest tomb examined above (SD). Two of these subjects are shown on tomb SA wearing a long-sleeved tunic, which descends to below mid-calf. Like the elite

Fig. 5. Busts from south necropolis tomb D, with possible junior elite figure between them (drawing by Joseph Wilkins based on photographs held in the Olwen Brogan Archive, Libyan Society Archive).

male on this monument, both figures have a mantle drawn across the body and over the left shoulder, but unlike him they are shown clean-shaven. They carry a basket and a curved stick or sickle (Brogan, Smith 1984, 184). Baskets appear, carried by apparently high-status figures shown sowing crops in agricultural scenes (Zanker 2008, 217–219), and by elite attendants in later ceremonial scenes at the site (pl. 16). One of the SA figures has the short hair associated with masculinity and a necklace, which was generally part of the construction of feminine identity at Ghirza (Fig. 2). He may be a youth exempt from elements of local gender codes, or this may be evidence for a more fluid construction of gender at the settlement than that usually presented in elite images. On the later tomb SD, a full-length figure is shown between the two principal busts (Fig. 5). It wears a short tunic and stands in front of a horse with a long stick in its left hand. The sculptor has punched a series of triangular marks across its shoulders, somewhat like the ruff shown on the elite male on this monument. It was perhaps a decoration to the neckline or may indicate a cloak; if the latter is the case, then it is the first depiction of this attire at the settlement. These figures are dressed similarly to their elite male counterparts. Their possession of a stick-like object or basket appears among junior elite subjects and attendants in the later tombs.

There are indications of change over time, even amongst these early tombs. The first tomb at Ghirza shows male and female subjects differentiated through the drape of their mantle, and perhaps also by female headwear not shown later at the settlement. On later tombs, the mantle is draped in a similar way for both genders, except that it is only ever shown drawn up over the head of a woman. Elite gender identities are constructed primarily through personal grooming and jewellery components. On the earliest monuments at the site, part of this gendered display could include the use of hairstyles worn by Roman emperors or empresses, a practice that is not indicated on the later monuments. The width of the mantle may have also diminished over time.

The male subjects at Ghirza may have been entitled to wear the toga of a Roman citizen following the passing of the *Constitutio Antoniniana* in AD 212, but it is not certain that all inhabitants of the frontier zone were included in this general grant, and the epigraphy from this site does not explicitly assert citizenship (Mattingly 1987, 80, n. 54). The absence of togas may be because the subjects were not entitled to this dress, or because the widening of enfranchisement caused this assertion of Roman citizenship to lose the earlier standing it had possessed in this region (e.g. Brogan, Reynolds 1985). We lack images of dress before the Roman presence, so it is possible that the fashions in draped adornment were a development that drew loosely on ideas about prestigious Roman clothing. Tunic and mantle were, in any case, certainly not styles that would have raised eyebrows in Roman society and are quite different from the stereotypes about un-girded or pelt-wearing Africans of the interior (Brennan 2008, esp. 262–263). Roman styles are, however, most clearly adopted at Ghirza in body technologies of personal adornment, most particularly in hairstyles.

The adoption of hairstyles embraced by the imperial family occurred around the Roman world, creating a phenomenon termed the 'period face', which was at its peak when the dissemination of imperial portrait types was widespread (Zanker 1982, 307–312; Zanker 1992, 348 Fittschen 2010, 235–241). The earliest tombs at Ghirza show that at this point an active engagement with these Roman styles could be desirable. This selective use of externally developed fashions has recent parallels in the way that people in Trinidad used the styles of American soap stars, alongside their own dress preferences, in order to compete in individual displays of personal style (Miller 1994, 245–255). A comparison from an age of mass media may seem irrelevant, but the people of Ghirza were also subject to images from elsewhere becoming part of their daily lives, through the dissemination of imperial portrait types. Their participation in a monetised economy meant that they saw these images on the coinage they used (Brogan, Smith 1984, 135, 151, 242), and at the coastal sites that the pre-desert was connected with. The images sent out from Rome, at the request of the provinces, provided a mechanism through which people were the recipients of up-to-date changing images of the imperial family, which showed hairstyles that could change frequently (e.g. Faustina Minor, see Fittschen 1982). This fostered an environment conducive to a 'fashion system', whereby people updated their images and showed awareness of new styles in order to gain prestige amongst peers (Craik 1994, x-xii, 3–10; Eicher, Roach-Higgins 1992, esp. 23; Entwistle 2000, 43–48). It seems that changing hairstyle fashions were used at Ghirza in the articulation of prized local gender values. In this context, they probably served to make their wearers look sophisticated and modern, rather than asserting an emphatically 'Roman identity'.

This selective use of personal styling developed in Rome was part of a wider contemporary negotiation of Roman power and culture. Ghirza's settlement prospered later, but these early tombs relate to the period when Roman economic incentives re-shaped the landscape by fostering an environment where sedentary agricultural practices were desirable, even on marginal land. Septimius Severus' addition of olive oil to Rome's *annona* saw third-century demands on production increase steeply in Tripolitania (Mattingly 1995, 144–159; Barker *et al.* 1996a, 278–290; Mattingly 1996, 321–328). Roman military presence was at unprecedented levels (Le Bohec 1989; Mattingly 1995, 80–89) and *ostraca* from the fort of Bu Ngem attest the army's close economic and diplomatic associations with local people (Marichal 1979, 448–450; Marichal 1992, esp. 99–114). The people who built these monuments were linked into a social and economic system that brought them into contact with Roman culture and consumables. Ghirza's tombs drew on Roman architectural forms and iconographies (Brogan, Smith 1984; Zanker 2008). In the first half of the third century, some people also absorbed changing Roman grooming fashions to assert gendered social prestige.

Ghirza's later tombs

In the fourth century, new forms of elite dress replaced the earlier draped styles. These innovative high-status personal styles showed subjects wearing cloaks and new headwear, and appeared at Ghirza as part of a package of changes in self-representation. The differentiation of gender on the monuments ceases to be emphasised, as female subjects do not appear on the later tombs, although they were referred to in the accompanying inscriptions (Brogan, Smith 1984, 135, 151). The practice of using statues and busts in relief was replaced by images showing elite individuals as active participants in scenes. This keys into a trend, seen around the empire, in the declining commission of new busts or statues (e.g. Smith 1985, esp. 218; Bauer, Witschel 2007a, 11; Smith 2007, 204–205; Witschel 2007). This shift in prestigious representation saw a greater emphasis upon the trappings of power and the retinue of people that surrounded the elite subject, a preference attested in other late Roman contexts from the third century (e.g. Elsner 1995, 159–189; Borg 2007). The new dress and image form are the products of the same changing cultural mores in self-representation; both served to further emphasise distinctions in social hierarchy. The novel, elite dress appears in its fully developed form, and there is little evidence for change over time in its appearance. For this reason, a detailed description of every occurrence of these dress styles is not given; rather, the objective here is to examine the contemporary significance of this important new styling choice.

The new dress forms appear on the next monuments in the series to be constructed: tombs NB and NC. These monuments depict consciously similar representations of a local ruler receiving gifts, consistently placed in proximity to a scene showing execution or punishment (Mattingly 2003, 163). Although the two reliefs share the same composition, that from NC is better preserved and provides the clearest information (pl. 16). This relief shows the local leader raised up on a dais and seated on an object that resembles a *sella curulis* (Brogan, Smith 1984, 153). He holds a goblet and volumen and is offered a wine jug and quiver by a man wearing a short tunic with a decorated belt. Behind the central figure, other subjects are shown standing on plinths and holding objects such as baskets and sticks or sceptres; attributes held by junior elites on the earlier tombs. The importance of these subjects is communicated through a descending hierarchy in scale as they stand further from the seated male at the centre, and also through differences in their dress. The seated male ruler and the man stood directly behind him wear the new styling choices that constituted the most prestigious dress on the later monuments.

The seated leader is shown with curly hair and beard. The focus of the sculptor's attention was upon indicating the intricate fabric of his clothes, perhaps suggesting richly woven fabric. The same figure on earlier tomb NB wears similar attire, although the carving lacks equivalent detail (Brogan, Smith 1984, fig. 63a). The subject wears what is probably a cloak, shown hanging straight from the shoulders, rather than being wrapped about the body as on earlier tombs. This attire falls further down the body than the mantles had, and the difference in body language, with arms shown outstretched rather than encased in fabric, is part of this change in dress. The likelihood that it is a cloak shown here finds further support in the increasing presence of this garment on the later tombs (e.g. Brogan, Smith 1984, figs 63a, 123b, 126a). It appeared in the early fourth century (perhaps first on SD, Fig. 5) and became a prominent feature in elite dress on later monuments. It seems that the way in which male prestige was being physically expressed had changed from a focus upon relatively plain cloth draped about the body, to an ornately woven cloak. While it is possible that this change in dress was simply a local innovation, separate from the wider Roman world, it is not safe to assume this.

A move towards increasingly elaborate dress styles was not unique to Ghirza: it was attested around the Roman world, both in traditional civic dress and in the tunics and cloaks that had become a prestigious way of asserting elite male identity (Goette 1990; Stone 1994; Harlow 2004). In the Roman world, the various types of cloak were customarily considered appropriate for 'the camp, the hunt and the journey' (Smith 1999, 177; see also Wild 1968, 223–226; Croom 2000, 52–56). However, from the early fourth century one particular form became used prominently: the *chlamys*. This was a long cloak with curved border, traditionally worn by high-ranking army officials and emperors; it became employed at this time by a wider range of prestigious individuals. Late Roman ideals of government considered administrative service as *militia*, so that figures such as provincial governors might wear it (Delbrueck 1929, 36–40; Ševčenko 1968; Smith 1999, 176–8; Smith 2002, 142–150). The military associations of this dress were paramount (e.g. *CT* XIV,10,1), with the presence of a scroll serving to articulate either the papers of office, the zealous pursuit of governmental duties, or learning

(Smith 1999, 177–178; Smith 2002, 142–144; Harlow 2004). Its wear was not restricted to officials (e.g. Smith 1999, 177), and although it was particularly useful in conveying Roman military authority, it was worn by others as a means of asserting personal status. Precise rank differentiation may have been expressed through the decorative detailing of the *chlamys*: with patches (*segmenta*), or with a rarer all-over pattern (Delbrueck 1929, 38–40, e.g. figs 62, 63, 65; Smith 1999, 142–143; Harlow 2004, 59–60).

The subject at Ghirza wears a patterned cloak, although other important details of his dress are not apparent. The fact that it was worn by a man shown holding a scroll and seated on a *sella curulis* might suggest that this personal style had not developed in complete independence from the decorated military cloaks embraced by a range of elite people around the Empire. Roman military styling at this time had generally become an articulate means of asserting social status around the Empire (Harlow 2004, 60–61, 66–68). In Tripolitania, it came at a period when the size of the Roman garrison had declined substantially (Mattingly 1995, 186–194; Mattingly 1996, 338). While local elites did not replace the army entirely (Rushworth 1992), sites like Ghirza were increasingly responsible for their own protection. There is no evidence to suggest that residents of Ghirza were recruited as *militia*, but it has been proposed that treaty relations with Rome were a contributing factor in Ghirza's success when the Tripolitanian economy was in a general decline (Mattingly 1996, 338–342). During the Byzantine re-conquest of the region, there existed the memory of an ancient custom where tribal units received 'tokens of office' from the Roman Emperor, comprising a range of rich clothes, including a cloak (Procopius *Vandal Wars* III, xxv, 1–10). It is conceivable that the cloak shown in the images relates to such a gift, but it is more probable that this was a styling choice that was actively developed by local elites, drawing upon wider Roman styles, rather than attire bestowed by Rome.

Roman military forms became drawn upon in a range of media as a source of prestige: the fortified *gsur*, attested at Ghirza in the fourth century, were architectural forms which seem to evoke Roman military architecture (Mattingly 1995, 147; Mattingly 1996, 328–329). Roman models were used in inscriptions that refer to local people with Roman military titles, such as 'tribune' and describe their residences with terms like *centenarium* (Buck *et al.* 1983; Brogan, Smith 1984, 79–80; Mattingly 1995, 194–197; Mattingly 1996, 326). In some cases these individuals may have been *gentiles* asserting treaty relations with the Roman frontier, but in others it is unlikely that the individuals played a role in wider strategic defence (Mattingly 1995, 102–103, 194–197). References to the Roman military may have been employed loosely as these elements were indigenised. Fashionable hairstyles were no longer useful, but shifting local power politics had created a cultural context in which it was advantageous for local elites to use Roman military personal styling when asserting their own authority (cf. Halsall 2000).

In the sculptural programme of the later tombs, the emphasis upon scenes of combat and armed men is much more pronounced. One image shows the subject wearing what appears to be armour (Fig. 6), but the dress evoking martial valour most frequently shown, is that worn by the subject standing behind the ruler in the ceremonial scenes (e.g. pl. 16). Damage to the sculpture prevents certainty about the precise number of times that this innovative dress occurs, but it is shown on at least seven occasions on fourth century tombs NB, NC, SF, SG. It does not occur on the final three monuments at the site, but they have little figurative detail so we cannot discount the possibility that this dress style continued. Colour image 16 shows this dress to comprise a long-sleeved tunic that falls to below the knee. An additional layer of fabric is shown above this, which on the counterpart figure on NB is clearly a long cloak, suggesting that this may have been the intention here, with the cloak covering arms that are indicated in outline (Brogan, Smith 1984, fig. 63a). The subjects in both versions of the scene wear distinctive headwear, which is usually represented as cone-shaped, but sometimes, as in pl. 16, it appears more lightly domed, possibly reflecting different attire, but more probably depending primarily upon how the artist chose to represent the same element of dress. The combination of this new and distinctive headwear, long tunic, sometimes worn with a cloak, appears in narrative contexts in prestigious positions next to the leader, and in proximity to combat, execution or armed horsemen. Subjects wearing these clothes are also depicted as separate from activities (e.g. pl. 17), suggesting that the dress itself conveyed an identifiable social identity. In such contexts, the subjects are usually shown carrying spears and sometimes a shield, indicating that their dress was a further means of evoking a military role for this subject.

The long girt tunic traditionally denoted higher status at the settlement. It is sometimes combined with a plain cloak, occasionally adorned with tassels, styling elements that had parallels in the dress of the Roman army (e.g. Brogan, Smith 1984, figs 123; Bishop, Coulston 2006, 184, 224). The inclusion of the hat or helmet was new and requires further examination. It may have been an entirely local development, which drew on dress forms that had not been depicted before at the site, but as military identity tended to engage with Roman models at Ghirza, it is worth considering whether this striking dress innovation was similarly connected. Arming caps worn under Roman helmets could be this sort of shape (James 2004, 101, no. 378, fig. 51), but this concealed component of their dress seems an unlikely model for local people to associate with military style. There are parallels with the conical helmets worn by those usually

Fig. 6. Figures on horseback wearing armour from north necropolis, tomb B, Ghirza (Istanbul Archaeology Museum).

identified as Syrian archers on Trajan's column, with long robes and cloaks (Coulston 1985, 279–280). If Syrian archers did wear such helmets, then the long-standing presence of the *I Cohors Syrorum Sagittariorum* in the region may be significant (Le Bohec 1981, 131; Mattingly 1985, 70–74; Le Bohec 1989, 449, 454–455, 488; Mattingly 1995, 85–88, 191; Le Bohec 2007, 242, 453–456, 460, 463). Their distinctive dress elements could have been referenced in local formulations of what constituted a prestigious military appearance. The gift of bow and quiver in homage scenes might support the idea of an association. However, the column reliefs are a problematic source for eastern archers' dress and first century reliefs show them dressed like other auxiliaries (James 1986, 129; Espérandieu 1922, nos. 6136–6137, 6125; Coulston 1985, 278–280; Coulston 1989; Sumner 2009, 40). A relief of an archer from the *Cohors Hamiorum* may show a conical helmet, but this has also been interpreted as a crest or a pointed cap (Webster 1969, 153; Robinson 1976, 29; Coulston 1985, 279; Coulston, Phillips 1988, 83). The evidence for the dress of Syrian archer units is too uncertain for a link with Ghirza's elite dress to be made, and even if these units were sometimes distinguished by conical helmets, it is unclear how far such traditions would have continued when the unit had been situated in the region for a long duration and had perhaps recruited locally (Le Bohec 2007, esp. 460–463).

Although the headwear worn by these figures does not find strong parallels in the most common Roman helmets worn in the third or fourth centuries (Southern, Dixon 1996, 91–6; Bishop, Coulston 2006, 173–178, 210–216), the shape of the headwear seen in the Ghirza images is comparable to *Spangenhelme*, which were worn by Roman cavalry on the arch of Galerius and attested in two finds from Egypt of possibly Tetrarchic date (Bishop, Coulston 2006, 215). However, these helmets also have cheek pieces and, in one case, a nasal guard suggesting that if technical borrowing had taken place at Ghirza, as occurred with the equipment of the Roman army (e.g. James 1986), it was of a very selective nature. Such a loose interaction seems rather consistent with what we see at Ghirza. Rome was one potential source of prestige that the people of this region interacted with, drawing upon elements of Roman personal styling in a way that seemed apt and resonant in this local context. The aim was not emulation and so Roman models might be absorbed directly or used more loosely in the creation of locally relevant expressions of power and prestige.

Using Rome: from fashion to military styling

The images of Ghirza are not detailed, polished pieces of work, but they nevertheless reveal changing preferences in elite personal styling, which were expressive to local audiences. These altering choices were the product of individuals actively engaging with the models of prestige around them when constructing their own physical expression of social values. The elite of Ghirza negotiated prestigious appearances for themselves, both through reference to personal styling known around the Roman world, and by using dress which was more specific to their locality. When elements of Roman dress were used, this was not passive emulation; rather these styles were employed selectively because they could be meaningful resources in expressing status to local people.

The altering style preferences were the product of Ghirza's elite striving to maintain high-status positions in changing local contexts. We see dress choices move from draped fashions and artful hairstyles to cloaks, and perhaps helmets. This reflects changing local needs as well as broader shifts in the Roman styling preferences, which had an enduring, but altering, significance for the people of this region. The earliest tombs' interaction with Rome is shown most clearly in the engagement, by some, with a fashion system of fast-changing personal grooming styles. This choice in styling consumption came at a time when Rome had a marked economic impact upon the region. It was attested alongside a local preference for draped dress adorning the body, which does not key into Roman styles as assertively as the fashionable hairstyles. Both components were oriented towards status expression in this locality. There was no polarisation between local or Roman dress: rather, Roman styles appear indigenised, employed to assert a prestigious elite identity. The later tombs show new styling preferences in response to changing contemporary needs. At this time, Roman dress served to evoke personal power and military authority. The difference was not simply that Roman styles had changed, but that local cultural contexts had altered. The agents for change were the local people, who used Rome in accordance with their needs, and in doing so they redefined elements of Roman culture to make it relevant to their contemporary context.

Lucy.Audley-Miller@ulb.ac.be

Bibliography

Barker *et al.* 1996a: G. Barker, D. Gilbertson, with C. O. Hunt, D. Mattingly, 'Romano-Libyan Agriculture: Integrated Models', in B. Jones (ed.), *Farming the Desert: The UNESCO Libyan Valleys Archaeological Survey* (Volume I: Synthesis), London, 265–291

Barker *et al.* 1996b: G. Barker, D. Gilbertson, B. Jones, D. Mattingly, *Farming the Desert: The UNESCO Libyan Valleys Archaeological Survey* (Volume II: Gazeteer), London

Bauer, Witschel 2007: F. A. Bauer, C. Witschel (eds), *Statuen in der Spätantike*, Wiesbaden

Bauer, Witschel 2007a: F. A. Bauer, C. Witschel, 'Statuen in der Spätantike', in Bauer, Witschel, 1–24

Bauer 1935: G. Bauer, 'Le due Necropoli di Ghirza', *Africa Italiana* 6, 61–78

Bishop, Coulston 2006: M. C. Bishop, J. N. C. Coulston, *Roman Military Equipment: from the Punic Wars to the Fall of Rome* (Second Edition), Oxford

Borg 2007: B. Borg, 'Bilder für die Ewigkeit oder glanzvoller Auftritt? Zum Repräsentationsverhalten der stadtrömischen Eliten im dritten Jahrhundert n. Chr.', in Bauer, Witschel, 43–77

Brennan 2008: T. C. Brennan, 'Tertullian's *De Pallio* and Roman Dress in North Africa', in J. Edmondson, A. Keith (eds), *Roman Dress and the Fabrics of Roman Culture*, Toronto, 257–270

Brogan 1971: O. Brogan, 'First and Second Century Settlement in the Tripolitanian Pre-Desert', in F. F. Gadallah (ed.), *Libya in History: Historical Conference*, Benghazi, 121–130

Brogan, Reynolds 1985: O. Brogan, J. Reynolds, 'An Inscription from the Wadi Antar', in D. J. Buck, D. J. Mattingly (eds), *Town and Country in Roman Tripolitania. Papers in Honour of Olwen Hackett*, Oxford, 43–46

Brogan, Smith 1984: O. Brogan, D. J. Smith, *Ghirza: A Libyan Settlement in the Roman Period*, Tripoli

Buck *et al.* 1983: D. J. Buck, J. R. Burns, D. J. Mattingly, 'Archaeological Sites of the Bir Scedua Basin: Settlements and Cemeteries', *Libyan Studies* 14, 43–54

Coulston 1985: J. C. N. Coulston, 'Roman Archery Equipment', in M. C. Bishop (ed.), *The Production and Distribution of Roman Military Equipment. Proceedings of the Second Roman Military Equipment Research Seminar* (BAR International Series 275), Oxford, 220–367

Coulston 1989: J. C. N. Coulston, 'The value of Trajan's Column as a source for military equipment', in C. Van Driel-Murray (ed.), *Roman Military Equipment: the Sources of Evidence. Proceedings of the Fifth Roman Military Equipment Conference*, Oxford, 31–44

Coulston, Phillips, 1988: J. C. N. Coulston, E. Phillips, *Corpus Signorum Imperii Romani, Great Britain: Hadrian's Wall West of the River North Tyne, and Carlisle* I, 6, London

Craik 1994: J. Craik, *The Face of Fashion: Cultural Studies in Fashion*, London and New York

Croom 2000: A. T. Croom, *Roman Clothing and Fashion*, Stroud

Delbrueck 1929: R. Delbrueck, *Die Consulardiptychen und verwandte Denkmäler. Studien zur spätantiken Kunstgeschichte*, Leipzig, Berlin

Di Vita 1964: A. Di Vita, 'Il "limes" Romano di Tripolitania nella sua concretezza archeologica e nella sua realtà storica', *Libya Antiqua* 1, 65–98

Eicher, Roach-Higgins 1992: J. B. Eicher, M. E. Roach-Higgins, 'Definition and Classification of Dress: Implications for Analysis of Gender Roles', in R. Barnes, J. B. Eicher (eds), *Dress and Gender: Making and Meaning in Cultural Contexts*, Oxford, 8–28

Elsner 1995: J. Elsner, *Art and the Roman Viewer: the Transformation of Art from the Pagan World to Christianity*, Cambridge

Entwistle 2000: J. Entwistle, *The Fashioned Body: Fashion, Dress and Modern Social Theory*, Cambridge

Espérandieu 1922: E. Espérandieu, *Recueil général des Bas-Reliefs, Statues et Bustes de la Gaule Romaine: Gaul Germanique* 2, 8 Paris

Fittschen 1982: K. Fittschen, *Die Bildnistypen der Faustina minor und die Fecunditas Augustae*, Göttingen

Fittschen 2010: K. Fittschen, 'The portraits of Roman Emperors and their families: controversial positions and unsolved problems', in B. Ewald, C. F. Noreña (eds), *The Emperor and Rome: Space, Representation, Ritual*, Cambridge, 221–246

Fittschen, Zanker 1983: K. Fittschen, P. Zanker, *Katalog der römischen Porträts in den Capitolinischen Museen und den anderen kommunalen Sammlungen der Stadt Rom*, Vol. 5, Mainz

Fittschen, Zanker 1985: K. Fittschen, P. Zanker, *Katalog der römischen Porträts in den Capitolinischen Museen und den anderen kommunalen Sammlungen der Stadt Rom*, Vol. 3, Mainz

Fontana 1997: S. Fontana, 'Il predeserto tripolitano: mausolei e rappresentazione del potere', *Libya Antiqua* 3, 149–163

Goette 1990: H. R. Goette, *Studien zu römischen Togadarstellungen*, Mainz am Rhein

Halsall 2000: G. Halsall, 'Archaeology and the Late Roman Frontier in Northern Gaul: The so-called 'Föderatengräber' reconsidered', in W. Pohl, H. Reimitz (eds), *Grenze und Differenz im früheren Mittelalter*, Vienna, 167–180

Harlow 2004: M. Harlow, 'Clothes maketh the man: power dressing and elite masculinity in the later Roman world', in L. Brubaker, J. M. H. Smith (eds), *Gender in the Early Medieval World: East and West*, Cambridge, 44–70

James 1986: S. James, 'Evidence from Dura Europos for the Origins of Late Roman Helmets', *Syria* 63, 1, 107–34

James 2004: S. James, *Excavations at Dura-Europos, Final Report VII, the Arms and Armour, and other Military Equipment*, London

Johns 2003: C. Johns, 'Art, Romanisation, and Competence', in S. Scott, J. Webster (eds), *Roman Imperialism and Provincial Art*, Cambridge, 9–24

Le Bohec 1981: Y. Le Bohec, 'Les marques sur briques et les surnoms de la IIIème Légion Auguste', *Epigraphica* 43, 127–60

Le Bohec 1989: Y. Le Bohec, *La Troisième Légion Auguste*, Paris

Le Bohec 2007: Y. Le Bohec, *L'Armée Romaine en Afrique et en Gaule*, Stuttgart

Lynch 1999: A. Lynch, *Dress, Gender and Cultural Change: Asian and American Rites of Passage*, Oxford

Marichal 1979: R. Marichal, 'Les Ostraca de Bu Njem', *Comptes-rendus de l'Académie des Inscriptions et Belles-lettres*, 436–452

Marichal 1992: R. Marichal, *Les Ostraca de Bu Njem*, Tripoli

Mattingly 1985: D. J. Mattingly, 'IRT 895 and 896: Two Inscriptions from Gheriat el-Garbia', *Libyan Studies*, 16, 67–75

Mattingly 1987: D. J. Mattingly, 'Libyans and the 'Limes': Culture and Society in Roman Tripolitania', *Antiquités africaines* 23, 71–94

Mattingly 1995: D. J. Mattingly, *Tripolitania*, London

Mattingly 1996: D. J. Mattingly, 'People as Agency', in G. Barker, *et al.* (eds), *Farming the Desert: The UNESCO Libyan Valleys Archaeological Survey*, Tripoli, 319–342

Mattingly 1999: D. J. Mattingly, 'The art of the unexpected: Ghirza in the Libyan pre-desert', in S. Lancel (ed.), *Numismatique, langues, écriture et arts du livre, spécificité des arts figures: Actes du VIIe colloque international sur l'histoire et l'archéologie de l'Afrique du nord*, Paris, 383–405

Mattingly 2003: D. J. Mattingly, 'Family Values: Art and Power at Ghirza in the Libyan Pre-Desert', in S. Scott, J. Webster (eds), *Roman Imperialism and Provincial Art*, Cambridge, 153–71

Mattingly 2011: D. J. Mattingly, *Imperialism, Power and Identity: Experiencing the Roman Empire*, Princeton and Oxford

Merighi 1948: A. Merighi, *La Tripolitania Antica*, Verbania

Miller 1994: D. Miller, *Modernity: an Ethnographic Approach*, Oxford

Moore 2007: J. P. Moore, 'The "Mausoleum Culture" of Africa Proconsularis', in D. L. Stone, L. M. Stirling (eds), *Mortuary Landscapes of North Africa*, Toronto, 75–109

Pratt, Rafaeli 1997: M. G. Pratt, A. Rafaeli, 'Organisational Dress as Symbol of Multilayered Social Identities', *Academy of Management Journal* 40, 4, 862–898

Robinson 1976: H. R. Robinson, *What the Soldiers Wore on Hadrian's Wall*, Newcastle upon Tyne

Romanelli 1922: P. Romanelli, 'Tomba Romana con Affrechi del IV secolo dopo cristo nella Regione di Gargáresh (Tripoli)', *Ministero delle Colonie Notizario Archeologico* 3, 21–34

Rushworth 1992: A. Rushworth, 'Soldiers and Tribesmen: the Roman Army and Tribal Society in Late Imperial Africa', University of Newcastle-upon-Tyne, unpublished PhD

Ševčenko 1968: I. Ševčenko, 'A late Epigram and the so-called Elder Magistrate from Aphrodisias', in A. Grabar (ed.), *Synthronon, art et archéologie de la fin de l'Antiquité et du Moyen âge, recueil d'études*, Paris, 29–41

Sjöström 1993: I. Sjöström, *Tripolitania in Transition: Late Roman to Islamic Settlement with a Catalogue of Sites*, Avebury

Smith 1985: R. R. R. Smith, 'Review: Roman Portraits: Honours, Empresses and Late Emperors', *Journal of Roman Studies* 75, 209–221

Smith 1998: R. R. R. Smith, 'Cultural Choice and Political Identity in Honorific Portrait Statues in the Greek East in the Second Century AD', *Journal of Roman Studies* 88, 56–93

Smith 1999: R. R. R. Smith, 'Late Antique Portraits in a Public Context: Honorific Statuary at Aphrodisias in Caria, AD 300–600', *Journal of Roman Studies* 89, 155–189

Smith 2002: R. R. R. Smith, 'The Statue Monument of Oecumenius: A New Portrait of a Late Antique Governor', *Journal of Roman Studies* 92, 134–156

Smith 2007: R. R. R. Smith, 'Statue Life in the Hadrianic Baths at Aphrodisias, AD 100–600', in Bauer, Witschel, 203–237

Southern, Dixon 1996: P. Southern and K. R. Dixon, *The Late Roman Army*, London

Stone 1994: S. Stone, 'The Toga: from National to Ceremonial Costume', in L. Sebesta and L. Bonfante (eds), *The World of Roman Costume*, Madison, 13–45

Sumner 2009: G. Sumner, *Roman Military Dress*, Stroud

Tarlo 1996: E. Tarlo, *Clothing Matters: Dress and Identity in India*, London

Webster 1969: G. Webster, *The Roman Imperial Army of the First and Second Centuries AD*, Chatham

Wild 1968: J. P. Wild, 'Clothing in the north-west provinces of the Roman Empire', *Bonner Jahrbücher des rheinischen Landesmuseums in Bonn* 168, 166–240

Witschel 2007: C. Witschel, 'Statuen auf spätantiken Platzanlagen in Italien und Africa', in Bauer, Witschel, 113–170

Zanker 1982: P. Zanker, 'Herrscherbild und Zeitgesicht', *Römisches Porträt. Wege zur Erforschung eines gesellschaftlichen Phänomens: Wissenschaftliche Konferenz 12–15 Mai 1981*, Berlin, 307–312

Zanker 1992: P. Zanker, 'Bürgerliche Selbstdarstellung am Grab im römischen Kaiserreich', in H.-J. Schalles, P. Zanker, and H. von Hesberg (eds), *Die römische Stadt im 2. Jh. n. Chr. Der Funktionswandel des öffentlichen Raumes. Kolloquium in Xanten vom 2 bis 4 Mai 1990*, Köln, Bonn, 339–358

Zanker 2008: P. Zanker, 'Selbstdarstellung am Rand der libyschen Wüste. Die Reliefs an den Häuptlings-Mausoleen in der Nordnekropole von Ghirza', in F. Pirson (ed.), *Austausch und Inspiration: Kulturkontak als Impuls architektonischer Innovation: Kolloquium vom 28.-30. 4. 2006 in Berlin anlässlich des 65. Geburtstages von Adolf Hoffman*, Mainz, 214–227

DRESSING THE DEAD IN THE CITY OF ROME: BURIAL CUSTOMS ACCORDING TO TEXTILES

SYLVIA MITSCHKE AND ANNETTE PAETZ GEN. SCHIECK

Our research project on Roman textiles, *Dress and Identities – New Perspectives on Textiles in the Roman Empire (DressID)*, had an apparent lack of Roman textiles found in Rome itself, so we decided to face the challenge of filling the *lacuna*.[1] Amongst other fields of research we focused on textiles in Roman catacombs, because they have never been investigated from a textile point of view, even though the burials contain numerous fragments and even complete items of clothing and soft furnishings. We were fortunate to be able to rely on Dr Alexandra Busch of the German Archaeological Institute (DAI), Rome. She was so kind to put us in touch with Dr Raffaella Giuliani, Ispettore delle Catacombe di Roma, Pontificia Commissione di Archeologia Sacra, who took care of our special interests. In November 2008 and 2009 Dr Giuliani made it possible for us to visit and investigate a selection of textile phenomena in Roman catacombs. We are deeply indebted to her for permission to analyse a burial from the Sant´Agnese catacomb at the Via Nomentana in the northeast of the city, to investigate the Santi Marcellino e Pietro catacomb in the Via Cassilina in the southeast of Rome, and to spend a whole day with the deceased buried in a sarcophagus at San Sebastiano in the Via Appia in the south (Fig. 1). We are also more than grateful for permission to take samples of the textiles for investigation of the fibres and for radiocarbon dating. Both types of analyses were performed by the Curt-Engelhorn Centre for Archaeometry at the Reiss-Engelhorn Museums in Mannheim, Germany.[2] Traces of resins were examined by Mathieu Boudin of the Royal Institute of Cultural Heritage (KIK/IRPA) at Brussels, Belgium.

In addition to the catacomb research, we were introduced to another amazing find by Prof. Dr Claudio Parisi Presicce, Director of the Capitoline Museums and the Antiquarium at Rome, and Prof. Dr Friedrich-Wilhelm von Hase. The find consists of a marble cinerary urn, which was found in the Via Ostiense in the south of the city (Fig. 1). It originally enclosed a large, and still complete, piece of textile, and the ashes of a cremated human. Both objects are kept in the Museo della Civiltà Romana (Sommella 1992, 145–150), and we are thankful to Dr Carla Martini for letting us investigate the piece of textile in the storage rooms.

Investigating textiles deriving from four different sites in the city of Rome enabled us to analyse three types of burial at the same time: cremation and burial in a cinerary urn, inhumation of human bodies wrapped in shrouds and bedded in the *loculi* of subterranean catacombs, and a sarcophagus-burial of a person dressed and also wrapped in shrouds, placed in a chamber beneath an early Christian church. These burial complexes in Rome (or, one might better say, beneath it) date to the period from the first to the third century AD.

Fig. 1. Rome and the sites of the investigation (drawing by A. P. g. Schieck).

Cremation was common practice in Rome before the second century AD (Koch, Sichtermann 1982, 27–30), and was mentioned by ancient authors like Vergil, Ovid, Martial, Propertius, and Lucan. Starting in the second century AD, however, inhumation became increasingly popular, but it was not until the mid-third century AD that it became general practice. The reasons for these changes cannot be definitely determined. Foreign influences are discussed as a factor, as well as the fact that the pre-existing practice of burying bodies in sarcophagi never actually stopped, but was continued by wealthy families.

As to the title 'Dressing the Dead', we understand the term 'dressing' in a broad sense, to include clothing as well as wrappings and shrouds employed to enclose and cover the dead body. The four complexes investigated will be introduced one by one, along with observed changes in burial practice. Our research aimed at tracing the standards of burial furnishing, not only in terms of textiles, but of burial ritual in general.

The cinerary urn found in the Via Ostiense

In 1928, a most remarkable cinerary urn was found in the course of construction work along the Via Ostiense, near Ponte Fratta (Fig. 2a) (Soler Villabella 1937; Tittoni 1992, 195 no. 441, 444). It was still closed by a lid, which is lost today. The airtight receptacle was opened on the spot and released an intense smell of camphor, which quickly evaporated under the influence of air. Inside, a remarkably well preserved textile was found (Fig. 2b), enclosing the ashes of a cremated person. No information is available on the exact find circumstances, site and original context. Due to the uniqueness of the urn and its contents, it has to be assumed that it once stood in an *arcosolium* of a *columbarium*, rather than being buried directly in the soil. The Via Ostiense region is famous for the *columbaria* of wealthy Roman families, such as those found near the basilica of the Apostle Paul. These subterranean burial buildings were constructed in late Republican times and remained in use until the late Empire (Della Portella 1999, 82–91 (Necropolis Ostiense, compare 115, 116); Koch, Sichtermann 1982, 44–45). While some of these chambers contain corpses buried in sarcophagi, others consist of *arcosolia* taking several urns.

The urn is made from one piece of marble, of Greek origin, according to Maddalena Cima (Tittoni 1992, 195). Its shape is rather heavy, consisting of a deep, hemispherical cup on a tiny, curved, circular foot. The shoulder bends sharply inwards at a near right angle, being separated from the cup by an incised line around the circumference. The sloping undecorated shoulder is surmounted by an everted lid-seat. Two handles of semicircular shape were carved out of the stone; one of them is missing today.

No inscription is provided and the cup is covered with S-shaped gadroons ('Riefeln'), carved into the ground. The upper edges are located at a slight distance from the line round the vessel at the shoulder, ending in a rounded form like *cannelures*. The gadroons are executed with great regularity and consistent depth, running all around the cup, and leaving sharply defined ridges between one another.

Since information on the find context is missing, and radiocarbon dating only works with organic material, stylistic analyses of the shape of the vessel and especially its decoration remain the only approaches to dating the urn. Urns made of marble with relief-decoration are typical for the city of Rome and have been produced in large quantities. Products of similar shape

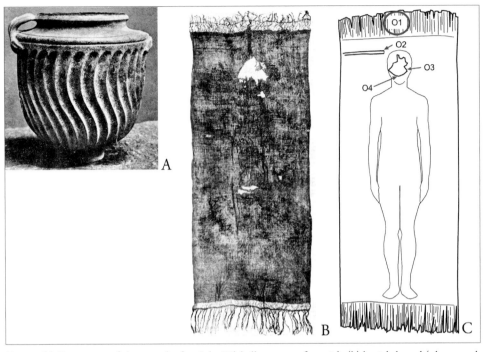

Fig. 2. (a) Cinerary urn (photograph after Soler Vilabella 1937, 75, fig. 1, 83); (b) burial shroud (photograph after Soler Villabella 1937, *ibid.*); (c) scheme of the shroud with human contour and sampling spots (drawing by A. P. g. Schieck, S. Mitschke).

and style are also attested in Ostia (Koch, Sichtermann 1982, 43, 45–54), but the chronology of marble urns has been established only by considering objects bearing inscriptions. Many of the urns are square-shaped, like simple boxes; others are simple tubes with a bottom. The Via Ostiense urn has been dated to the middle of the first century AD by Ramón N. Soler Vilabella, without listing the arguments. Since no comparable object can be named, however, even by Friederike Sinn, who collected 714 urns, a definite date can hardly be suggested (Soler Villabella 1937, 76; Sinn 1987). Two urns, however, dating to the Augustan period or slightly later (Sinn 1987, 94 no. 14, pl. 7, 96 no. 20, pl. 8), exhibit very general features which hint at the middle of the first century AD: a heavy, hemispherical cup, a tiny stand, two tiny handles and a vertical lid. These two urns, however, are completely covered with ivy leaves and berries or branches of laurel. Another approach would be to compare the urn with other kinds of vessel. The only type that combines a comparable shape and decoration is a group of bronze vessels found in northern Germany and Scandinavia, as goods imported from Rome into Free Germania: they are the so-called 'Hemmoor buckets' (Eggers 1951, nos 44–47), dating to the early second century AD.

Gadroon decoration was very popular and was mainly applied to sarcophagi in the late second and third centuries AD. Sarcophagi with this decoration even form an individual type, named after the decoration (Koch, Sichtermann 1982, 73–76 esp. 74 fig. 2, 241–245). The S-curved ornamentation is combined with architectural elements that subdivide the decorative scheme on the front face of the sarcophagus, but gadroons are seldom found on urns, even though Guntram Koch and Hellmut Sichtermann mention vessels dating back to the first and early second century AD (Koch, Sichtermann 1982, 242). A cinerary urn of a different shape, but decorated with gadroons, was found incorporated into the walls of the hallway leading down to the Sant'Agnese church building (Fasola 1974, 175–205, esp. 203). It is also made of Greek Pentelic marble and measures 40 cm in diameter, 20 cm in height. It bears an inscription, dated to the second or third century AD by Umberto M. Fasola.[3]

While stylistic classification of the vessel tends to be rather difficult, its organic content provides a better opportunity to employ scientific methods of analysis in order to date the ensemble. After opening the lid, a large and complete piece of linen textile came to light. A sample (O1, MAMS 11205), was taken from the fringes for radiocarbon dating (Fig. 2c), revealing a possibility range of 95.4 per cent (at 2 sigma) for AD 55 to AD 210, and of 68.2 per cent (at 1 sigma) for AD 79 to AD 126. When all the information on the urn is combined, the suggestion by Maddalena Cima of a possible date in the middle of the first century AD bears repetition, and may even be confirmed (Tittoni 1992, 195) – if we consider the ensemble to be genuine, and the piece of textile not to have been stored for too long before it was used for this burial.

The fabric is of rectangular shape, measuring 72.5 cm by 183 cm, and still has its four original edges (Figs 2b, 2c), the longer ones (the selvedges) being the returning weft threads. The threads projecting from the narrower transverse edges were arranged into fringes for decorative purposes as well as to prevent the fraying of the ground-weave. The fringes on one end measure 12.5 cm, and those on the other, 22 cm.

The fabric is woven in tabby; the threads of the ground-weave have a count of about 14 to 17 threads per centimetre in both warp and weft direction. Using these figures, the textile can be described as of medium quality. Accompanying the fringed edges, self-bands made of thicker weft threads were woven to form a regular system of bands (compare Soler Villabella 1937, 78, fig. 3; Volbach 1942, pl. III T4, T6; pl. V T7, T11; pl. VI T8, T10, medieval according to Volbach). Additionally, each end of the sheet is flanked by one section of interlace pattern, one measuring 4 cm and the other 5.5 cm (compare Huber 2007, 35 fig. 31). Two pairs of purple-coloured wool weft threads, about 25 cm in length and about 1.5 cm apart, were woven into the ground, close to just one of the corners (Fig. 3a).

The warp threads have a diameter of about 0.2 mm to 0.3 mm, and are spun in S-direction, whilst the coloured weft threads are Z-spun and range between 0.8 mm to 1 mm in width. The spinning is quite weak in general. According to Lise Bender Jørgensen's theory of spinning

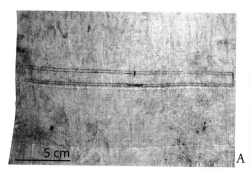

Fig. 3. (a) Detail of the woollen purple weft-threads; (b) fibrous surface with resinous stains (photos by S. Mitschke).

traditions (Bender Jørgensen 1992), the S-spun yarns in the ground-weave could indicate a provenance in the eastern Mediterranean.

Analysis of samples O 3 + 4 (Fig. 2c) confirmed the optical impression that there are no differences in material and quality of the threads employed in the ground-warp and weft. They are both made of fine, half-bleached flax (*Linum usitatissimum* L.), showing fibre diameters of minimum 4 µm, maximum 15 µm, mean 9 µm (Fig. 4a). The coloured weft thread (sample O 2) (Fig. 2c) turned out to be sheep's wool (OVIS), with a fibre diameter of minimum 15 µm, maximum 45 µm, mean 25 µm (Fig. 4b). Whether these woollen weft threads were merely decorative or whether they transmitted some sort of information, such as the signature of a weaving workshop, cannot be determined in this case. Similar 'signatures' have been observed on Pharaonic and especially late Roman Egyptian textiles, also carried out in red wool yarn (Vogelsang-Eastwood 1995, 40–41; Fluck *et al.* 2000, 20; Wulff, Volbach 1926, 152–154, pl. 124, no. 41244; Huber 2007, 51 fig. 30).[4] The same features can also be observed on burial shrouds from Egypt in the collection of the Egyptological Institute of the University of Heidelberg (inventory number 3081) and the monk's grave no. 10 in the necropolis of Epiphanius monastery in Thebes-West, dating to the sixth and seventh century AD (Gessler-Löhr 2010, 311 fig. 2; Crum, Winlock 1926, 49). Differing slightly from the Egyptian examples, are two pieces of textile from Palmyra in Syria, which show the same characteristics as the Via Ostiense textile in terms of design and technique, i.e. a ground-weave of S-spun linen thread, coupled with decoration in self-bands, and again Z-spun, red woollen weft threads that do not extend across the whole fabric width (Schmidt-Colinet *et al.* 2000, 149 no. 259, pl. 31b, 161 no. 432, pl. 19b). Some undecorated textile finds from Palmyra of the same material and quality seem to have had an original width of about 108 cm in the weft direction (Schmidt-Colinet *et al.* 2000, 161 no. 340, pls 24a.c, 28d, Va). The width of the Via Ostiense textile at 72.5 cm thus corresponds better to the general width of Egyptian linen textiles (Huber 2007, 55; Schieck 2009, 120). Taken with the other characteristics of the Roman fabric, this rather indicates an Egyptian, rather than a Syrian, provenance.

In the light of its loosely woven and fibrous appearance (Fig. 3b), the textile can be characterised as muslin-like. Muslins were already mentioned in the *Periplus Maris Erythraei*, dating to the first century AD (Casson 1989). This text lists muslins among the valuable goods traded in Roman times along the Red Sea, from India to Rome via Egypt (Albaladejo,

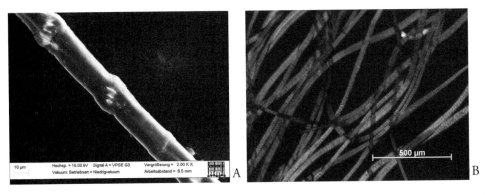

Fig. 4. Fibres of the burial shroud: (a) linen fibres in ground-weave, (b) coloured weft-thread of sheep's wool (photos by S. Mitschke).

Mitschke (in press)). We do not know from what material those muslins were made, but cotton (*Gossypium* sp.) is the most likely. The Roman linen shroud, therefore, could also be understood as an attempt to imitate Indian muslins.

Another striking feature was observed and needs to be mentioned. The textile showed the outline of a human body, as a shadow, created by substances employed in the burial rites (Fig. 2b).[5] It measures 130 cm in length, and this suggests that the burial was of a juvenile. The fabric can thus be identified as a burial shroud, in the sense of being a textile that was ultimately wrapped around the body for burial, but it also played a part in the preparation of the deceased for cremation. The preparation stages can be reconstructed as follows:

1. When preparing for the cremation, the textile was spread out and sprinkled all over with a paste-like, dark, substance, and then dried. The substance possibly included camphor.
2. The body was embalmed with a fluid of an oily or fatty consistency. Once embalmed, it was then either laid in the centre of the shroud, supine and extended, with the textile drawn up over its flanks, or it was covered by the shroud, the sides of which were stuffed beneath the body.
3. The corpse was unwrapped again and cremated. The remains were then collected in the textile. The bundle was put into the cinerary urn, which was then transferred to the burial location, perhaps a *columbarium* as described above.

The documented wrapping and unwrapping of the body possibly relates to the time when the embalming media were applied, before the corpse was dressed again, laid out publicly and later accompanied by a procession of mourners to the destined cremation or burial location (Kierdorf 1997, 89, 90). The use of embalming substances of different consistencies seems to have been common practice during funeral ceremonies, as observed also for some late Antique burials in Trier (Reifarth 2011, 104). Future comparative investigations on the shroud from the Via Ostiense hold much promise.

Taking all of the information about the Via Ostiense assemblage into account, the following conclusions can be drawn: all of the elements and components of the burial, particularly the costly embalming substances, the imported textile from the Eastern Mediterranean or even India, and the marble vessel, characterise this complex as the burial of a member of a wealthy, upper-class family during the second half of the first century or the early second century AD.

Catacombs beneath Sant'Agnese, Via Nomentana 351

The catacombs, named after the martyr Agnes, are located on the Via Nomentana in the north of the city, about 2.5 km from the city walls. Agnes was born in AD 237, and executed in AD 250 for her Christian beliefs. Her grave was located in the cemetery of the Praetorian Guard in the Via Nomentana. It became highly attractive to pilgrims, who laid out their necropolis around the saint's grave, and even attracted the attention of Constantine the Great and his daughter Constantina, who erected several buildings in the neighbourhood. In the fifth century, another small basilica was built over the previous structures, and the final building was erected by Pope Honorius I in AD 625–638. All of these edifices impinged in some respect on the catacombs, which are located just beneath foundation level, and have to be entered via the church building.

Written sources do not provide much information about the beginnings of the catacomb burials (Cianetti, Tavolini 2004; Deichmann 1946, 1–4, 213–234). The earliest section, however, may be located in the area accessible through the sacristy. It was built in about AD 250, like the *Coemeterium Maius*, another catacomb located on the Via Nomentana. The nucleus of the catacomb of Sant'Agnese, the Regio I, is located just beneath the northern corner of today's basilica, and it extends under the Via di Sant'Agnese (Fiocchi Nicolai *et al.* 1989, 28 fig. 23; Rasch, Arbeiter 2007). This section consists of major hallways and cross-passages, cut into the soft bedrock and arranged roughly in a radial pattern. Along the aisles, columns of three to six *loculi* were carved into the bedrock, taking one or two corpses per compartment. They were closed off with tiles, bricks, or plasterwork. Today, most of these *loculi* have been opened and cleaned out, except for three burials in Regio I, which we were allowed to investigate. Due to the high temperature and humidity, the working conditions in the catacomb of Sant'Agnese have to be characterised as 'suboptimal': camera lenses steamed up immediately, and textile fragments adhered unavoidably to tweezers and sampling vessels.

The first compartment to be examined was located in gallery 2, next to the cross-section no. 10; it was the central *loculus* out of five. Its measurements are 121 cm in length and 28 cm in height. It contains the mummy package of an individual of about 103 cm in length, quite probably a child, the wider end defining the head, pointing to the right. The corpse was completely wrapped in a textile, giving it a smooth shape. It is relatively well preserved, except for the foot end, which broke off in part, probably due to visitors passing by the intersection of the galleries and touching it. The textiles of the mummy package have a whitish colour, which can be attributed to an added powder, probably gypsum ($CaSO_4$), lime or chalk ($CaCO_3$), spread all over the package. This material is evidence for the practice of plaster burial, where desiccating substances were spread over the deceased. The powdered material was used alone or as a mixture (Sparey-Green 1993, 422, 423; Reifarth 2011, 104). During the archaeological deposition, mineralisation, i.e. calcination, of associated organic substances, such as textile, may occur. In the course of this substitution with metallic components from various minerals, the textiles turn stiff and lose all of their textile qualities, except for their appearance. In some parts of the package investigated, therefore, textile structures are still visible: in the region of the hip particularly the impression of folds of textile, diagonally stretched, can be traced. A small sample was taken from there (sample A 1), carefully dried, and investigated in the laboratory at Mannheim. Decomposition had already progressed to a high degree and so the material could no longer be identified.

A second *loculus* was investigated deeper in the labyrinth, located in gallery 28, next to the corner of gallery 27/28. Three compartments were arranged one above the other; the compartment in the middle was the one investigated. It measured 180 cm in length, 38 cm in height, and about 80 cm in depth (pl. 18a), and again contained the mineral-packed bodies of two adults, who lay on their backs, side by side, in an extended position, with their skulls pointing to the corner of gallery 27/28. The skeleton in front is in poor condition and also largely destroyed by visitors grasping at the human remains. The size of the body could not be recorded due to decay, but it seems to have been smaller than the second one. The latter, at the back, measures about 175 cm in length. Even though the rear skeleton is better preserved than the one at the front, it must be noted that both have nearly disintegrated. Only the heavier bones, such as the skulls and parts of the arms and legs, survive in a highly degraded amalgam of obviously different textiles (pl. 18b). Because of the darkness of gallery 28, the narrowness of the entrance of the *loculus*, and the fact that the better preserved corpse was positioned at the back, it was quite difficult to carry out further investigations on the spot. Four samples of the textile remains, therefore, were taken (Fig. 5). One sample was obtained from the right lower part of the leg of the person in front (sample A 2), one from the hip of the person at the back (sample A 3), and two from the latter's thoracic region (sample A 4 and 5).

Microscopic observation proved sample A 2 to contain a fibrous substance, but again, the decay was much too advanced to identify the kind of organic material. Sample A 3 was also rather damaged, but the textile structure of two systems of threads crossing each other at a right angle could be seen; a fine diagonal line revealed a twill weave. Both warp and weft showed no clear torsion (but there might have been a slight s-twist), and a thread diameter of between 0.1 mm and 0.2 mm. The longitudinal view of the fragmented fibres in the scanning electron microscope (SEM) was smooth, with a roundish to triangular cross-section. The fibres' fineness varied from between 10 μm and 15 μm. These features can be assumed to be characteristic of real silk, which derives from the domesticated silkworm *Bombyx mori* L.

Even though the upper and lower sides of samples A 4 and A 5 could no longer be identified, both showed the same structure and were obviously made of the same organic residues; there was always one greyish-blackish side, lying opposite a beige-coloured side. The black layer may be a result of dirt or micro-organisms, and its hard consistency points to embalming substances. Adhering to this was a decomposed tabby-woven textile fragment in a veil-like medium quality. The S-spun threads were 0.4 mm to 0.5 mm thick. The blackish covering could also be seen on the cracked single fibres under the microscope. Apart from that, they also showed a smooth surface with a fineness of about 10 μm, which again indicates silk.

The third *loculus* to be investigated is located just opposite to the second, in gallery 28, next to the corner of gallery 27/28. It is the central compartment of five, and is still half closed off with two tiles. It contains the burial of an adult, with its feet pointing to the corner of gallery 27/28. The skeleton is in better condition than the ones in the other graves, and the fragments

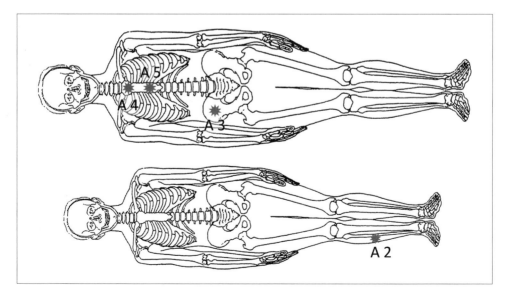

Fig. 5. Scheme and overview of the sampling spots of *loculus* 2 in Sant'Agnese (drawing by S. Mitschke).

of the skull, the spine, hips, and bones from the legs are still preserved. Some tiny bits of textile could be observed sticking to them, and two samples were taken, one paravertebral from just below the chin (sample A 6), and another one from the top of the skull (sample A 7). Both turned out to have disintegrated into small, weak, fragments of short brownish fibres, which lack distinguishing features.

Summing up, the burials investigated in the catacomb of Sant′Agnese (dating to the second half of the third century AD) reveal information on the practices employed when preparing the deceased for burial. The evidence of white minerals, together with the fact that some of the samples bear thin layers of obviously resin-like substances, prove that embalming procedures took place to preserve the body of the deceased.

Taking into account the difficult preservation and sampling conditions, the meagre remains from *loculus* 2 still reveal various qualities of fine textile made from precious and expensive silk. The character of the elaborate textiles and textile techniques, as well as the presence of precious imported silk, and the resins, indicate the deceased to have been relatively wealthy persons.

Santi Marcellino e Pietro, Via Cassilina 641

The catacombs named after the martyrs Santi Marcellino e Pietro are located on the Via Cassilina, about 2.5 km from the Roman city wall. The catacombs extend beneath the large mortuary building erected by Constantine to house the remains of his mother Helena, who died in AD 328. Long before that, the area, which belonged to the Emperor, had been used as a training ground by the *equites singulares Augusti*. The place had also been used as a necropolis by these troops. Several of their gravestones have been found at the site.

Below ground-level here, the catacombs have been carved into the tufa. The core of the subterranean burial site was Regio X. Later, the relics of Marcellinus and Petrus were buried in this area as well. Both were imprisoned for their Christian beliefs during the time of the Diocletianic persecution. In prison they started baptising other inmates, for which they were then decapitated in AD 299 or 304, and buried in the catacombs of the Via Cassilina. While Paul Styger explicitly stated in 1933 that there was no reason to date the catacombs earlier than the fourth century (Styger 1933, 205), modern research tends rather to date the beginning of the construction work to the third century (Fiocchi Nicolai *et al.* 1989, 30–31 figs 27, 29, 61, 68–69, 98, 103, 131,144; Guyon 1987). The latest excavations in Regio X started in summer 2003, and were carried out by the Pontifical Commission for Sacred Archaeology under the aegis of Dr Raffaella Giuliani, in cooperation with the École Française at Rome and anthropologists from the University of Bordeaux, France, led by Professor Dr Dominique Castex (Giuliani 2009). Investigations were undertaken near the crypt of the eponymous martyr, revealing the original location of the chest that housed the relics of Marcellinus and Petrus in the sixth century. Just behind this spot, an amazing burial site was revealed, which had been forgotten about until this excavation: several chambers filled with human corpses, of which at least 1200 could be identified (Blanchard *et al.* 2007). The individuals must have died within a very short period of time and there seems to have been a need for quick burial. This interpretation rests on the fact that the bodies had been piled up without individual preparation, except for being dressed and in some cases wrapped in textiles. The only substance added in the course of burial was gypsum. It was spread over the deceased, probably for hygiene reasons, to reduce the smell of decay. The humidity evaporating from the bodies reacted with the gypsum to form casts enclosing the textile remains. The general impression given is that there was no time to spend on rituals, in view of the sheer number of dead. It is quite likely that the death of such a large number of persons was due to a plague, and that the highly infectious corpses needed fast removal in order to avoid spreading infection. Laboratory data and numismatic finds date this event to the first half of the third century.

A lump of gypsum from this part of Regio X with calcified textile fragments (MP 06 14-02-06 X 81) (pl. 19) was handed over to us by Dr Raffaella Giuliani. Unfortunately, the exact find-context is not recorded and the piece has to be considered unstratified, but as we were interested in different qualities of Roman textile from Rome in general, the find was important. The gypsum object investigated measured 5 cm to 8 cm in length and 5 cm in height. The dimensions are evidence that the mineral was employed on a large scale. One side of the sample revealed textile structures with an open appearance. They were preserved almost solely as impressions, but further scanty remains of fibres could be seen. This textile was called sample MP 1 (pl. 19a). In the SEM, the heavily degraded structures were identified as a loose weave made of silk. Both warp and weft had a count of 8 threads per centimetre; one system proved to be Z-spun, the other S-spun. Small pieces which crumbled off the main gypsum fragment were also examined, and a remarkably fine piece of textile came to light (sample MP 2) (pl. 19c). This sample turned out to be a 2-over-1 or possibly a 3-over-1 twill weave, which was also made of silk. In both directions, the weak S-spun threads showed a diameter of 0.2 mm to 0.3 mm. The density of the weave in warp and weft is about 40 threads per centimetre. In both samples the fineness of the fibres was very difficult to determine, as the fibres were practically liquefying: the diameter range lay between 10μm and 15μm.

To sum up: although the unstratified find from the mass grave in the catacomb of Santi Marcellino e Pietro cannot be assigned to a particular person, the quality of the samples investigated indicate the burial of an individual belonging to the upper social class in the third century AD.

San Sebastiano, Via Appia 130

The church and catacombs named after the martyr Sebastian are located of about 2 km from the Porta Sebastiano, on the Via Appia, heading south-east. This area was exploited for its Pozzuolan earth, and the quarry formed a deep depression in the landscape. The latter feature gave the area its name in antiquity, *ad catacumbas*, and the nomenclature was later extended to all Roman burials of this kind (Mancinelli 2007, 32–37; Styger 1933, 177–184). The region and this basin in particular, were owned by former slaves and freedmen from the imperial court. They dug here *coemeteria*, subterranean burials of individual families, during the first century AD. By the mid-third century, the whole terrain was covered and back-filled with earth, and in the period AD 306–337, a large funerary hall was erected on top of it, initiated by Constantine the Great. The building spread across all of the existing structures, covering the catacombs with its eastern end and a villa and courtyard with its western end. The building exhibits the same characteristics as other funerary halls, such as those at Sant'Agnese, and Santi Marcellino e Pietro, which were used for funerary banqueting; all of the halls share a U-shape plan. The place was a famous burial centre up until the seventh century, being named

Basilica Apostolorum after the two Apostles Peter and Paul, whose relics had been transferred to San Sebastiano by the Emperor Valerian between AD 253 and 260, in a time of Christian persecution. After the seventh century, the church began to be identified with, and named after, Saint Sebastian, who became a Christian martyr in the second half of the third century.

In 1915, excavations were carried out in the church building. The floor was removed almost completely and several burials were revealed beneath, which are accessible through the catacombs today. The ones of greatest interest for the purpose of this paper were the three Roman sarcophagi found at a depth of 1.70 m beneath the church floor (Styger 1915, 100–105, figs 12, 15; *idem* 1933, 177–184, 331–351). They were arranged parallel to the longitudinal axis of the basilica, positioned in the north-east of the church, in the centre of the aisle (Nieddu 2009, 104 figs 100, 124, 133–135). A narrow chamber embraced the three sarcophagi, and the room was given the number C.D.A.S.M cm XXII. No electricity is available in this room: only portable gas-lamps serve as illumination and work was quite difficult in such conditions.

The sarcophagi were set side by side, leaving very narrow aisles between them. The three are of about the same size, and made of marble. While the outer ones (nos 5 and 7) are plain, without decoration, the one in the centre (no. 6) shows a decorated front, an undecorated back, and two narrow ends, which have minor relief-decoration of incised oval shields arranged diagonally, crossing one above the other. The elaborate relief on the front side is oriented towards sarcophagus no. 5, and in view of this decoration, it may be concluded that the sarcophagus was intended to stand against a wall and to be approached from one side only. The design was very common from the second century onwards. It consists of two pilasters, a bottom and top framing line, and gadroons ('Riefeln') in S-curves running in opposite directions, but meeting at the central motif of a *tabula ansata* (Koch, Sichtermann 1982, 73–76 fig. 2, type 6). The marble lid of this sarcophagus was removed in 1915, and still leans against the wall of the chamber. It has a roughly carved lower surface made to fit into the opening (Nieddu 2009, 125 fig. 136). Basically, it consists of a flat lid, but in front it turns at a right angle, showing a decorated area of gadroons along the main side of the sarcophagus. The sarcophagus seems to be empty today, but sarcophagus no. 5 contains the simple bones of a skeleton, and is covered with a plain, undecorated, stone panel.

Tomb no. 7 was of most interest to us, for it still contains a complete inhumation burial (Fig. 6a). The sarcophagus measures 62 cm in width and 205 cm in length on the outside, leaving a chamber of 45.5 cm by 199 cm with rounded corners on the inside. Its marble is of coarse grained quality. One of the long sides has been neatly smoothed, while the other one was quite roughly made, like the two narrow sides. The marks of workmen's tools, such as the claw chisel and the smoothing iron, are visible, as well as incised working sketches to be followed. In the centre of the narrow side to which the feet point, a straight groove was carved into the top of the wall, and into the upper edge of the rear wall of the sarcophagus. At a distance of 62.5 cm, and again at 85 cm, from the foot-end, two vertical holes were drilled into the wall on the long side, measuring 2.2 cm and 2.5 cm in diameter. Both holes were filled with a metallic substance, which was sampled (sample S 4) (Fig. 6b). It proved to be made of iron and was probably part of a clamp to secure the lid.

The sarcophagus still contains the burial of an individual, whose feet point eastwards. The body was positioned in the centre, on a bed of powdery brownish, whitish material, about 1 cm thick, mixed with stone chippings that had fallen into the sarcophagus while it was being

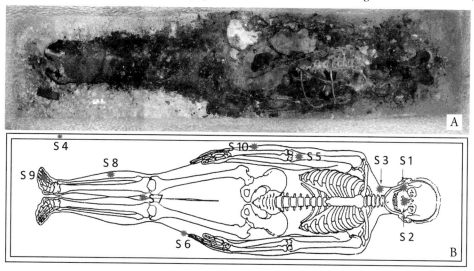

Fig. 6. (a) Sarcophagus beneath San Sebastiano; (b) scheme with sampling spots (photos by A. P. g. Schieck, S. Mitschke).

produced. The cadaver lies on its back, the feet parallel, close together, and it measures 176 cm in total length. Given the size, it is most likely that the person was male, but the poor state of preservation allows no precise interpretation for the moment. Computer tomography might one day be helpful here.

The human package is seriously damaged; the thorax is broken, the spine and the ribs are lying open and in disorder, as is the hip region. The human flesh and textiles have vanished and turned to dust. But the region below, embracing both legs, is in much better shape, though the latter are broken off at the level of the knee.

The whole bundle appears to be more or less covered with a hard, smooth substance of reddish or black colour. In the broken part of the face especially, the layer is thick enough for the solid pieces of this material to appear. Again, the use of incense and resins in different combinations seems likely. The resinous, almost tarry-looking matter could have been applied during the burial ceremony, but the availability of pre-soaked shrouds is also under discussion at the moment (Reifarth 2011, 104). Two samples were taken of this substance, one from the right cheek (sample S 1) (Fig. 6b), and the other one from the nose (sample S 2) (Fig. 6b). Back in Mannheim, the composition of both looked similar under the microscope. For that reason, only one was sent to KIK/IRPA Brussels for gas chromatography with attached mass spectrometry (GC/MS). There, cinnamic acid and p-hydroxy cinnamic acid were found. These components are amongst those typical for benzoe or storax balsam, which is obtained from the bark of several species of trees and shrubs of the genus *Styrax* L. (Modugno *et al.* 2006). Fatty acids were also discovered. Mathieu Boudin calculated the ratio of palmitic acid to stearic acid as 1.51, and he concludes that this could probably indicate the use of linseed oil, although contamination from the lipids of the body cannot be discounted.

The body was completely covered by several layers of textile. Traces of sewing lines suggest that the fabrics were not only wrapped around the body, but packaged, at least in part, in order to give them a shape. There is no indication that material was wound around the arms region, for example, whilst the legs were still wrapped in only one large piece of textile. The direction of winding can still be traced, especially at the ankles. Along these diagonal folds several sections of hemmed edging can be observed for up to 4 cm.

A whitish bloom on the textiles – possibly caused by the unequal hygroscopicity of different materials – indicates that the feet are shod in 'ballet-shoes', so-called *campagi*, always worn with stockings, *udones*. The material and colour of the shoes is not determinable, as they are still hidden in the package, although the tips of the shoes have broken off and expose the disintegrating feet. A seam runs around the feet, binding the sole and upper part of the shoe together. The sole shows a linear structure, most likely reflecting a papyrus insole, and inside the shoe, a yellowish silky material is exposed, possibly the stockings or foot-wrappings worn inside the shoes. Remains of a constructional line are visible (pl. 20). Open shoes for men, enclosed over the toes and heels, have been described by Alexandra T. Croom. Amongst other depictions she refers, for example, to the late antique mosaic in San Vitale, Ravenna, on which the Emperor Justinian and his court all wear this type of shoe (Croom 2000, 62, 63, 65, colour pl. 1; compare Braun 1964, 385–388).

Although the exact construction of the whole bundle was only partly determinable *in situ*, there was evidence of at least five different kinds of textiles (Fig. 6b):

Sample S 3 derives from the cervical area of the deceased. There, we found some multi-layered material, in a winding form, showing a textile structure. Under magnification the sample was identified as very fine 2/1 twill, which is completely sealed with the blackish substance mentioned above. The warp is slightly Z-spun, whilst no torsion of the weft is detectable. The diameter of the yarns in both thread-systems measures around 0.1 mm to 0.2 mm; the density of the weave ranges between 50 and 60 threads per centimetre. In the SEM, silk fibres were again identified.

Sample S 5 was taken from the breast, where hardened textile fragments of a beige colour could be seen. Due to the advanced degradation the analysis was quite difficult, but a fine twill could be recognised, most likely 2/1 again. The count in both directions was 30 threads per centimetre, with a yarn fineness of 0.2 mm to 0.4 mm. One system – probably the warp – was Z-spun, whereas the weft had no apparent twist. The analysis in the SEM again proved the use of silk.

In the lower part of the corpse, a fragmentary purple-coloured textile was found (samples S 6–8), which seemed to be wrapped around the body from the hip to the feet. This fabric belongs to a group of fewer than twenty published Roman silk block-damasks (De Jonghe 2001; Foulkes 2010; Reifarth 2011; Schrenk, Reichert 2011), to which this example can now be added. The group is often classified under the Latin term *scutulatus*, which means something like 'chequered' (Wild 1964). A special loom type for weaving silk damasks is mentioned in Diocletian's 'Edict on Maximum Prices' (Wild 1987, 465), but we do not know exactly what it looked like (compare Schrenk, Reichert 2011, 223, 224). Also the regions where damask manufactures have been located are still under discussion (Schmidt-Colinet *et al.* 2000, 53; Schrenk 2007), but from a technical point of view, Syria seems most likely to have been the place of origin (Becker 2009, 258). First datable pieces made of unspun Chinese silk yarns come from tower-tombs of Iamblik and Elahbel in Palmyra, Syria, which were dedicated in the years AD 83 and AD 103 (Schmidt-Colinet *et al.* 2000, 159 no. 319, pl. 13b, 80a, 178 no. 453, pl. 13a, 79b-c). This marks a *terminus post quem* for the deposition of the textiles.

During our one-day survey it was not possible to draft the exact repeat of the pattern, but it is clear that it is based on a 3/1 (1/3) twill with geometrically alternating warp- and weft-faced zones, the subtle design of which only becomes visible through contrasting light reflections. An assignment to the phases of block-damask technique according to D. De Jonghe and M. Tavernier (De Jonghe, Tavernier 1977/78, 149–156) could therefore not be accomplished. However, the overall impression of the fragmentary fabric looked in fact chequered. In the admittedly poorly lit condition, no indication of the later types of block-damasks, with complex diamond- or lozenge-shaped patterns, could be seen. While the warp could be characterised as slightly Z-spun, the weft shows no torsion at all. Both warp and weft threads have a fineness of about 0.1 mm, their density ranging between 50 and 60 threads per centimetre. As could be seen in the SEM, the single silk fibres were from 5 μm to 10 μm in diameter, which is very fine. The texture of the fabric looked almost identical to the damask weave from grave 174 at St Maximin, Trier (Reifarth 2011, 104, fig. 5); its thread-count may be compared to one of the examples from Palmyra (Schmidt-Colinet *et al.* 2000, 178 no. 453, pl. 13a, 79b-c).

In addition to this, another very fine textile with a veil-like appearance was found underneath the block-damask in samples S 7 and S 8 (Fig. 7a). The fabric had disintegrated into very small pieces, so its weave could not be determined. The threads showed a remarkable fineness, about 50 μm in diameter. One system seems to be Z-spun, while the other does not show any twist at all. As expected, in the SEM both warp and weft turned out to be being made of silk (Fig. 7b).

The next sample (sample S 9) was taken from the right foot of the deceased, where under the outer purple-coloured layer another yellowish-reddish textile appeared (pl. 20a). In the light of its position and the fact that it was carefully sewn together from at least two cut sections, it can be assumed that it belongs to some kind of stockings, as already stated above. It is also another block-damask in 3/1 (1/3) twill (pl. 20b). Its exact pattern repeat could also not be determined during our field work. With 50 to 60 threads per centimetre and a yarn diameter of about 0.1 mm to 0.15 mm, the fineness of this fabric is comparable to the purple-coloured block-damask from the outer layer. Once again, only the warp shows a weak Z-spin, while the weft has no torsion at all.

Radiocarbon dating of the last sample, taken from the right arm of the deceased (sample S 10), assigns its entombment to the years between AD 143 and 344 at 95.4 per cent possibility range (at 2 sigma), and AD 236 to 323 at 68.2 per cent possibility range (at 1 sigma).[6] This time-frame seems to be relatively wide, but the simple check-pattern of both block-damasks suits a production date at the end of the second or beginning of the third century AD. This links the

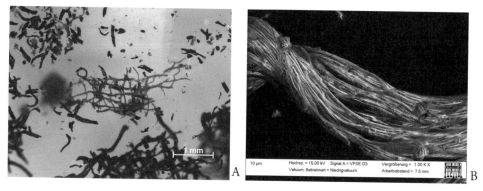

Fig. 7. (a) Veil under reflected light microscope; (b) silk fibres of the veil in the SEM (photo by S. Mitschke).

textiles of the burial in San Sebastiano to Syria, which is the most likely place of manufacture of this special type of textile.

Summing up, we can suggest that the face of the deceased was covered by a very fine twill fabric, stained with benzoe or storax balsam. A second, fine quality textile was discovered in the chest region, but due to the great damage in this area it cannot be said whether it belonged to a specific garment or whether it was just a sheet of textile. The much better preserved hip and leg region was wrapped in a purple block-damask with hemmed edges, but here again it was not possible to identify a garment. Below, we found a very fine veil-like textile, which could possibly belong to a sort of undergarment. The feet were clad in yellow stockings, sewn from a second kind of block-damask, and the deceased wore shoes of a material which could not be determined. The total ensemble was covered, in addition, by the purple block-damask.

It can be said that in San Sebastiano, as in the other burials in the catacombs in Rome, there is evidence for the use of embalming media and very expensive silk textiles. The open shoes were the mark of high officials and churchmen, and so the high status of the deceased is assured.

Conclusions

Our investigations have led us along roads (with their accompanying graves) from the north-east to the south-east of the ancient city of Rome, and thence to the far south. We were deeply impressed by the variety of the archaeological finds and records that we came across.

Our aim was to gain information about Roman textiles from Rome itself, and we have achieved that; but this can only be regarded as a starting point. Our research work on textiles has enabled us to evaluate the archaeological record, not only in terms of technical and technological data, but also with reference to the sociological background of the deceased. All of the inhumation burials investigated by us have a common factor: they are located in the oldest sections of the catacombs. This probably mirrors the wish of the deceased to be buried near to the saints, with whom they wanted to be associated. It was their social status that enabled them to be buried in this neighbourhood, and their status was also manifested in their expensive grave-furnishings, consisting of imported textiles and costly resins. This goes back to a tradition that is attested for the first time by a cremation burial coming from the Via Ostiense.

Textiles, moreover, have turned out to be transmitters of burial customs. By this means, a precise impression of how the deceased was prepared and arranged for his burial can be gleaned. Regardless of the type of burial, we could demonstrate that the deceased was treated with embalming substances in order to preserve and deodorise the mortal remains. The practice may have resulted from recognition of the disinfecting properties of such substances, and the same may be said of the application of gypsum or other minerals in a funerary context.

These insights were all gained by the investigation of just tiny fragments. They would not have been achievable without the support of modern scientific methods, such as ^{14}C, morphological and chemical analysis.

sylvia.mitschke@mannheim.de
annette.schieck@cez-archaeometrie.de

Notes

1. The DressID research project on clothing and identities in the Roman world is funded with the support of the European Commission. For further information, visit www.DressID.eu.
2. For details of the microscopes used for fibre analysis and the accelerator mass spectrometer for dating purposes, visit www.cez-archaeometrie.de.
3. The museum of the island of Reichenau in Lake Constance has a marble urn of a rather similar shape. This vessel was taken to Lake Constance by the Greek monk Simeon in about AD 900. He considered it to be a cup that was used at the wedding at Canaan. It can only be mentioned as a parallel for shape, it does not provide any clue to dating.
4. For weavers' marks see John Peter Wild (forthcoming).
5. Shadows of human corpses have so far only been known from Egyptian burial shrouds of Late Roman times such as the shroud inventory number 3081 of the Egyptological Institute of the University of Heidelberg collection (Gessler-Löhr 2010, 311 fig. 2) and the rectangular linen textile with loop weave decoration of the Katoen Natie collection at Antwerp, inventory number 515 (DM34) (De Moor *et al.* 2008, 11, fig. 5, 164–165). These shadows originate from the desiccating substances of the mummified bodies they enveloped and held for inhumation burial.
6. Compare also with the latest investigations of the 2/1 block-damask found attached to the relics of Saint Severin at Cologne, Germany. The ornament appears to be more complex. Taking this fact into account, in combination with the slightly later radiocarbon date of the Cologne textile, there evolves a chronology in technological features and possibilities (radiocarbon date: 250 to 390 AD at 68.2 per cent possibility range (at 1 sigma), 230 to 420 AD at 95.4 per cent possibility range (at 2 sigma). See Tegtmeier *et al.* 2011, 133–134.

Bibliography

Albaladejo, Mitschke (in press): M. Albaladejo, S. Mitschke, 'Der Import exotischer Textilien nach Rom', in *Ausstellungskatalog DressCode im alten Rom*, Reiss-Engelhorn-Museen, Mannheim

Becker 2009: J. Becker, *Pattern and Loom: A Practical Study of the Development of Weaving Techniques in China*, Western Asia and Europe, Copenhagen

Bender Jørgensen 1992: L. Bender Jørgensen, *North European Textiles until AD 1000*, Aarhus

Blanchard *et al.* 2007: P. Blanchard, D. Castex, M. Coquerelle, R. Giuliani, M. Ricciardi, 'A mass grave from the catacomb of Saints Peter and Marcellinus in Rome, second-third century AD', *Antiquity* 81, 989–998

Braun 1964: J. Braun, *Die liturgische Gewandung im Occident und Orient nach Ursprung und Entwicklung, Verwendung und Symbolik*, Darmstadt

Casson 1989: L. Casson, *The Periplus Maris Erythraei. Text with Introduction, Translation and Commentary*, Princeton

Cianetti, Tavolini 2004: M. M. Cianetti, C. Tavolini, *La Basilica Costantina di Sant'Agnese. Lavori Archeologici e di Restauro*, Rome

Crum, Winlock 1926: W. E. Crum, H. E. Winlock, *The Monastery of Epiphanius at Thebes I*, New York

Deichmann 1946: F. W. Deichmann, 'Die Lage der Constantinischen Basilika der Heiligen Agnes an der Via Nomentana', *Rivista di Archeologia Cristiana* XXII, 1–4

De Jonghe, Tavernier 1977/78: D. De Jonghe, M. Tavernier, 'Die spätantiken Köper-4-Damaste aus dem Sarg des Bischofs Paulinus in der Krypta der St.-Paulinus-Kirche in Trier', *Trierer Zeitschrift* 40/41, 145–174

De Jonghe 2001: D. De Jonghe, 'From the Roman horizontal loom to the 3/1 twill damask loom of the early medieval period', in P. W. Rogers, L. Bender Jørgensen, A. Rast-Eicher (eds), *The Roman Textile Industry and its Influence: A Birthday Tribute to John Peter Wild*, Oxford, 137–147

Della Portella 1999: I. Della Portella, *Roma Sotterranea*, Venice

De Moor *et al.* 2008: A. De Moor, C. Verhecken-Lammens, A. Verhecken, *3500 Years of Textile Art. The Collection Headquarters*, Tielt

Fasola 1974: U. M. Fasola, 'La "Regio IV" del cimiterio di S. Agnese sotto l'atrio della Basilica Constantiana', *Rivista di Archeologia Cristiana* 50, 175–205

Fiocchi Nicolai *et al.* 1989: V. Fiocchi Nicolai, F. Bisconti, D. Mazzoleni, *Roms christliche Katakomben. Geschichte – Bilderwelt – Inschriften*, Regensburg

Fluck *et al.* 2000: C. Fluck, P. Linscheid, S. Merz, *Textilien aus Ägypten I*, Staatliche Museen Preußischer Kulturbesitz Bestandskatalog 1, Wiesbaden

Foulkes 2010: S. J. Foulkes, 'Roman silk block damasks', *Journal for Weavers, Spinners and Dyers* 233, 1–9

Gessler-Löhr 2010: B. Gessler-Löhr, 'Two child mummies and some grave goods of the Byzantine Period from the Egyptian collection at Heidelberg University, Germany', in A. Wieczorek, W. Rosendahl (eds), *Mummies of the World, Catalogue Exhibition USA 2010–2013*, Mainz, 310–315

Giuliani 2009: R. Giuliani, *Recent Excavations in the Central Region of the Catacomb of Sts Peter and Marcellinus*, Pamphlet by the Pontifical Commission of Sacred Archaeology, Vatican

Guyon 1987: J. Guyon, *Le Cimetière aux Deux Lauriers. Recherches sur les Catacombes romaines*, Rome

Huber 2007: B. Huber, 'The textiles of an early Christian burial from el-Kom el-Ahmar/Šaruna (Middle Egypt)', in A. De Moor, C. Fluck (eds), *Methods of Dating Ancient Textiles of the 1st Millennium AD from Egypt and Neighbouring Countries. Proceedings of the 4th Meeting of the Study Group 'Textiles from the Nile Valley', Antwerp, 16–17 April 2005*, Tielt, 36–65

Kierdorf 1995: W. Kierdorf, 'Totenehrung im Alten Rom', in M. Witteyer (ed.), *Des Lichtes beraubt: Totenehrung in der römischen Gräberstraße von Mainz-Weisenau*, Wiesbaden, 86–92

Mancinelli 2007: F. Mancinelli, *Führer zu den Katakomben in Rom*, Florence

Modugno *et al.* 2006: F. Modugno, E. Ribechini, M. P. Colombini, 'Aromatic resin characterisation by gas chromatography – mass spectrometry', *Raw and Archaeological Materials: Journal of Chromatography* A, 1134, 298–304

Nieddu 2009: A. M. Nieddu, *La Basilica Apostolorum sulla Via Appia e l'Area Cimiteriale Circostante, Monumenti di Antichità Cristiana*, Pontificio Istituto di Archeologia Cristiana II Serie XIX, Vatican

Oepen *et al.* 2011: J. Oepen, B. Päffgen, S. Schrenk, U. Tegtmeier (eds), *Der hl. Severin von Köln*, Studien zur Kölner Kirchengeschichte Band 40, Siegburg

Rasch, Arbeiter 2007: J. J. Rasch, A. Arbeiter, *Das Mausoleum der Constantina in Rom, Spätantike Zentralbauten in Rom und Latium* 4, Mainz

Reifarth 2011: N. Reifarth, 'Textiles in their scientific context – interdisciplinary cooperation during the evaluation of burial textiles', in C. Alfaro, J.-P. Brun, Ph. Borgard, R. Pierobon Benoit (eds), *Purpureae Vestes III. Symposium Internacional sobre Textiles y Tintes del Mediterráneo en el Mundo Antiguo*, Valencia, 101–107

Schieck 2009: A. Paetz gen. Schieck, 'Late Roman cushions and the principles of their decoration', in A. De Moor, C. Fluck (eds), *Clothing the House. Furnishing Textiles of the 1st Millennium AD from Egypt and Neighbouring Countries. Proceedings of the 5th Meeting of the Study Group 'Textiles from the Nile Valley', Antwerp, 6–7 October 2007*, Tielt, 115–131

Schmidt-Colinet *et al.* 2000: A. Schmidt-Colinet, A. Stauffer, K. al-As'ad, *Die Textilien aus Palmyra*, Mainz

Schrenk 2007: S. Schrenk, 'Die spätantiken Seidengewebe in Trier', in A. Demandt, J. Engemann (eds), *Konstantin der Große: Imperator Caesar Flavius Constantinus*, Mainz, 416–417

Schrenk, Reichert 2011: S. Schrenk, U. Reichert, 'Die Textilien aus dem hölzernen Schrein in St. Severin', in Oepen *et al.* 2011, 220–326

Sinn 1987: F. Sinn, *Stadtrömische Marmorurnen*, Mainz

Soler Villabella 1937: R. N. Soler Villabella, 'Una stoffa romana', *Bullettino della Commissione archeologica comunale di Roma* 65, 73–82

Sommella 1992: A. M. Sommella, 'L'Antiquarium Comunale e le raccolte Capitoline da "Roma Capitale" ai progetti per la loro sistemazione 1870/1992', in M. E. Tittoni (ed.), *Invisibilia. Rivedere i Capolavori, Vedere i Progetti, Catalogue of the Exhibition at the Palazzo delle Esposizioni, February 19 to April 12, 1992*, Rome, 145–150

Sparey-Green 1993: C. Sparey-Green, 'The rite of plaster burial in the context of the Roman-British cemetery at Poundbury, Dorset (England)', in M. Struck (ed.), *Römerzeitliche Gräber als Quellen zu Religion, Bevölkerungsstruktur und Sozialgeschichte*, Archäologische Schriften des Instituts für Vor- und Frühgeschichte der Johannes Gutenberg-Universität Mainz 3, Mainz, 421–432

Styger 1915: P. Styger, 'Scavi a San Sebastiano. Scoperta di una memoria degli Apostoli Pietro e Paolo e del corpo di San Fabio Papa e Martire', *Römische Quartalschrift für christliche Altertumskunde und für Kirchengeschichte* 29, 73–110

Styger 1933: P. Styger, *Die römischen Katakomben*, Berlin

Tegtmeier *et al.* 2011: U. Tegtmeier, K. Van der Borg, A. de Jong, P. Grootes, M.-J. Nadeau, 'Die AMS-Datierungen an Materialien aus dem Holzschrein des Hl. Severin', in Oepen *et al.* 2011, 133–134

Vogelsang-Eastwood 1995: G. M. Vogelsang-Eastwood, *Die Kleider des Pharao. Die Verwendung von Stoffen im Alten Ägypten*, Katalog der Ausstellung, Leiden

Volbach 1942: W. F. Volbach, *I Tessuti. Catalogo del Museo Sacro della Biblioteca Apostolica Vaticana* 3, 1, Rome

Wild 1964: J. P. Wild, 'The textile term *scutulatus*', *Classical Quarterly* New Series 14, 263–266

Wild 1987: Wild 1987: J. P. Wild, 'The Roman Horizontal Loom', *American Journal of Archaeology* 91.3, 459–471

Wild, forthcoming: J. P. Wild, 'The textiles', in C. Thomas, *Report on Excavation of a Cemetery at Spitalfields, London*, forthcoming

Wulff, Volbach 1926: O. Wulff, W. F. Volbach, *Spätantike und koptische Stoffe aus ägyptischen Grabfunden in den Staatlichen Museen*, Berlin

The Roman child clothed in death

Maureen Carroll

Introduction

In an article on infant and maternal mortality in Tanzania in the *New York Times* in May 2009, a striking photograph by Béatrice de Géa showed the burial of a stillborn baby. The women had wrapped the corpse in a *kanga*, a brightly coloured wrap of cotton normally worn by Tanzanian women, and they scoop the excavated earth back into the little grave dug by the men of the family and neighbourhood.[1] As an archaeologist studying both the death and burial of Roman infants and newborn children and the use of clothing and textiles in the funerary sphere of that period, the photo prompted me to wonder what, in a couple millennia, might be left of the shroud of this Tanzanian child in the archaeological record. Would we be able to recognise that the baby had been wrapped at all, and how could we possibly know about the gendered division of care invested in giving the child its last rites?

Such questions are pertinent to a study of attitudes towards infant death and the mortuary treatment of children in the Roman period, given that ancient authors convey the impression that children up to the age of three were afforded minimal, if any, ritual attention when they died. As I have demonstrated elsewhere in a study on infant death and burial, however, Roman texts, penned by men who upheld restraint and self-control as an aristocratic virtue, are to be used with caution in assessing Roman attitudes towards childhood and child death (Carroll 2011). Plutarch (*Consolation to his Wife* 11), on the death of their two-year-old daughter, wrote to his wife: 'Our people do not bring libations to those of their children who die in infancy, nor do they observe in their case any of the other rites that the living are expected to perform for the dead, as such children have no part in earth or earthly things; not do they linger where the burial is celebrated, at the graves, or at the laying out of the dead, and sit by the bodies. For the laws forbid us to mourn for infants' (Baltussen 2009). What Plutarch meant by 'laying out' the dead must relate, among other things, to the process of dressing or wrapping and adorning the body in preparation for burial. To test the reliability of such comments on the lack of attention to the body of a child, it is vitally important to examine the archaeological evidence for wrappings and textiles in child burials, especially those of a very young age, from newborn to a few years old. This includes the physical remains of textiles and fibres, metal clothing accessories, textile impressions on gypsum and plaster or coins, as well as the skeletal evidence for textile containment of the corpse (Green 1977; Angelini *et al.* 2008). These diverse sources of information will be the main focus of the following discussion, but I also would like to explore the portraits of infants and young children on Roman funerary monuments to gain insight into the role of clothing in the construction and expression of status, citizenship and gender in this age group of Roman society.

Textiles in child burials

In Roman art, there are few extant depictions of adult bodies prepared for burial, and even fewer of children. An interesting series of tomb paintings of the fourth century BC from Paestum preserves several images of the deceased lying in state (*expositio*), probably at home, with mourners present. The dead body, always that of a woman, is enveloped in a white shroud, leaving only the face and shoe-clad feet uncovered (Cipriani, Longo 1996, 123, 126–127, 130; Pontrandolfo, Rouveret 1996). Late Roman depictions of the final stage of burial preparation show the corpse tightly wrapped from head to toe and tied up with bands or ropes. A fourth-century image scratched into the walls of the catacomb of Commodilla in Rome, for example, is that of a *fossor*, or grave digger, standing over a dead body bound in this way and ready for interment in the catacombs, the same kind of wrapping prevalent in scenes of the raising of Lazarus (Mazzoleni 1999, 161, fig. 164; Carroll 2006, 262, fig. 76; Jensen 1995; see cover image). An exceptional archaeological discovery of wrapped corpses was made in burial chambers on the grounds of the later church of Saints Peter and Marcellinus in Rome. Here, hundreds of bodies of men, women and children, possibly linked to the garrison of the imperial bodyguard, were buried in the late second or early third century AD in plaster-covered sheets or shrouds that had been wound tightly around the body, leaving impressions of the fabric in the plaster. Residual gold threads associated with these burials suggest that the bodies might have been clothed in garments of expensive gold-shot brocade before they were undressed to be wrapped in shrouds (Blanchard *et al.* 2007, 993–994; Martorelli 2000).

Of course, in Egypt there is considerably more surviving evidence for shrouds, as in the east cemetery at Kellis, where adults, children and even foetuses were wrapped in linen shrouds bound with cords or linen bandages from the first to fifth century AD (Bowen 2003; Tocheri *et al.* 2005).

Archaeology indicates that the dead might also be buried in their clothes. At Martes-de-Veyre in the Auvergne, for example, the garments of a twenty-year-old woman buried in the second century AD were in a remarkable state of preservation. She was dressed in a sleeved tunic of brown linen with traces of blue decoration, brown linen stockings, and beige linen shoes (Audollent 1923, 285, 316–319, pls 8.1, 9.1, 10.3; see Mitschke and Schieck, this volume).

Dead children were wrapped in shrouds too, just like adults. Evidence for a shroud is provided by the (modern) plaster cast of a death mask of a ten-year-old girl named Claudia Victoria who died in Lyon about AD 100 (Dasen 2010, 125, Figs 5.4a-b; Carroll 2006, 38–39, fig. 13). An impression of her face had been made from which to fashion a portrait after her death. This mould, buried with the girl, shows that a shroud had been wrapped around her head and under her chin, leaving only her face exposed. A very recent (unpublished) discovery at Mill Mount in York, is the late Roman burial of a child between eleven and fourteen years of age, interred in a stone sarcophagus and covered by liquid gypsum that had hardened.[2] The underside of the gypsum preserved an impression of the corpse, showing that the upper part of the body, and the face, had been tightly bound in a shroud; the position of the skeleton's arms confirm this textile confinement of the corpse.

A depiction of a shroud more akin to a blanket survives in a relief scene on a marble sarcophagus of the early second century AD in Agrigento, Sicily (Fig. 1) (Amedick 1991, 73, 121, Cat. 2, pl. 53.1; George 2000, 195, fig. 3). The child in this *expositio* scene, already a few years old and mourned by his mother, father and child-carers, lies supine on his funerary bed, his body covered by a blanket pulled up to his chin. Like the adult corpses lying in state in the Paestum paintings, the contours of the body and the extended arms can be seen clearly, perhaps suggesting that the child is already wrapped for burial underneath the shroud.

Physical remains of a combination of shrouds and blankets survive at Martres-de-Veyre where the body of a girl about six years of age in a pine coffin was excavated in the nineteenth century (Audollent 1923, 285–287). No photographs were taken of this second-century burial, but the body is described as having been wrapped in a shroud of finely woven linen and lying on another layer of the same fabric, folded over several times, as if to make a thin mattress. The body was entirely covered with a fringed blanket of white wool, and at the girl's feet were boxwood branches with intact leaves. Leaves of plants could have various properties, and the physician Soranus, one of our best ancient sources on childbirth and matters pertaining to child care, recommended placing bay or myrtle leaves under a baby's mattress to keep it smelling sweet (*Gynaecology* 2.16.85). Leaves are also found in adult burials, as in London where box leaves and textile remains at the top end of a late Roman lead sarcophagus suggest that the head of the twenty-year-old female occupant rested on a bay leaf cushion (Thomas 1999).

A spectacular set of textiles and clothing are amongst the contents of a lead sarcophagus of the later third century at Naintré in western Gaul (Desrosiers 2000; Barago-Szekeres, Duday 2008). The approximately twelve-year-old child in the sarcophagus had her legs and torso wrapped in fabric, and she wore a cap or headdress. She appears also to have worn a purple and gold tunic, over which her body was completely enveloped from shoulder to feet in a tapestry

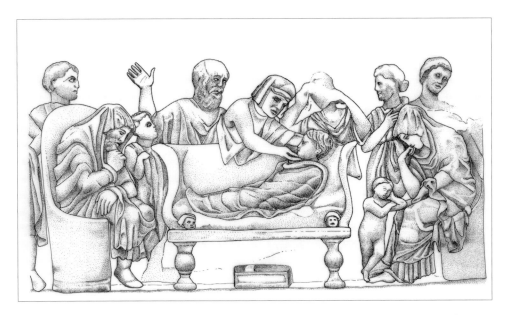

Fig. 1. A dead child is wrapped in a shroud on a sarcophagus in Agrigento, early second century AD (drawing by J. Willmott).

of purple and gold fabric 2.5 metres in width. On top of all this, several layers of damask silk covered the body, and two other items of clothing, probably tunics, were placed across the legs. It is uncertain whether the purple and silk fabric might have come from Palmyra or was produced in Gaul. These textiles and garments were clearly precious and costly, and they attest to the affluence of the family and the investment of wealth in the burial of a loved child. The silk damask buried with a very young child in Kent further attests to such investment (Wild 1965, 246).

Evidence for much simpler clothing used to dress dead children survives elsewhere. At Bourges in central Gaul, for example, the body of a young boy between two and three years of age was buried in the third century AD, and survived in a mummified state, in a simple wool tunic with sleeves (Roche-Bernard 1993, 8–9; Coulon 2004, 122–123, 165–166). This garment is the most common one shown in depictions of children on Gallo-Roman tombstones. The tunic worn by the boy in Bourges was made to measure, the dullness of the monochrome garment being alleviated by two green vertical stripes from shoulder to the knee-length hem that were painted on, rather than woven into, the fabric.

The wrapped and swaddled infant in life and death

From birth, Roman children were wrapped in swaddling clothes, and they remained so for the first 40–60 days of their lives, or even slightly longer. The following excerpt from the *Gynaecology* (2.14.83) of Soranus contains instructions on how to swaddle an infant:

> The midwife ... must take soft woollen bandages which are clean and not too worn out, some of them three fingers in breadth, others four fingers. 'Woollen', because of the smoothness of the material and because linen ones shrink from the sweat; 'soft', so as not to cause bruises when covering the body which is still delicate; 'clean', so that they may be light and not heavy, nor of evil smell, nor irritate the surface by containing natron; and 'not too worn out': for whereas new ones are heavy, worn out ones are too cold, and sometimes rough as well and very easily torn. They must have neither hems nor selvages, otherwise they cut or compress unevenly. [After wrapping the legs separately, the midwife] should lay the arms along the sides and the feet one against the other, and with a broad bandage she should wrap up the whole infant circularly from the thorax to the feet ... the little head should be covered by bandaging it circularly with a soft clean cloth or piece of wool.

The broad bandage referred to here is held and unrolled by one of the triad of mother goddesses in Gallo-Roman statuettes; the second holds a swaddled infant and the third holds a jug of water with which to wash the baby (Fig. 2) (Coulon 2004, fig. p. 67; Dasen 2009, 214, fig. 9). Daily care of the newborn child was a labour-intensive procedure. Each day the baby was unwrapped, washed, massaged and oiled, and then re-wrapped from head to toe. After being 'imprisoned' in swaddling bands 'to the very tips of the toes' for up to sixty days or longer, the child, was gradually freed, one hand and one foot at a time, with several days in between each step (*Gynaecology*, 2.15.84, 2.42.111).

We have abundant evidence for the appearance of swaddling clothes, primarily from Italian votive terracottas of the third to first centuries BC (Fig. 3). These life-size figures, deposited in

Fig. 2. The middle mother goddess on a stone relief from Bibracte unrolls a broad bandage used to swaddle infants (drawing by J. Willmott).

the sanctuaries of deities such as Mater Matuta and Juno, are a visible reminder of the personal and emotional investment in the conception, birth and well-being of children and the need to seek divine assistance for their survival (Baggieri, Rinaldi Veloccia 1996; De Casanove 2008). Votive dedications of swaddled children carved in limestone and deposited in healing shrines are also fairly popular in Roman Gaul where they might even be depicted resting and firmly wrapped in a cradle (Fig. 4) (Deyts 2004, 227–235; Coulon 2004, 49–50). In all cases, cloth bands are wrapped either horizontally or diagonally around the baby's whole body, and the head is also enclosed in a cap-like cloth. Even children this young sometimes wear a necklace strung with apotropaic amulets or with a *bulla*, the disc-shaped locket acting as a protective device and a symbol of Roman citizenship for pre-pubescent boys (Fig. 3).

If so much effort was made to clean and protect the newborn in the first months of its life, was there also an effort made to wrap and swaddle the child if it unfortunately died at this early stage? Roman written sources would have us believe that very young children were regarded as not worthy of the usual funerary rites. According to the jurist Ulpian (*FIRA* 2, 536): 'children younger than three are not formally mourned, but are mourned in marginal form; a child less than a year receives neither formal mourning nor marginal mourning'. Plutarch (*Numa* 12) tells us that the early Roman king Numa 'regulated the periods of mourning... Over a child of less than three years there was to be no mourning at all; over one older than that, the mourning was not to last more months than it had lived years, up to ten'. Regulations such as these, however, relate to the manifestation of funerary ritual in public which may have nothing to do with sentiments of grief and loss expressed, or activities conducted, in private. The archaeological evidence for the burial of infants offers a better chance to explore the physical treatment of children this young and to explore what role textiles and clothing might have played in final gestures of familial care in mortuary ritual.

This evidence is varied. Plaster or gypsum occasionally has preserved the impression of infants wrapped in textiles. A remarkable find is a late Roman sandstone sarcophagus from York in which the occupants were deposited and covered with gypsum (Henshall 1962). The impressions in the plaster indicate that three adult bodies had been wrapped in textiles, and it

Fig. 3. Terracotta and limestone votive figures in the form of swaddled infants, from various sanctuaries in Satricum and Tarquinia in Italy and Mt Auxois in Gaul (drawing by J. Willmott).

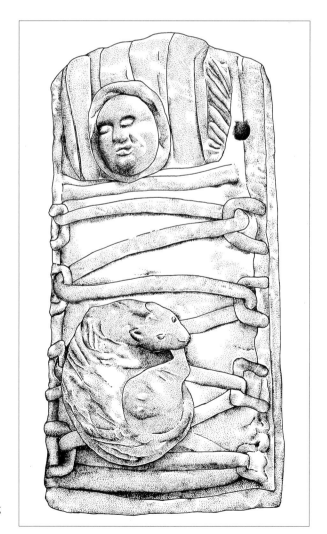

Fig. 4. The infant in this stone votive figure from Nuits St George is wrapped tightly in his cradle (drawing by J. Willmott).

is particularly clear that the sarcophagus contained a swaddled infant placed between the legs of one of them, possibly its mother who died after having given birth (pl. 21). This baby had been wrapped in bandages that encircled its body, head (and possibly face), legs and feet. Also surviving in late Roman Trier, as a result of a similar process of pouring gypsum or spreading lime on bodies in sarcophagi, is the negative form of a small child (Cüppers 1984, 212). As a plaster cast of this form showed, the infant was tightly and completely wrapped in diagonally wound bands from head to toe, and its face was also enveloped in fabric.

Plaster preserved the face of a baby only a few months old in another late Roman burial in Paris, but this was an intentional product of the practice of taking a mould in order to produce a portrait in another material such as stone or bronze (Dasen 2010, 131–133, figs 5, 8a-b; Carroll 2010, 68–69, fig. 4.2). A cast having been made of the mould, the negative plaster form was then buried with the child. The baby's head was wrapped around the face and under the chin, much as it is in depictions of swaddled infants held by mother goddesses or depicted in votive statuettes.

There is also indirect evidence for the use of swaddling when an infant was buried. One of the features of the stone figurines of swaddled infants from Roman Gaul, for example, is the use of a ring placed centrally on the child's chest through which ropes or cords are drawn to hold the bandages in place and increase the immobility of the baby (Fig. 3). Just such a ring, made of iron, was excavated among the contents of an inhumation burial of an infant at Argenton in central Gaul, the ring providing evidence for the use of swaddling clothes, even though no textile fragments had survived (Allain *et al.* 1992, 95, fig. 27; Dasen 2003, 202–203). Furthermore, the positioning of the limbs of a skeleton parallel to the body might be evidence for the child having been buried in swaddling bands. One of the thirteen infants buried under the floor of a Roman pottery workshop at Sallèles d'Aude was probably interred in this way, and another infant three to four months old, likely just past the age of being swaddled, might have been wrapped in a shroud or sheet, the fibula found at the shoulder perhaps indicating that it was fixed with this brooch (Duday 2009, 63–69). The use of shrouds for children closer to the age of one year, and therefore too old to be swaddled, may be recognised by the inclusion of bone pins in the burial goods. At Vagnari in Puglia, for example, a child nine to twelve months old was in possession of such a pin that could have held the shroud together (Small and Small 2007, 195, fig. 36). In children's graves elsewhere in Roman Italy, bone and bronze pins found at the level of the knee or ankle may also be indicative of shrouds (Cipollone 2000, 202, fig. 198).

One burial of the second third of the second century AD in Britain, in particular, allows us to seriously question the veracity of Plutarch's statement that children who died in infancy were not laid out with special care. In this grave on Ermine Street near the Roman posting-station at Arrington Bridge, a costly lead sarcophagus contained the body of a child of ten to eleven months old, suffering from hydrocephalus; the child was buried in woollen wrappings dyed with madder and indigo (Taylor 1993, 203–204). Perhaps these colours were chosen specifically for their protective qualities regarding young life, as Quintilian (*Institutes of Oratory* 11.1.31) wrote that purple and red were not suitable for the elderly (Sebesta 1994, 47). So much for the lack of care in burying infants, even physically handicapped ones, under the age of one!

The clothed child on Roman funerary monuments

It is extremely rare to find an infant portrayed, on its own, as the prime focus of a grave *stele*, and this rarity is a vivid reflection of the importance of children, whose portraits were commissioned, to their families. Although babies can be depicted naked, as in the case of the infant daughters of Telesphoris in Mainz, they also can be shown wrapped in swaddling clothes (Selzer 1988, 177–178, Cat. No. 126–127; Carroll 2006, 169–170, figs 56–57). On a gravestone commemorating the infant Aeliola from Metz, the child is shown wrapped in criss-crossing bands with her face visible (Coulon 2004, 46, fig. on p. 45; Dasen 2009, 206, fig. 6). Another baby from Chauvigny in western Gaul appears on its gravestone to wear a tunic-like undergarment reaching to and flaring out at its feet, the tunic, and the child's limbs, being held in place by rather coarse ropes that are intertwined across the torso (Deyts 2004, 236, fig. 9; Coulon 2004, 47, fig. on p. 46).

Tiny infants also are sometimes depicted on gravestones with their mothers, the motif possibly having been chosen to commemorate women who died giving birth to a child or shortly thereafter (Gourévitch 1987; Carroll 2006, 153–154). The eighteen-year-old Scaevina Procilla from Ravenna, for example, is commemorated by her parents rather than her husband, and she is shown as a young woman gazing at a swaddled infant in her arms (Mansuelli 1967, 143–144, fig. 48). Flavia Aiulo from Aquincum on the Danube, only twenty years old, holds an infant wrapped from head to toe in her arms on her grave *stele* of the late first or early second century AD (pl. 22) (*CIL* III, 14352). There is no mention of the child (or the father) in the inscription; we learn only that baby's mother was commemorated by her brother and cousin. Further poignant examples of mothers and tiny babies in the clothing appropriate for such young children are known from a number of Roman sites such as Poitiers, Metz and Cologne, the swaddling bands actually highlighting the extreme youth and vulnerability of the child, as well as increasing the pathos evoked by its untimely demise (Coulon 2004, figs pp. 66, 157; Carroll 2006, 6, 154, fig. 3). The tightly wrapped child becomes a symbol of tragic, early death in Roman funerary commemoration.

Older children are far more prominent in Roman funerary imagery (Huskinson 1996; Rawson 1997; Rawson 2003a, 17–94; Diddle-Uzzi 2005). What they wear in their funerary portraits can be informative about status, citizenship and gender, their clothing also revealing parental and social expectations of the young. The marble sarcophagus of Cornelius Statius from Ostia is a so-called biographical sarcophagus, decorated with relief scenes of the boy at various stages of his short life (Amedick 1991, 140, Cat. 114.4, pl. 53; George 2000, 192, fig. 2; Rawson 2003a, 106, fig. 2.2). In each of these stages, attention is paid to the changing clothing appropriate for the developing child. When, as an infant, he is being breastfed by his mother, he seems already partly released from the swaddling bands he wears; sitting on his father's shoulder as a toddler he is clothed in a short tunic; and later, when standing and reciting what he has learned, he is dressed in the *toga praetexta*, the garment worn by freeborn citizen boys who had not yet come of age (Fig. 5).

For the offspring of freedmen and for children who were free born and, therefore, Roman citizens from birth, the display of particular clothing and accessories as clear symbols of citizenship and legal status is extremely important in funerary art. Freeborn sons of freedmen parents can be conspicuously dressed in the badges of civic honour which had been inaccessible to their fathers in their own servile childhood. On a relief from the family tomb of the Servilii

Fig. 5. Cornelius Statius is shown in various stages of his childhood on this sarcophagus of the mid-second century AD from Ostia (drawing by J. Willmott).

in Rome, for example, the freedman father Q. Servilius Hilarus wears the toga (Stone 1994; Davis 2005) that he is entitled to after his manumission as an adult, but his young son P. Servilius Globulus, born free after the manumission of his parents, had every right to wear this garment from birth (Fig. 6) (Rawson 1997, 211–212, fig. 9.1; Rawson 2003a, 29–31, fig. 1.5). His portrait, highlighting the toga and the *bulla* or locket on a strap around his neck, also occupies the extreme left of the relief and is separated from the portraits of his parents by a pilaster, as if to further stress the fact that the child is special and privileged in status.

Girls, too, could be depicted wearing the toga until they reached maturity. The freedwoman mother on a high relief panel in Rome is seen in the *pudicitia* pose and heavily clad in layered garments to symbolise wifely chastity and piety, like a good free-born Roman matron (George 2001). As a slave, she would not have been entitled to wear a toga when she was a child, but her free-born daughter is formally dressed in the *toga praetexta*. The daughter embodies her parents' accomplishments and change in legal and social status, but she also acted as a symbol for a greater future and upward social mobility. Her toga was worn explicitly as a childhood item of clothing; it was intended that, once in her teens, she would exchange her age-specific attire for the *stola* and *palla* of the adult and married women to dress like her mother (Sebesta 1998; Olson 2008).

Even if the child was a slave and of the lowest social status, the commemorator of that child might 'improve' reality and have it depicted as a Roman citizen in death. A funerary altar of the early second century AD in Rome is a most appropriate monument to consider here, especially since it commemorates children under the age of one (those supposedly not mourned at all) and just a bit older than one (those supposedly only marginally mourned). In the funerary portraits decorating this altar, Nico, the son of Publicia Glypte, may be free-born, but the other little boy Eutyches, the house-born slave of Publicia Glypte, is not, as the inscription makes clear, yet both boys wear the *toga praetexta* (Fig. 7) (Rawson 2003b, 286–288, fig. 2). This perhaps is an indication of what had been the woman's intention: to free Eutyches and raise him as a citizen and brother to Nico. In this instance, the Roman child clothed in death conveyed clear messages about status and citizenship.

Ethnicity, gender and age roles also can be articulated through children's clothing and dress in funerary art. On the Danube frontier in the territory of the Celtic Eravisci in Pannonia, women from the first to third centuries AD, are often depicted in their ethnic costume

Fig. 6. The young Publius Servilius Globulus, free-born son of a former slave, wears the toga and *bulla* to advertise his status as a Roman citizen on this family funerary relief of the late first century BC from Rome (drawing by J. Willmott).

Fig. 7. Two little boys, a son and a slave of Publicia Glypte, wear the *toga praetexta,* on this funerary altar of the second century AD in Rome (drawing by J. Willmott).

consisting of a long-sleeved tunic and a pinafore, worn with large shoulder fibulae, neck rings and bracelets, as well as a headdress of turban and veil (Lang 1919; Facsády 2001). Sometimes these women are accompanied by their daughters who dress in the same costume, but a simpler version of it. Magio, a non-Roman citizen man in Budapest, for example, set up a stone in the first half of the second century AD with funerary portraits of his twenty-five-year-old wife Brogimara and his daughter Iantuna who lived for only two years (pl. 23) (Schober 1923, Cat. No. 277; *CIL* III.3594). Unlike her mother, who wears a headdress, the little girl is bare-headed. Images such as these make it clear that ethnic costume and traditional dress were handed down maternally, with youthfulness and maturity being recognisable in slight differences in attire, particularly in the type (or lack) of headdresses. Boys' clothing could also reflect gendered behaviour. Vitalus, a boy who died at the age of three years, eleven months and eighteen days in Aquincum in the late second or early third century, is depicted in emulation of his father, an officer of Legio II Adiutrix, in a short tunic, a military belt, and the cloak, or *sagum*, that formed a typical and recognisable part of the Roman soldier's attire (Schober 1923, Cat. No. 158; *CIL* III.15159). The boy was obviously too young to have served in the Roman army, but his clothing symbolised a masculine career, even if, in this case, only a virtual one.

Conclusions

The evidence for the clothed child in the context of burial and commemoration is of importance in exploring Roman attitudes towards childhood and the role of children in the family and society. This study has focused on the archaeological, visual and textual evidence for the role that clothing and textiles played in the burial of infants and children, particularly in the expression of social belonging and identity. Ancient written sources might give the impression that the Romans invested little effort in the burial of the youngest children, but the archaeological evidence from Italy and the European provinces indicates that special care often was taken to bury them in clothing appropriate to their ages, and to wrap them with shrouds and coverlets of different materials. Even babies could be interred in the swaddling clothes they wore during the first forty to sixty days of their brief lives. Furthermore, dead children sometimes were portrayed on funerary monuments in various types of dress and bodily adornment, their clothing being a reflection of status, gender, ethnicity and citizenship. When untimely death robbed a child of a future, the funerary portrait of the clothed child could function as a vehicle to express the family's wishes and aspirations for upward social mobility, projected careers and acceptable familial roles.

p.m.carroll@sheffield.ac.uk

Acknowledgement

I should like to thank Jerneja Willmott for the beautifully drawn illustrations, and the Hungarian National Museum in Budapest for permission to reproduce photos taken in the museum. I am grateful to the EU-funded project *Clothing and Identities. New Perspectives on Textiles in the Roman Empire (DressID)*, of which the University of Sheffield is a co-beneficiary, for the financial support for travel to European museums.

Notes

1. http://www.nytimes.com/2009/05/24/health/24birth.html?_r=1; http://www.nytimes.com/packages/html/world/2009-maternalmortality/index.html
2. http://www.archaeologicalplanningconsultancy.co.uk/blog/

Bibliography

Allain *et al.* 1992: J. Allain, I. Fauduet, M. Tuffrau-Libre, *La nécropole gallo-romaine du Champ de l'Image à Argentomagus (St-Marcel, Indre)*, Saint-Marcel

Amedick 1991: R. Amedick, *Die antiken Sarkophagreliefs. Die Sarkophage mit den Bildern aus dem Menschenleben: Vita Privata*, Berlin

Angelini *et al.* 2008: M. Angelini, G. Bandini, O. Colacicchi, J. Polakova and I. A. Rapinesi, 'Il recupero di oggetti mobili da ambiti funerari di età romano-imperiale', in J. Scheid (ed.), *Pour une Archéologie du Rite. Nouvelles Perspectives de l'Archéologie Funéraire*, Rome, 305–336

Audollent 1923: A. Audollent, 'Les tombes gallo-romaines à inhumation des Martres-de-Veyre (Puy-de-Dôme)', *Mémoires présentés à l'Académie des Inscriptions et Belles-Lettres* 13.1, 275–328

Baggieri, Rinaldi Veloccia 1996: G. Baggieri and M. L. Rinaldi Veloccia (eds), *Speranza e Sofferenza. Nei votivi anatomici dell'Antichità*, Rome

Baltussen 2009: H. Baltussen, 'Personal Grief and Public Mourning in Plutarch's *Consolation to his Wife*', *American Journal of Philology* 130, 67–98

Barago-Szekeres, Duday 2008: B. Barago-Szekeres and H. Duday, 'Les tombes fastueuses de Naintré', *Dossiers d'Archéologie* 330, 120–127

Blanchard *et al.* 2007: P. Blanchard, D. Castex, M. Coquerelle, R. Giuliani and M. Ricciardi, 'A Mass Grave from the Catacomb of Saints Peter and Marcellinus in Rome, Second-Third Century AD', *Antiquity* 81, 989–998

Bowen 2003: G. E. Bowen, 'Some Observations on Christian Burial Practices at Kellis', in G. E. Bowen and C. A. Hope (eds), *The Oasis Papers III: Proceedings of the Third International Conference of the Dakhleh Oasis Project*, Oxford, 167–179

Carroll 2011: M. Carroll, 'Infant Death and Burial in Roman Italy', *Journal of Roman Archaeology* 24, 99–120

Carroll 2010: M. Carroll, '*Memoria* and *Damnatio Memoriae*. Preserving and Erasing Identities in Roman Funerary Commemoration', in M. Carroll and J. Rempel (eds), *Living through the Dead. Burial and Commemoration in the Classical World*, Oxford, 65–90

Carroll 2006: M. Carroll, *Spirits of the Dead. Roman Funerary Commemoration in Western Europe*, Oxford

CIL: Corpus Inscriptionum Latinarum, Berlin, 1963

Cipollone 2000: M. Cipollone, 'Gubbio (Perugia). Necropoli in loc. Vittorina. Campagne di scavo 1980–1982', *Notizie degli Scavi* (Serie 9) 11, 5–372

Cipriani, Longo 1996: M. Cipriani and F. Longo (eds), *Poseidonia e i Lucani. I Greci in Occidente*, Naples

Coulon 2004: G. Coulon, *L'enfant en Gaule romaine*, Paris

Cüppers 1984: H. Cüppers, *Trier. Kaiserresidenz und Bischofssitz. Die Stadt in spätantiker und frühchristlicher Zeit*, Mainz

Dasen 2010: V. Dasen, 'Wax and Plaster Memories: Children in Elite and non-Elite Strategies', in V. Dasen and T. Späth (eds), *Children, Memory, and Family Identity in Roman Culture*, Oxford, 109–146

Dasen 2009: V. Dasen, 'Roman Birth Rites of Passage Revisited', *Journal of Roman Archaeology* 22, 198–214

Dasen 2003: V. Dasen, 'L'enfant malade', in D. Gourévitch, A. Moirin and N. Rouquet (eds), *Maternité de petite enfance dans l'Antiquité romaine*, Bourges, 178–217

Davies 2005: G. Davies, 'What made the Roman Toga *Virilis*?', in L. Cleland, M. Harlow and L. Llewellyn-Jones (eds), *The Clothed Body in the Ancient World*, Oxford, 121–130

De Casanove 2008: O. De Casanove, 'Enfants en langes: pour quels voeux?', in G. Greco and B. Ferrara (eds), *Doni agli dei. Il sistema dei doni votivi nei santuari*, Pozzuoli, 271–289

Desrosiers 2000: S. Desrosiers, 'Textiles découverts dans les deux tombes du Bas-Empire à Naintré (Vienne)', in D. Cardon and M. Feugère (eds), *Archéologie des Textiles des Origines au Ve Siècle: Actes du Colloque de Lattes, Oct. 1999*, Montagnac, 195–207

Deyts 2004: S. Deyts, 'La femme et l'enfant au maillot en Gaule. Iconographie et épigraphie', in V. Dasen (ed.), *Naissance et petite enfance dans l'Antiquité. Actes du colloque de Fribourg, 28 novembre – 1er décembre 2001*, Fribourg, 227–237

Diddle Uzzi 2005: J. Diddle Uzzi, *Children in the Visual Arts of Imperial Rome*, New York

Duday 2009: H. Duday, *The Archaeology of the Dead. Lectures in Archaeothanatology*, Oxford

Facsády 2001: A. R. Facsády, 'La parure et le costume traditionnels', *Romains de Hongrie, Ier-Ve siècles après J.-C.*, Lyon, 42–47

FIRA: *Fontes Iuris Romani Anteiustiniani*, Florence, 1940–1943

George 2001: M. George, 'A Roman Funerary Monument with a Mother and Daughter', in S. Dixon (ed.), *Childhood, Class and Kin in the Roman World*. London, 178–189

George 2000: M. George, 'Family and *Familia* on Roman Biographical Sarcophagi', *Römische Mitteilungen* 107, 191–202

Gourévitch 1987: D. Gourévitch, 'La mort de la femme en couches et dans les suites de couches', in F. Hinard (ed.), *La mort, les morts et l'au-delà dans le monde romain. Actes du Colloque de Caen 1985*, Caen, 187–193

Green 1977: C. J. S. Green, 'The Significance of Plaster Burials for the Recognition of Christian Cemeteries', in R. Reece (ed.), *Burial in the Roman World*, York, 46–52

Henshall 1962: A. S. Henshall, 'Cloths in Burials with Gypsum', *An Inventory of the Historical Monuments in the City of York 1: Eburacum, Roman York*, London, 108–109

Huskinson 1996: J. Huskinson, *Roman Children's Sarcophagi: Their Decoration and its Social Significance*, Oxford

Jensen 1995: R. M. Jensen, 'Raising Lazarus', *Bible Review* 11.2, 20–29

Lang 1919: M. Lang, 'Die pannonische Frauentracht', *Jahreshefte des Österreichischen Archäologischen Institutes* 19, 209–260

Mansuelli 1967: G. A. Mansuelli, *Le stele romane del territorio ravennate e del Basso Po*, Ravenna

Martorelli 2000: R. Martorelli, 'Clothing in Burial Practice in Italy in the Early Christian Period', in J. Pearce, M. Millett and M. Struck (eds), *Burial, Society and Context in the Roman World*, Oxford, 244–248

Mazzoleni 1999: D. Mazzoleni, 'Inscriptions in Roman Catacombs', in V. Fiocchi Nicolai, F. Bisconti and D. Mazzoleni (eds), *The Christian Catacombs of Rome. History, Decoration, Inscriptions*, Regensburg, 147–185

Olson 2008: K. Olson, *Dress and the Roman Woman. Self-presentation and Society*, London

Pontrandolfo, Rouveret 1996: A. Pontrandolfo and A. Rouveret, 'Le necropoli urbane e il fenomeno delle tombe dipinte', in Cipriani and Longo, 159–183

Rawson 2003a: B. Rawson, *Children and Childhood in Roman Italy*, Oxford

Rawson 2003b: B. Rawson, 'Death, Burial and Commemoration of Children in Roman Italy', in D. L. Balach and C. Osiek (eds), *Early Christian Families in Context*, Grand Rapids, 277–297

Rawson 1997: B. Rawson, 'The Iconography of Roman Childhood', in B. Rawson and P. Weaver (eds), *The Roman Family in Italy. Status, Sentiment, Space*, Oxford, 205–232

Roche-Bernard 1993: G. Roche-Bernard, *Costumes et Textiles en Gaule Romaine*, Paris

Schober 1923: A. Schober, *Die römischen Grabsteine von Noricum und Pannonien*, Vienna

Sebesta 1998: J. L. Sebesta, 'Women's Costume and Feminine Civic Morality in Augustan Rome', in M. Wyke (ed.), *Gender and the Body in the Ancient Mediterranean*, Oxford, 105–117

Sebesta 1994: J. L. Sebesta, 'Symbolism in the Costume of the Roman woman', in Sebesta and Bonfante, 46–53

Sebesta and Bonfante 1994: J. L. Sebesta and L. Bonfante, *The World of Roman Costume*, Madison

Selzer 1988: W. Selzer, *Römische Steindenkmäler. Mainz in römischer Zeit*, Mainz

Small and Small 2002: A. M. Small and C. M. Small, 'Excavations in the Roman Cemetery at Vagnari in the Territory of Gravina, Puglia, 2002', *Papers of the British School at Rome* 75, 123–229

Stone 1994: S. Stone, 'The Toga: from National Costume to Ceremonial Costume', in Sebesta and Bonfante, 13–45

Taylor 1993: A. Taylor, 'A Roman Lead Coffin with Pipeclay Figurines from Arrington, Cambridgeshire', *Britannia* 24, 191–225

Thomas 1999: C. Thomas, 'Laid to Rest on Pillow of Bay Leaves', *British Archaeology* 50, 8–11

Tocheri *et al.* 2005: M. W. Tocheri, T. L. Dupras, P. Sheldrick and E. Molto, 'Roman Period Fetal Skeletons from Kellis, Egypt', *International Journal of Osteoarchaeology* 15.5, 326–341

Wild 1965: J. P. Wild, 'A Roman Silk Damask from Kent', *Archaeologia Cantiaca* 80, 246–250

DEATH AND THE MAIDEN: REPRISING THE BURIALS OF ROMAN GIRLS AND YOUNG WOMEN

MARY HARLOW

This paper grew from a desire to combine two research strands: the Roman life course and dress, and a recognition of how far an understanding of each would enhance the other. At the time of the *Dressing the Dead* conference in May 2010, Ray Laurence and I had been working on Roman betrothal and the role it played in the life courses of all of those involved in the process: the bride and groom to be, the parents of both families and the wider social group (Harlow, Laurence 2010). Life course studies examine ways in which attitudes to age, ageing and expectations of age-related behaviour, underpin ideas of how society might work and how social groups interact. Age can be defined simply chronologically, in years lived, but also in biological, social and cultural ways. These are not necessarily the same. Society can use chronological age to define parameters of behaviour such as the age of majority, the age of criminal responsibility, or more relevant here, the age of marriage. Social and cultural rites of passage, moving from one stage of life to another, demonstrate moments a society deems worthy of marking publicly. In 'Betrothal, mid-late childhood and the life course', Ray Laurence and I argued, among other things, that for a young girl, betrothal formed part of the extended transition to womanhood, a rite of passage that moved her towards marriage and motherhood, and which marked her eventual translation into full social adulthood. It is, however, very difficult to get any sense of the process from the point of view of the young girl herself. The dress and accessories of the later stages of a young woman's life – her bridal outfit and the traditional dress of the citizen wife – have been discussed by several scholars (see for example, Hersch 2010; La Follette 1994, 54–64; Olsen 2008, 21–42). A series of young female burials have been identified by various scholars as particularly marking out unmarried status (Bordenache Battaglia 1983; Martin-Kilcher 2000); this chapter picks up on that research and focuses on the adornment of a young girl on the occasion of the *sponsalia* (celebration day of betrothal) – a moment that is arguably best displayed by, and known from, the burials of those young women who never achieved the next transition to adulthood through marriage.

A (first) betrothal for young Roman girls tended to take place sometime during their childhood. Marriage was legal after the age of twelve for girls and fourteen for boys, but the work of Saller and Shaw has shown the more likely age of first marriage for young girls was the late teens (Saller, Shaw 1984; *Digest* 23.1.14; 32.2.4.). After Augustus, marriage had to take place within two years of betrothal, which meant that the minimum age for an engagement was officially the age of ten (although there is evidence that betrothals continued to be made at an earlier age: *Digest* 23.1.14; Fayer 2005, 74–87). Much of the information we have about betrothal comes from legal texts, most of which date to the latter part of the second century AD or later. As we might expect, the picture that emerges from the legal texts gives practically no impression of how the young girl might receive the news that she is to be betrothed, or if she was consulted in the choice of partner. A daughter did have to consent to her parent's choice of partner, but silence is deemed to mean acceptance (*Digest* 23.1.1, 4, 11, 12). The young girl's role in the whole process was relatively minimal and to us she remains a cipher. Legal texts stress the dominance of the role of the *paterfamilias* in arranging the match through the advice and negotiations of his family and friends, in developing an association with the potential son-in-law (and his father, if still alive), and in organising the dowry. While there is evidence that mothers and other female members of the family also played an active part in the choice of partner, betrothal often appears as a purely business arrangement between men. This dominance of the older generation and the nature of the sources converge to make the young girl, who is the centre of negotiations, virtually invisible. Yet, betrothal was clearly a major change in her social status, even if she was very young; it marked her out as 'spoken for.' For her parents, or more probably her father, it meant the cementing of a relationship with the groom-to-be and his family, and, as such, it had public (and often political) implications. The impact on the girl herself was part of the private domestic world but it can be deemed a social rite of passage, it signalled the coming end of childhood in a future marriage. Her future would be mapped out in a concrete way (for discussion of the legal aspects of betrothal see Fayer 2005; Treggiari 1991, 83–160; and for life course approach Harlow, Laurence 2010).

A major difference between betrothal and marriage in the Roman world was that betrothal was characterised by gift giving, a practise that was forbidden in marriage (*Digest* 24.1.1, 3, 27, 32.27; Treggiari 1991, 152–153). On marriage, the groom (or his father) received a dowry from his new wife's family and, before the marriage, it appears customary for him to give some gifts to his bride-to-be to mark the engagement. Such gifts could include property, land, livestock or slaves, but jewellery, including finger rings, was more common (*Digest* 24.1.36.1). Finger rings featuring images of hands joined in the *dextarum iunctio* gesture, or figures of couples facing each other in full body or profiled heads, and/or featuring *concordia* (*homonia* in Greek), are known throughout the Roman empire, from Britain, Gaul, Italy and the Balkans (for examples see Marshall 1907, nos. 272, 275–277, 423, 514, 541, 561, 1181; for Britain, see Johns 1996, 62–65; for the Rhineland, see Henzel 1913; Henig and MacGregor 2004, 113, 114–115; for the Balkans, see Ruseva-Slokoska 1991, cat. nos. 168, 217). For Tertullian, in second-century AD North Africa, this ring, the *annulus pronubus* was made of gold (*Apologia* 6.4). Pliny the Elder noted that women in his time were still sent iron rings as engagement presents (*Natural History* 33.12). These are the only clear literary references to betrothal rings in the Roman period (Treggiari 1991, 149). This does not mean that such rings were not given (the quantity of finds seems to belie that idea), but they cannot all be certainly identified as betrothal rings. The acknowledgement that gift giving from the groom-to-be (*sponsus*) to the bride-to-be (*sponsa*) was customary, suggests that rings were part of the panoply of presents, but they may not have been particular signifiers of betrothal (Fayer 2005, 69; 102–120). In the late fourth-century *Historia Augusta*, we find a list of gifts given by Toxotius to Junia Fadilla: 'a necklace of nine pearls, a net-work cap [*reticulum*] with eleven emeralds; a bracelet with a row of four sapphires and besides these, gowns worked with gold, all of them royal, and other betrothal pledges [*insignia sponsaliorum*]' (SHA *Maximi duo* 27; Fayer 2005, 103). Note, there are no rings specifically identified in this list. Furthermore, in the context of arguments offered below we should note that the *Digest* (39.5.1) makes the point that gifts could come in two forms, and this applies specifically to *insignia sponsaliorum:* gifts made from affection and liberality cannot be reclaimed, but if the marriage does not take place the groom could ask for their return.

In literary evidence, the young betrothed girl is almost invisible, despite the significance of the moment in her life course. However, she is arguably more visible in the archaeological record. There are a number of furnished burials found near or around Rome that have been noted by several scholars for their particularity – girls or young women buried with a number of relatively precious grave goods, mostly jewellery and what we might term female accoutrements, and dolls (e.g. Bordenache Battaglia 1983; Bedini 1995; Chioffi 1998; Martin-Kilcher 2000; Rapinesi 2004). These have been variously interpreted, and are most commonly viewed as marking out girls dying before or just after marriage – representatives of the 'non-attained wedding', to use Stefanie Martin-Kilcher's phrase (2000, 67). The rest of this paper is a reprise of this evidence, and I also suggest yet another way in which we might read it in terms of the life course of the deceased and her family.

Arguably one of the most famous of this group of graves is that of Creperia Tryphaena uncovered in 1889 in the newly dug foundations of the Palazzo di Giustizia on the right bank of the Tiber in Rome (Lanciani 1892; Bedini 1995; Chioffi 1998, 81–84; Denzey 2007, 2–9; Martin-Kilcher 2000, 64, 69) (Fig. 1). Rodolfo Lanciani records the finding and opening of the coffin which, as it had filled with water over the years, was considered both too heavy and too destructive to its contents to move (Lanciani 1892, 265–266). There was an immediate shock for those observing the opening as trailing algae in the water gave the impression of being long brown locks of hair. Once the water dispersed, however, the body was revealed with its associated finds (for most recent images see Bertelli *et al.* 2008, 116–117).

The skull was inclined towards the left shoulder, where a carved oak doll lay on the shoulder blade. The young body was buried adorned with jewellery and accompanied with a variety of precious goods. On each side of the head were pearl drop gold earrings. There was also a gold chain with thirty-seven green jasper pendants and a brooch with amethyst intaglio, found mingled with the vertebrae of the neck. Four gold rings were found in the area of the

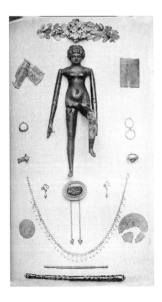

Fig. 1. The grave goods found in the coffin of Creperia Tryphaena in Rome in 1889 (from Lanciani 1892).

left hand, one of which shows the *dextrarum iunctio* (joined hands) engraved in red jasper, identified by Lanciani (1892, 266) as an engagement ring. The second had the name 'Philetus' engraved on the stone, the others were plain gold. Close to the right hip was a wooden box inlaid with bone, ivory and coloured wood. This had come apart but contained two combs, a small mirror of polished steel, a silver box (for cosmetics), an amber hair pin, an oblong piece of soft leather and some fragments of sponge (Lanciani 1892, 266). And, to quote Lanciani, 'the most impressive discovery was made after the removal of the water and the drying of the coffin. The woman had been buried in a shroud of fine white linen, pieces of which were still encrusted and cemented against the bottom and sides of the case, and she had been laid with a wreath of myrtle fastened with a silver clasp about the forehead. The preservation of the leaves is truly remarkable' (Lanciani 1892, 267).

Lanciani interpreted the finds thus: at the time of her death Tryphaena was on the eve of her marriage. The *dextrarum inctio* ring is read as a betrothal ring with the Philetus ring suggested to name her fiancé. Lanciani (1892, 268) believed that she was buried in her 'full bridal costume and then covered with the linen shroud because there are fragments of clothes of various textures and qualities mixed in with those of the white linen', and the myrtle wreath, which he claims is part of the traditional bridal dress. He also suggests that the presence of the doll supports this assumption, as dolls would not be present in the graves of married women (see below). While this emotive interpretation is seductive, it is also problematic. Creperia Tryphena's body showed clear signs of deformity in the ribs, identified as scrofula, which may not have made her an attractive marriage partner. As regards the myrtle wreath, we know from literary sources that the bridal crown was usually made of flowers, *verbenae* (leafy twigs from aromatic shrubs) and herbs which, according to Festus (56.1.L), the bride picked herself (but he would also have every bride weaving her own *tunica recta* as well). The crown is certainly meant to be sweet smelling. Catullus mentions flowers associated with Venus, so we may also assume it has associations of fertility (Catullus 61. 6–7 cited in La Follette 1994, 56). More recently Martin-Kilcher (2000, 69) has identified them as box leaves and associated them with the underworld, which rather changes the dynamic of the interpretation.

The case of Tryphaena is exceptionally well documented, but she is not the only example of such burials. Others have been found around Rome and the empire, all with jewellery, some with dolls, but very few with surviving clothing (see Table 7.1 in Martin-Kilcher 2000, 64; Rinaldi 1956). Unfortunately, many of these were discovered at a time when conservation techniques were either not available or simply not used effectively. For instance, at Mentana in 1954, a sarcophagus was uncovered full of water, but inside could be seen the corpse of a very young woman wearing a white tunic with a gold embroidered band. There was a necklace of granite around the neck and a gold ring on the finger with a crystal surface, under which one could see a gold depiction of the Capitoline wolf feeding Romulus and Remus. Unfortunately, the water was removed and both the corpse and most of the tunic disintegrated before being conserved, with only a few pieces of the gold thread being saved (Bordenache Battaglia 1983, 40–48; Chioffi 1998, 87–88). Another discovery, now displayed in the Museo Nazionale Palazzo Massimo, is from Tomb 2 from Vallerano (on the Via Laurentina beyond E.U.R), a large cemetery dating to the middle imperial period, excavated in the early 1990s. This grave contained the body of a young woman aged about sixteen or seventeen, as the bone analysis revealed. With the body were found traces of a gold hair net (see below), six rings, including one of sapphire and gold, two necklaces, three brooches (one of gold and amethyst), a pair of armbands, a silver mirror, a silver compact in the shape of a scallop shell, and an ivory doll (pl. 24, Fig. 2). Gold thread and beads, which were originally thought to have decorated her dress, were also found (Bedini 1995, figures 7.1–8; Oliver 2000, 115–116; Rapinesi 2004, 36–39).

The burial of another young woman, aged by dentition to about twenty, was uncovered by chance at Vetralla in 1887. The finds had been somewhat dispersed around collections in Rome, but over time were reclaimed as part of a single collection. This assemblage is extensive and is now said to include a range of objects: the remains of a hair net of gold thread; two necklaces of gold and emeralds; one gold ring; a further ring of pearls and gold with two emerald squares; decorated bone or ivory pins; fine pins of gold; a gold needle; various amber figures, including a hooded figure and shells; little tubes; eight little spatulas; spindles; a rock crystal bowl (*skyphos*) and perfume vase; a small glass vase; a miniature cameo; six white glass paste studs with putti heads stamped on them; a miniature ointment flask with a long neck; miniature perfume blasks (*bombylios*); ivory spindles; and two little wooden boxes with silver fixings (Bordenache Battaglia 1983, 49–78).

Another furnished burial, but of unknown provenance, is recorded by Bordenache Battaglia (1983, 79–90; see also Chioffi 1998, 44–47). This is a female grave that contained two gold rings, or possibly three, according to the correspondence of Ficorini in 1732 (Bordenache Battaglia 1983, 85), a silver vase and glass perfume bottles. It also contained seven ounces of tangled gold thread, which was originally interpreted as being a veil decorated with gold thread, but more recently has been identified as a hair net (*reticulum*) (Chioffi 1998, 44–46).

While this is not meant to be a comprehensive list of young girls' graves and their contents, three other well documented examples should also be included. At Tivoli, the tomb of a woman identified as the Vestal Cossinia, was excavated in 1929. In this was found an ivory doll that had traces of decoration, including tiny gold bracelets and a gold necklace. In the first interpretations, this doll was deemed symbolic of the continued virginal innocence of Cossinia, who, according to the inscription, died aged 60 (Bordenache Battaglia 1983, 130; Rinaldi 1956, 117–119; Martin-Kilcher 2000, 67) (Fig. 3). Further investigation proved the doll to come from the burial of a young girl whose tomb lay alongside and overlapped that of Cossinia (Bordenache Battaglia 1983, 124–38; Chioffi 1998, 88–9). The tomb of fifteen-year-old Julia Graphide in Bruscello contained a minature dinner service. Martin-Kilcher describes these of low quality and unlikely to have been played with (2000, 69) but without close examination of wear it is hard to tell if such objects are solely votive.

A final, and rather anomalous example which is worth including, at least for the sake of discussion, is the body of a seven- or eight-year-old girl found in a mummified state on the Via Cassia in the commune of Grottarossa (see Ciuffarella 1998; Chioffi 1998, 47–50) She had been wrapped, probably in a shroud of linen and silk, and objects had been placed on her body in appropriate places: a sapphire and gold necklace; a little gold ring incised with an image of victory, bent to fit a small finger; gold earrings; an ivory doll (Fig. 4); little amber pots shaped like shells; a miniature amber vase; a jug and ladle; and tiny amber dice. As with Tryphaena, the doll was found near the head (Bordenache Battaglia 1983, 100–122).

These graves are interesting because of the types of finds and their relationship to the age and sex of the deceased. Andrew Oliver (2000, 117) argued that jewellery is rarely found in funerary contexts in Rome, or in highly Romanised areas, but that when it is found it is precisely in the context of burials of girls/young women. The graves of older women contain far less jewellery and fewer toilet items. Oliver uses evidence from law codes to suggest the reasons that lie behind

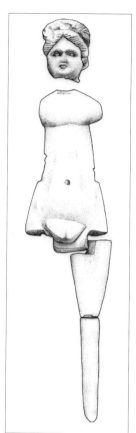 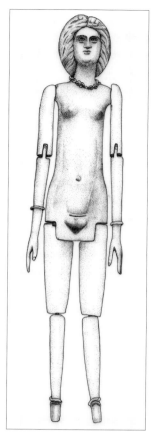 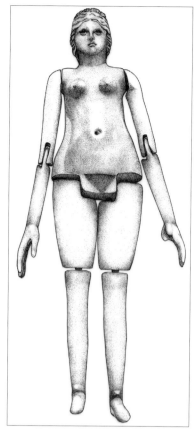

Above left: Fig. 2. Fragmentary ivory doll from the burial of a girl in Vallerano (drawing by J. Willmott).

Above middle: Fig. 3. Ivory doll from the burial of a young girl in Tivoli (drawing by J. Willmott).

Above right: Fig. 4. Ivory doll from the burial of a young girl on the Via Cassia in Grottarossa (drawing by J. Willmott).

this are twofold: that women traditionally passed down their jewellery to their daughters or other female relations and retainers, so it would not be buried with the woman at her death but stay in circulation, and that the jewellery and other accoutrements we find buried with young women/girls represent the dowry they have not used – either by not yet being married or the return of the dowry after their deaths. A wide range of jewellery is found in these graves, often made of gold with precious and semi-precious stones. As far as I can ascertain, no (published) research has been carried out on the extent to which any of these objects show signs of wear or damage, or how many of them were in pristine condition and unused when deposited. Any such evidence might allow us to debate whether the jewellery buried with these young women was made up of heirlooms – objects handed down from mother to daughter – or given as new as gifts to the young woman in life, or even provided especially for the burial ritual. This all begs questions as to why the graves of some young women are arranged with such apparent care and what families were attempting to express through this unusual addition of objects, and what those objects may have symbolised. Moreover, the regalia may not have been simply presented for the after-life; the body was also open to view at a Roman funeral, and the presence of these objects may have held specific social connotations.

The presence of dolls has also led to a lot of speculation (Figs 2–4). A number of dolls have been found in Roman-period graves from across the empire. They are made of wood, bone and ivory, and are all in the shape of young women, more 'Barbie' than 'baby' doll. All are found without clothes but often with jewellery, sometimes of gold, in the form of bracelets or anklets. They are rarely considered simply as playthings, or items of special affection for the deceased. Ida Anna Rapinesi makes the suggestion that the presence of the dolls might mark out girls who died before fulfilling their potential as mothers. Others have argued that the dolls signify the unmarried status of these girls and are a symbol of the ritual wherein girls laid aside their dolls before their wedding day, or that they might have had some hitherto unknown religious meaning (Rapinesi, 2004; Chioffi 1998, 28; Denzey 2007, 4, following Lanciani 1892, 268; on dolls more generally see Elderkin 1930, 455–479; Manson 1987, 1991, 1992; Ricotti 1995, 51–62; Rinaldi 1956). These arguments are persuasive and suit the overall thesis of this paper very neatly, but it would be better to be suspicious of the dedication of dolls as part of a traditional ritual. I am aware of it only being mentioned five times in the literary sources (and three of those are 'antiquarian': Persius, *Satires* 2.69; Varro in Nonius, *De compendiosa doctrina* 863.15 L; Arnobius, *Adversus Nationes* 2.67; *Palatine Anthology* 6.280 (for recent discussion of the ritual and sources see Hersch 2010, 65–68). The idea that such a ritual existed seems to have become generally accepted and is seen as a parallel to the male rite of passage where boys laid aside their *bulla* as part of the ritual of entering manhood. Thus, girls were seen to be laying aside childish things before marriage – the female rite of passage to adulthood. Others have argued that the dolls are not toys at all and, like the other miniature objects found among the grave goods (above) and *crepundia*, they serve symbolic and/or apopotraic purposes (Martin-Kilcher 2000, 67–69; Bordenache Battaglia 1983, 116–117). Dolls and other miniature items could, of course, have served multiple purposes. As with the jewellery, marks of wear and repair might mean that they were used (played with) in life, but this does not preclude their ritual and symbolic meaning in death.

There are very few items of dress surviving in these burials, despite Lanciani's speculation over Creperia Tryphena being buried in her wedding outfit. We know from literary and visual sources that changes of dress, or at least of public dress, marked different stages of the life course. This is most apparent for males who underwent a public ceremony when they laid aside their *bulla*, took off the child's *toga praetexta* and assumed the adut *toga virilis* to mark the beginning of adulthood (see Harlow, Laurence 2002, 67–72; Dolanksy 2008, 47–70). For a young citizen woman, the wedding day was marked out by a special costume, featuring a *tunica recta* (traditionally woven by the bride herself), a girdle tied with a special knot, a special hair arrangement (*seni crines*), a wreath of flowers and herbs (see above), and the veil (*flammeum*) over it all (for bridal wear and its symbolism see Sebesta 1994, 48; Hersch 2010, 69–114; Olsen 2008, 21–25; La Follette 1994). As children among the upper classes, both boys and girls were said to wear the *toga praetexta* but there are considerably fewer representations of togate girls than boys (Goette 1990, 80–82; 158–159; Olsen 2008, 17; Sebesta 2005, 113–120). Images of children at play on sarcophagi or wall paintings show them far more often in loose unbelted tunics, with girls tending to wear garments that are longer and reaching to the feet (Huskinson 1996). As a young girl grew, it can be assumed she learnt appropriate behaviour and clothed body language by emulation of women in the family and around her. Her dress may have become more constrained and sedate, at least in public. Particular items of underclothing are attributed by (male) antiquarians to the wardrobe of young unmarried women – the *strophium* (breast band) and the *supparus* (perhaps a shift-like garment). The *strophium*, according to Nonius (863 L; Terrence, *Eunuch* 313–17), restricted the growth of pubescent breasts, and it is mentioned among the items dedicated to the Lares by young girls before their wedding (Varro in Nonius 863 L). The *supparus* is rather harder to define, but it is described as a linen garment for girls, worn either underneath the tunic or like a night gown (Nonius 866L; Festus 407L; Olsen 2008, 16). According to Lucan (*Pharsalia* 2.364), it was part of the bridal outfit, a narrow tunic which partly covered the arms. Unfortunately, we have practically no surviving clothing (that I am aware of) from these graves, but interestingly we do have at least two, and possibly three, *recticula* (hair nets) which Varro, and the author of the extract from the *Palatine Anthology*, mention as being part of the items dedicated before the wedding. According to Festus (364L) a bride wove her hair net as she wove her *tunica recta*. She wore it the night before her wedding, dedicated it to the Lares, and replaced it with the *flammeum*, the wedding veil. The *reticulum* was made of wool dyed the colour referred to as *luteus*. This is a difficult colour to define, but like the *flammeum* was akin to bright yellow/orange/saffron (see Hersch 2010, 10–18 on the difficuties of this interpretation). The remains of gold thread, probably silk, and tiny ornaments, have been reconstructed as a *reticulum* for tomb 2 from Vallerano. The grave of unknown provenance listed above also appears to have a potential *reticulum*. Chioffi also records a tomb of a girl aged between twelve and fourteen that contained jewels and a gold *reticulum* (1998, 66–68). This was uncovered in 1485 and, while it is difficult to be clear about what was actually present, there appears to have been a green silk ribbon around the head, and a diadem with a golden hair net. The most well known visual example of such a hair net from the Roman period is the Pompeian wall painting from a building in Regio IV (Insula Occidentalis) of the young girl known as Sappho; she wears a delicate gold *reticulum*.

Conclusions

The evidence laid out above is seductive but not unproblematic. Ray Laurence and I have argued that betrothal marked out a young girl as ready for the, often extended, transition to adulthood. Not all of the bodies listed above can be securely aged, but where they can be, the majority fit the idea that these are young girls/women are in puberty or on the cusp of it, ready to be betrothed in Roman law, if not married. The tradition of gift giving at betrothal, highlights the young girl as different from non-betrothed girls and the gifts both mark the moment and the promise of marriage in the future. At this stage, she is still a virgin but one who had entered a liminal stage in which she was neither a child nor a married woman, but clearly in transition, only now for her the transition is suspended, and instead of childhood and marriage the transition was between life and death. The wealth of 'feminine' grave goods not only represents compensation for a life not fully lived, but also allowed mourners, who presumably would have viewed the body, to see the young girl at her finest moment so far in the life course. Presumably the laying out of the body, and the choice of grave goods, was decided by her parents, and, probably, by custom. The richness of some of the jewellery and the range of dolls, sometimes exquisite miniatures, toilet items, spindles, needles and so on, which make up *mundus muliebris* (women's toilette articles), must have been chosen for a reason, or several reasons. These objects appear to reflect both childhood lived and unachieved maturity, and they indicate the recognition of what had been and what would never be. Parents may have thought it was important to advertise the coming, but unattained, wedding to mourners, as it gave their child a social identity close to adulthood – a stage more highly valued than childhood in the Roman mind. It also kept alive, if only for a short time, the relationship between the betrothed couples' families. It may also have been thought important to enter the afterlife as near to the married state as possible, and the laying out of the young body with jewellery, signifying the betrothal, the dolls and miniatures from her fading childhood, the perfume bottles and spinning implements symbolising her skills for adulthood, meant that the deceased would appear as symbolically complete. We have very rare glimpses into the clothed life of non-adults, but these burials perhaps give us some insight into a moment in a girl's life where she might have been the centre of family attention. Dressed for her appearance at the *sponsalia*, wearing her best dress and her finest jewellery (gifts from her husband to be), the burial recalls that pinnacle moment, for her and her family.

m.e.harlow@bham.ac.uk

Bibliography

Bedini 1995: A. Bedini, *Mistero di una fanciulla: Ori e gioelli della Roma di Marco Aurelio da una nuova scoperta archaeologica*, Rome

Bertelli *et al.* 2008: C. Bertelli, L. Malnati, G. Montevecchi, *Otium: L'arte di vivere nelle domus romane di età imperiale*, Milan

Bordenache Battaglia 1983: G. Bordenache Battaglia, *Corredi Funerari di Età Imperiale e Barbarica nel Museo Nazionale Romano*, Rome

Chioffi 1998: L. Chioffi, *Mummificazione e imbalsamazione a Roma ed in altri luoghi del mondo Romano. Opuscula Epigraphica 8*

Denzey 2007: N. Denzey *The Bone Gatherers: The Lost Worlds of Early Christian Women*, Boston

Dolanksy 2008: F. Dolanksy, '*Togam virilem sumere*: Coming of Age in the Roman World' in J. Edmondson, A. Keith (eds), *Roman Dress and the Fabrics of Roman Culture*, Toronto, 47–70

Elderkin 1930: K. Elderkin 'Jointed Dolls in Antiquity', *American Journal of Archaeology* 34, 455–479

Fayer 2005: C. Fayer *La Familia Romana. Aspetti Giuridici ed Antiquari Sponsalia Matrimonio Dote Parte Seconda*, Rome

Goette 1990: H. R. Goette, *Studien zu römischen Togadarstellungen*, Mainz

Harlow, Laurence 2002: M. Harlow, R. Laurence, *Growing Up and Growing Old at Rome: A life course approach*, London

Harlow, Laurence 2010: M. Harlow, R. Laurence, 'Betrothal, mid-late childhood and the life course', in L. Larsson Lovén, A. Strömberg (eds), *Ancient Marriage in Myth and Reality*, Newcastle upon Tyne, 56–77

Henig, MacGregor 2004: M. Henig, A. MacGregor, *Catalogue of Engraved Finger Rings in the Ashmolean Museum II: Roman* (BAR International Series 1332), Oxford

Henkel 1913: F. Henkel, *Die Romischen Fingerringe der Rheinlande und der Benachbarten Gebeite*, Berlin

Hersch 2010: K. Hersch, *Roman Wedding: ritual and meaning in antiquity*, Cambridge

Huskinson 1996: J. Huskinson, *Roman Children's Sarcophagi*, Oxford

Johns 1996: C. Johns, *Jewellery in Roman Britain*, London

La Follette 1994: L. La Follette, 'The Costume of the Roman Bride' in Sebesta, Bonfante, 54–64

Lanciani 1892: R. Lanciani, *Pagan and Christian Rome*, Rome

Manson 1987: M. Manson, 'Le bambole romane antiche', *Ricerca Folklorica* 16, 15–26

Manson 1991: M. Manson, 'Les poupées antiques', *Jouer dans L'Antiquité*, Marseille, 54–59

Manson 1992: M. Manson, 'Les Poupées Antiques', *Les Dossiers d'Archaeologie* 168, 48–57

Marshall 1907: F. Marshall, *Catalogue of Finger Rings, Greek, Etruscan and Roman in the Department of Antiquities, British Museum,* London

Martin-Kilcher 2000: S. Martin-Kilcher '*Mors Immatura* in the Roman world – a mirror of society and tradition', in J. Pearce, M. Martin, M. Struck (eds), *Burial, Society and Context in the Roman World*, Oxford, 63–77

Oliver 2000: A. Oliver, 'Jewelry for the Unmarried', in D. E. Kleiner, S. B. Matheson (eds), *I Claudia II. Women in Roman Art and Society*, Austin, Texas, 115–124

Olsen 2008: K. Olsen, *Dress and the Roman Woman: Self Presentation and Society*, London.

Rapinesi 2004: I. A. Ripanesi, 'Il lusso a Roma', in D. Candilo (ed.), *Moda Costume e Bellezza nella Roma Antica*, Rome, 33–40

Ricotti 1995: E. S. Ricotti, *Giochi e Giocattoli*, Rome

Rinaldi 1956: M. R. Rinaldi, 'Richerche sui giocattoli nell'antichità a proposito di un'iscrizione di Brescello', *Epigraphica* 18, 104–129

Ruseva-Slokoska 1991: L. Ruseva-Slokoska, *Roman Jewellery*, Sofia

Saller, Shaw 1984: R. Saller, B. Shaw, 'Tombstones and Roman family relations in the Principate: civilians, soldiers, slaves', *Journal of Roman Studies* 74, 124–156

Sebesta 2005: J. Sebesta, 'The *toga praetexta* of Roman children and praetexate garments', in L. Cleland, M. Harlow, L. J. Llewellyn-Jones (eds), *The Clothed Body in the Ancient World*, Oxford, 113–120

Sebesta, Bonfante 1994: J. Sebesta, L. Bonfante (eds) *The World of Roman Costume*, Madison

Treggiari 1991: S. Treggiari, *Roman Marriage*, Oxford

KEYWORD INDEX